Unless Recalled Earlier

DATE DUE

Worlds Enough *and* Time ─────────

Recent Titles in Contributions to the Study of Science Fiction and Fantasy

Worlds Enough *and* Time

Explorations of Time in Science Fiction and Fantasy

Edited by Gary Westfahl,
George Slusser, and David Leiby

Contributions to the Study of Science Fiction and Fantasy, Number 101
Donald Palumbo, Series Adviser

Greenwood Press
Westport, Connecticut • London

Library of Congress Cataloging-in-Publication Data

Worlds enough and time : explorations of time in science fiction and fantasy / edited by
  Gary Westfahl, George Slusser, and David Leiby.
      p.   cm.—(Contributions to the study of science fiction and fantasy,
    ISSN 0193–6875 ; no 101)
    Includes bibliographical references and index.
    ISBN 0–313–31706–2 (alk. paper)
    1. Science fiction—History and criticism.   2. Fantasy fiction—History and criticism. 3.
Time in literature. I. Westfahl, Gary. II. Slusser, George Edgar. III. Leiby, David. IV.
Series.
PN3433.6.W67   2002
809.3′87609384—dc21   2002016106

British Library Cataloguing in Publication Data is available.

Library of Congress Catalog Card Number: 2002016106
ISBN: 0–313–31706–2
ISSN: 0193–6875

First published in 2002

Greenwood Press, 88 Post Road West, Westport, CT 06881
An imprint of Greenwood Publishing Group, Inc.
www.greenwood.com

Printed in the United States of America

The paper used in this book complies with the
Permanent Paper Standard issued by the National
Information Standards Organization (Z39.48–1984).

10 9 8 7 6 5 4 3 2 1

Contents

Acknowledgments

We thank the many people who contributed to the long process of assembling this volume, including Darian Davies, Sara Fitzpatrick, Carl Freedman, Susan Korn, Sheryl Lewis, Joseph D. Miller, Gladys Murphy, Joe Sanders, Milton T. Wolf, and especially Melissa Conway and Donald E. Palumbo. For guidance and assistance during the final stages of preparation, we thank George F. Butler, Audrey Klein, Terri M. Jennings, and their associates at Greenwood Press; and finally we thank friends, family members, and colleagues too numerous to name who have provided encouragement and support while we worked on completing this project.

1

Introduction:
The Quarries of Time

Gary Westfahl

"Time is the funniest thing, sir. It ties a man in knots."
— Clifford D. Simak, *Time and Again*[1]

One trait that distinguishes human beings from other animals is our keen and far-ranging awareness of time. After the invention of language, people possessed the unique power to convey knowledge and narratives to their descendants, first through oral traditions and later in written records. Absorbing the accumulated wisdom of distant ancestors, early human civilizations came to conceive of the past as a distant realm quite different from their mundane present—a Golden Age when humans walked with gods and magical events were part of everyday life. Cultures all over the globe developed rich mythologies filled with fabulous stories occurring in this idealized past. And as a mirror image to these ancient worlds, some religions projected a future when the ancient paradise would be restored, suggesting that time itself moved in an immense cycle analogous to the monthly cycles of the moon and annual cycles of the seasons.

In later, more secular times, the myths and legends of a Golden Age have metamorphosed into the literary genre now known as fantasy. It is a truism to suggest that virtually all fantasies, either explicitly or implicitly, take place in an imagined past and are infused with tropes and props from various ancient and medieval cultures. One foundation of fantasy appears to be a longing to return to the past, accompanied by the sense that the passing of time has brought humanity only decline and degeneration. This leads to numerous stories of people magically transported to romantic or idealized past eras, as in Katharine Burdekin's *The Burning Ring*, Diana Gabaldon's Outlander novels, and the play and film *Berkeley Square*. There are also visions of lands separate from our own reality where time moves more slowly or stands still, such as J. M. Barrie's Neverland; the timeless town of the play and film *Brigadoon*; J. G. Ballard's "The Garden of Time," where plucking magical flowers can temporarily suspend the passing of time; and the strange zone of "eternity" in Flann O'Brien's *The Third Policeman*. And without the trappings of scientific rationales, fantasies can wistfully contrast worlds of what happened with worlds of what might have happened, as in Alan Brennert's *Time and Chance*, where a man who looks back ruefully on his decision to abandon an acting career for marriage and a family encounters his unmarried *döppelganger* who decided to stay the course and become a successful actor in an alternate world.

If the literature of fantasy derives from an ancient human awareness of the past as a distinct world, one might argue that the literature of science fiction derives from a more recent awareness that the future might become another distinct world, not merely a continuation of the present or reinstatement of the past. Science suggested that time moved in a linear, not cyclical, fashion, so that humans had the power to create new and different societies as a result of scientific and social progress. Paul K. Alkon's *Origins of Futuristic Fiction* traces the growing number of texts in the eighteenth and nineteenth centuries that imagined such future civilizations, and envisioning such places led inexorably to tales about present-day humans traveling there.

While science fiction is sometimes regarded as a literature primarily focused on space travel, then, one can argue that time travel is actually its principal fascination, and that the genre first emerged in response to a growing interest in the future more than a growing interest in outer space. While the nineteenth-century writers viewed as the genre's progenitors did not all write about traveling through space, they all produced stories involving distant and unfamiliar futures, or even the transportation of people or documents to or from the future, such as Mary Shelley's *The Last Man*, Edgar Allan Poe's "Mellonta Tauta," Jules Verne's "In the Twenty-Ninth Century," Edward Bellamy's *Looking Backward, 2000–1887*, and Mark Twain's "From the *London Times* of 1904." The growth of science fiction in the early twentieth century accompanied no new breakthroughs in astronomy, but rather the growing realization that time could be characterized as the universe's fourth dimension, creating the possibility of time travel achieved through scientific means—a concept brilliantly exploited by H. G. Wells's *The Time Machine* and other works of its era. And virtually all authors associated with science fiction during the subsequent century produced tales of time travel, indicating that the conquest of time is a theme just as ubiquitous in the genre as the conquest of space.

The deeper generic origins of science fiction are more hotly debated than those of fantasy, but two broadly acceptable premises may account for the genre's connections to time and time travel. First, while Hugo Gernsback was unsuccessful in his efforts during the 1920s and 1930s to make science fiction primarily a forum for presentations of scientific facts and explorations of new scientific concepts, he legitimized the notion that science fiction is a "literature of ideas," allowing some later authors to create stories that focused more on scientific speculations than literary values. Second, however, science fiction is principally an outgrowth not of scientific textbooks and journals but of previous literary genres such as the travel tale, melodrama, utopia, Gothic horror, and satire. For both reasons, time travel has emerged as a central trope in science fiction.

Considered as topics for scientific inquiry, time and time travel open up innumerable avenues for speculation. If time travel to the past is allowed, one encounters the famous Grandfather Paradox: If you went back in time to kill your grandfather and prevent your own birth, would you instantly eliminate yourself from existence, create a parallel universe where you did not exist, or find yourself mysteriously unable to carry out the cosmos-changing murder? Such questions were argued in the letter columns of Gernsback's *Amazing Stories* during the 1920s, at a time when scientists generally dismissed time travel as impossible, and they are still argued today, at a time when physicists like Kip Thorne can envision in some detail precisely how the Theory of General Relativity would allow for the construction of time machines by manipulating wormholes in space. Contemporary writers can stay within the boundaries of scientific plausibility and explore such possibilities as alternate universes generated by time travelers altering the past, time loops in which a person with a time machine endlessly repeats the same sequence of events, or the creation or discovery of universes where time moves backward or at a dizzyingly rapid velocity.

Considered as a valuable device in generating narratives, time travel would be attractive to writers of many different temperaments. After all regions of the Earth had been exhaustively explored, allowing no room for posited lost civilizations in deep jungles or on remote islands, writers who simply yearn to create new travel tales about imagined realms can employ a time machine or time portal to instantly transport protagonists to inaccessible regions of the past, like the prehistoric times visited in Michael Bishop's *No Enemy but Time*, to strange futuristic environments, like the exotic future of John Taine's *The Time Stream*, or to parallel universes where differing historical events have generated significant different present-day worlds, as in the television series *Sliders*. If writers wish to produce exciting melodramatic adventures, time travel opens up a vast and multifaceted new arena for tales of good guys battling bad guys who range back and forth in time through our universe or alternate universes each striving to preserve their own existence, as seen in Jack Williamson's *The Legion of Time*, Clifford D. Simak's *Time and Again*, Fritz Leiber's *The Big Time*, and John Barnes's *The Timeline Wars*. And for writers who seek to depict a utopia, time travel can imbue their visions with special impact by placing the ideal society in the future, rather than a faraway island or planet, so that authors can portray their utopias as natural outgrowths of their own cultures, provided that recommended policies are followed. Thus, when Bellamy transported a nineteenth-century man into an ideal future America in *Looking Backward*, he immediately inspired the formation of "Bellamy Clubs" dedicated to making his dream a reality.

While such colorful and positive visions are a part of science fiction, the genre has a darker side as well, which can also make effective use of time travel. For writers seeking to make a satirical point about the inadequacies of our own society, time travel can bring visitors from other eras into our world or transport modern protagonists into other eras; thus, Twain's *A Connecticut Yankee in King Arthur's Court* illustrates the violence and brutality of modern civilization by having the time-traveling Hank Morgan transform stately Camelot into a bloody war zone. For the effect of horror, time travel can bring ancient menaces back into the world, as Robert Bloch's "A Toy for Juliette" places the murderous Jack the Ripper into a tranquil future city; exile protagonists into eternal timelessness, as in Harlan Ellison's "Jeffty Is Five"; or force time travelers into endlessly repeating time loops, as in Philip K. Dick's "A Little Something for Us Tempunauts." To convey the grim warning of dystopia, time travel can inadvertently lead to a totalitarian society, as occurs in Ray Bradbury's "A Sound of Thunder," or shock time travelers with disheartening visions of pampered future humans drifting into helplessness and extinction, as observed in Wells's *The Time Machine* and later works like John W. Campbell, Jr.'s "Twilight" and Brian W. Aldiss's "Ahead."

These brief comments cannot, and are not intended to, epitomize all the narrative possibilities that time and time travel bring to fantasy and science fiction. But one further point should be made. The gaudy magical effects of fantasy, and to an even greater extent the machinery and jargon of science fiction, can be intimidating and alienating to many readers. Dragons, spaceships, and robots may seem utterly divorced from people's everyday concerns and problems. But considerations of time strike closer to home. All humans experience time on a daily basis, engaged in their own measured time travel from yesterday to tomorrow, constantly recalling the past and planning for the future, feeling that time at various moments either moves too fast or moves too slowly. Stories about disruptions or dislocations in time can thus seem more intimate, more personal, than other fantastic narratives. And when readers think about which stories reveal the most about their authors's personalities and attitudes, the answers are often stories about time and time travel—Isaac Asimov's "The Ugly Little Boy," Octavia E. Butler's *Kindred*, Orson Scott Card's *Pastwatch: The Redemption of Christopher Columbus*, William Gibson's "The Gernsback Continuum," Robert A. Heinlein's "By His Bootstraps," Mary Shelley's "The Mortal Immortal," and Theodore Sturgeon's "Microcosmic God" being only a few works that come to mind.

Two other stories that belong on that list—Philip K. Dick's "A Little Something for Us Tempunauts" and Clifford D. Simak's *Time and Again*—invite discussion as examples of how time travel stories can both stimulatingly play with scientific ideas and establish visceral, personal connections between author and reader.

In Dick's story, three American time travelers find themselves trapped in an endlessly repeating time loop. They live through one week while the world mourns their deaths and scientists attempt to figure out a solution to their problem; they are then captured by a time machine and transported back in time one week; upon their return, an explosion kills all three of them, leaving bodies to be buried, but also preserves an identical set of three living men who will again experience the same week of events leading up to the same return, the same explosion, and the same subsequent week of events. They finally realize, of course, that it is not simply they, but the entire world around them, that are trapped in this unending cycle. Such perpetually replicating time loops are one of the paradoxical phenomena now thought to be sanctioned by the Theory of General Relativity, although physics cannot explain how one might create such a loop; Dick's idea of a causal explosion resulting because "No two objects can occupy the same space at the same time" is as plausible as any.[2]

Yet scientific considerations were clearly not Dick's priority in writing this story; rather, the situation he develops serves as a powerful metaphor for the ways that people can trap themselves in repetitive cycles, making the same bad decisions over and over again, creating the sense that they are constantly moving but getting nowhere. The story begins with the adverb "Wearily" (259), ends with the phrase "The dreadful and weary miracle of eternal life" (282), and conveys throughout an overwhelming feeling of exhaustion and frustration:

We're in a closed time loop, he thought, we keep going through this again and again, trying to solve the re-entry problem, each time imagining it's the first time, the only time . . . and never succeeding. Which attempt is this? Maybe the millionth; we have sat here a million times, raking the same facts over and over again and getting nowhere. He felt bone-weary, thinking that. And he felt a sort of vast philosophical hate toward all other men, who did not have this enigma to deal with. (262; author's ellipses)

Given what we know of Dick's life in the early 1970s, as he spiralled downward into paranoia and frustration, this reads almost like a journal entry, and Dick manifestly identified with the plight of his time travelers, as he confessed in an afterword to the story in *Final Stage*: "In writing this story, I felt a weary sadness of my own and fell into the space (I should say time) that the characters are in, more so than usual." He proceeds to explain the value of science fiction: "We, when we're depressed, are fortunately imprisoned within our heads; once time-travel becomes a reality, however, this self-defeating psychological attitude could spell doom on a scale beyond calculation. Here again, science fiction allows a writer to transfer what usually is an internal problem into an external environment" (283). Indeed; and the time travel story in this case allowed Dick to convey an individual human predicament on a grand and evocative scale.

The work of a very different author in a very different mood—a natural optimist approaching the peak of his career—Clifford D. Simak's *Time and Again,* first published in magazine form under the title *Time Quarry,* may qualify as the quintessential Simak novel. Six thousand years in the future, a space traveler named Asher Sutton discovers that every creature in the universe is accompanied throughout its life by an invisible being, referred to as its "destiny," which subtly oversees and guides the creature in the right directions. After visiting the home world of these beings, Sutton intends to write a book explaining what he has learned, which will begin:

We are not alone.
No one ever is alone.
Not since the first faint stirring of the first flicker of life on the first planet in the galaxy that knew the quickening of life, has there ever been a single entity that walked or crawled or slithered down the path of life alone. (105; author's italics)

The revelations in that book will in the future trigger a vast war through space and time between humans, determined to maintain their control over the galaxy, and the androids they created, who will take Sutton's words as evidence of their rights to complete equality. While androids from the future work to protect Sutton so that he can write the book he plans to write, humans from the future seek to kill him, so the book will never be written, or attempt to influence him to write a slightly different book more amenable to claims of human superiority.

Reading *Time and Again*, we recognize first that Simak is an author constantly preoccupied with the mental time travel that all people engage in. Like other Simak heroes, Sutton repeatedly goes over past events in his mind, reliving them, pondering their implications, trying to clarify and sort things out for himself and for readers; he also plans for the future, carefully crafting and refining his plans before taking action. In this novel, one of Sutton's priorities is to figure out the ramifications of time travel. Just as Simak seeks to philosophically embrace all living creatures as equally important and worthwhile, he also seeks through Sutton to reconcile the conflicting theories regarding the potential paradoxes of time travel. He is inclined to reject the notion that altering the past might generate parallel universes: "Alternate futures? Maybe, but it didn't seem likely. Alternate futures were a fantasy that employed semantics twisting to prove a point, a clever use of words that covered up and masked the fallacies" (164). He instead wishes to believe in a single, unalterable past, but recognizes that time travelers would necessarily possess some power to alter past events. He commonsensically settles upon a compromise position, concluding that time can be altered, but only in small and subtle ways: "The past cannot be changed, he argued with himself, in its entirety. It can be twisted and it can be dented and it can be whittled down, but by and large it stands. . . . somewhere, somewhen he had written a book. The book existed and therefore had happened, although so far as he was concerned it had not happened yet" (194–195). Then, recognizing the inevitability of his message being promulgated, Sutton enjoys ten peaceful and recuperative years working on a twentieth-century Wisconsin farm, calmly returns to the future to confront his chief nemesis, and finally travels to a faraway planet to live with an old family robot while he writes his history-making book.

Thus, while time travel brings only pain and weariness to Dick's heroes, time travel brings a sense of serenity and fulfillment to Simak's protagonist. As time goes on, he confidently believes, benevolence will inexorably win out over evil, and traveling through time cannot prevent, and might even hasten, its final victory. In Simak's universe, one might say, kindness is the sword that cuts the Gordian "knots" of time paradoxes that the novel references (229), and Simak's answer may strike readers as both scientifically defensible and personally satisfying.

The fact that imagined time travel can generate stories as starkly divergent as Dick's and Simak's suggests just how potent and far-ranging this narrative device can be, and the chapters in this volume will further demonstrate the astonishing vitality of time travel as a theme in science fiction and fantasy. In the first section, "Time's Arrows," George Slusser and Robert Heath, Richard Saint-Gelais, and

David A. Leiby explore in various ways the forms and complexities of time travel narratives, while Andrew Sawyer investigates the fascinating subtopic of stories involving the reversal of time. In the second section, "Timescapes," contributors consider broader aspects of the interface of time and literature: Kirk Hampton and Carol MacKay survey visions of humanity's far future, Susan Stratton ponders time in the context of posited psychic powers, Susan Kray contemplates the relationship between time and Jewish people in fantasy and science fiction, and Jefferson M. Peters employs a famed manga series to assess Japanese attitudes toward time. In the final section, "Time Capsules," contributors focus on particular works that provocatively deal with time, with Pekka Kuusisto's exegesis of the cosmology in Dante's *The Divine Comedy*, Larry W. Caldwell's examination of historical time in George Orwell's *Nineteen Eighty-Four*, Andrew Gordon's consideration of time travel as reincarnation in Ken Grimwood's *Replay* and two films, Bradford Lyau's appraisal of Stephen Baxter's *The Time Ships* as a commentary on projected limits of scientific inquiry, and Erica Obey's analysis of Diana Gabaldon's Outlander novels and other time travel romances. A concluding bibliography lists science fiction novels and stories, films and television programs, and nonfiction works related to time and time travel.

In producing this volume, we recognize that valuable contributions to this field of study have already been made by works such as Bud Foote's *The Connecticut Yankee in the Twentieth Century* and Paul J. Nahin's *Time Machines: Time Travel in Physics, Metaphysics, and Science Fiction*. Still, time and time travel in science fiction and fantasy remain subjects in need of thoroughgoing analysis, given the ubiquity of time travel in literature and its growing prominence in scientific thought. Without claiming to be exhaustive in our coverage, we hope that this volume will inspire other scholars to visit the rich quarries of time, where many more treasures are ready to be unearthed.

Notes

1. Clifford D. Simak, *Time and Again* (New York: Ace Books, 1951), 229. Later page references in the text are to this edition.
2. Philip K. Dick, "A Little Something for Us Tempunauts," in Edward L. Ferman and Barry N. Malzberg, editors, *Final Stage: The Ultimate Science Fiction Anthology* (1974; New York: Penguin Books, 1975), 263. Later page references in the text to the story and to its authorial afterword are to this edition.

Part I

Time's Arrows

2

Arrows and Riddles of Time: Scientific Models of Time Travel

George Slusser and Robert Heath

To Count the Clock that Tells the Time

What is time? We must have some sense of what time and the passage of time is before we can characterize time travel in science fiction stories. The steady tick-tock of a clock demonstrates the passage of time, but how is that passage meaningful in terms of physical laws? Indeed, to use time as a unit to measure travel, one would need to know how to modify its passage. The dictionary defines time as a period, but this is not especially helpful. One might say that "time is what happens when nothing else happens," or "time is that which prevents everything from happening simultaneously," or perhaps "time is how long we wait for something to happen." The most scientific definition is that time is the cumulative sum of a series of repetitions of a periodic event, something that happens over and over, in a regular manner. In the tick-tock of a clock, the escarpment forces some of the energy contained in a wound-up spring to be transformed into the repetitive back-and-forth motion of a pendulum. Each back-and-forth movement is measured by the movement of the circle of an arm, the second hand. After sixty seconds the hand repeats itself, but causes the minute hand to move 1/60th of a rotation, and so on. Before the invention of the clock, the daily passage of the sun across the sky or the rhythm of the human pulse were used to measure the passage of time—both are periodic events with characteristic periods of repetitions. Today, the vibrations of atoms generate a periodic event that is counted. But have we progressed in our definition of time as it applies to time travel?

The formation of a periodic event and the counting of that periodic event are crucial to the measurement of time—but are they crucial for our understanding of the formation of time in the physical universe? Here we must deal with the direction and rate of such metaphors as the "flow" of time. Using a different (yet equally directional) metaphor, Stephen Hawking argues that there are at least three different "arrows of time": the thermodynamic arrow, the cosmological arrow, and the psychological arrow. Given these different realms of displacement, how can something be said to "travel" in time? We all travel in time at a velocity of one second per second of time. That is, each second we and everything associated with us in our field of perception have "moved" one second in time. This is not what is meant by time travel in sf. Time travel is the ability to move forward in time at a "velocity" greater than one second per second, so that, like H. G. Wells's Time Traveller, over a few minutes of your clock time you move centuries of time forward or positively into the future. On the other hand, you can move negatively but rapidly backward in time in order to visit your past. But how is this to be done?

Insofar as "time happens" in stories of time travel, let us return to Hawking's arrows of time to classify these stories. Essentially, we will deal with two arrows: the thermodynamic arrow and psychological arrow. The cosmological arrow of time seems to underlie stories of spacetime displacement, like Poul Anderson's *Tau Zero*. On this macroscale, the initial explosion and direction of entropy increase drives the period from the "big bang" to the "heat death," giving us the time direction for the entire universe. Local time reversal through a "time machine" could be possible, but the ultimate end of the universe could not be influenced from inside. Writers like Anderson, however, use this end of time not as a final end, but rather as a hesitation in the movement of travelers who leap through the end to a new beginning, witnessing the "big bang" and finding that the universe repeats itself very much like before.

The thermodynamic arrow underlies many time travel stories. It is posited that time is related to how energy is transferred from one system to another without loss of usable or storable energy. The thermodynamic arrow of time is due to energy transformations within, and entropy increase of, the universe. From another angle, entropy has been linked to the organization of a given system. As the system becomes more disorganized, the entropy of that system increases. This increase in entropy is said to follow the natural movement of time. A vase falls from the table and shatters. The organization of the vase is decreased, time moves normally, and the entropy of the vase has increased. In this field, all events are linked. The broken vase does not reassemble on the ground and leap back to the table fully formed. Time and entropy increase. To make the reassembly of the vase event occur, energy must be added to the system, and this must come from another system in which entropy increases. It is thus clear that, if time travel to the future moves with the entropy slope, time travel to the past would require much energy to induce the current entropy of the machine and traveler to decline. Perhaps energy could be extracted from the increased entropy of the system moving into the future. Thus in the film *Back to the Future* (1985), the car with the dog Einstein travels one minute into the future and becomes very cold, presumably by "pulling energy" out of the car during its travel.

The psychological arrow is equally important in time travel stories. The physical flows of time (the thermodynamic and cosmological arrows of time) have their own movement, but our perception of these movements is not uniform. We inhabit only a small slice of time, called the "now," before which is our past and memories, after which lies our future and its desires. There are a number of stories that exist on the cusp of the physical arrows and the psychological arrow of time. It is in this sense that we interpret Robert Silverberg's remarks in *Up the Line* that if one can travel anywhere in *the* future, one cannot travel anywhere at all in *one's own* future, except along one's natural biological timeline at one second per second. Future travel in this sense becomes mind travel. In like manner, we can reverse Silverberg's formula and say that, though one can travel anywhere one wishes in *one's own* past, one cannot travel at all in *the* past, for reasons of the energy problem described earlier. Many time loop stories play upon this disparity between time travel along different time arrows: thermodynamic on one hand, psychological on the other.

Models of Time Travel: Definitions

The majority of time travel stories operate at what we might call the human interface, where the thermodynamic and psychological arrows of time interact. On one vector, time is said to "progress" objectively, on the other, subjectively. Human beings experience time as a slice of time called "now," a period of short but not infinitely short duration. In terms of this "now," normal time progress is defined as the series of events that occur as time progresses from "now" to "now," events that can either be altered or not altered by the person(s) who inhabit these time slices. Time travel offers "freedom" from this normative time progression. The question then becomes: What sort of time structures does one meet with when, like Wells's Time Traveller, one moves away from the human norm, be it physical or psychological, that has up till now characterized human activity and the narratives that tell of such activity? It matters less perhaps, in terms of psychological rather than physical time, whether such travel is to the future or the past. More important, in modeling the experience of time displacement, is the nature of the progress of time in the world where a given traveler operates. In terms of temporal structures, we offer three basic models:

(A) *The Time Machine Model.* In such a universe, the time traveler is, in Silverberg's words, "in transit," "a drifting bubble of now time ripped loose from the matrix of the continuum, immune to the transformations of paradox."[1] Time progress in such a universe is fixed, a continuum as in Wells's "universe rigid" or "block universe." It can be moved on or through without altering the current history or future, for the traveler, as with Wells's protagonist crossing the exact trajectory of Mrs. Watchett upon his return from the far future, must somehow reintegrate with his or her own biological timeline as an event on this fixed temporal progression. These are the tales of the loop, tales that reaffirm the fixity of events on this continuum, events whose temporality is vectored by the laws of thermodynamics.

(B) *The Sound of Thunder Model.* In such a universe, time progress is branched. The time traveler merely moves to another branch when he/she disturbs the normal progress of the timeline on which he/she is initially located. If in the first category, the traveler must go home, to the exact or near exact moment when initial detachment occurred, here the traveler cannot go home again. These stories of alternate timelines and temporal disjunction are generally associated with travel to the past, where alteration of fixed events results in branching. Under sway of the thermodynamic arrow, time goes forward, but on an alternate path.

(C) The Solipsism Model. Here time progress is an individual protocol where events happen only for the individual "traveler." In this category, we must distinguish between false solipsisms from true ones. An example of the first category is Heinlein's " 'All You Zombies—.' " Here, despite the fact that the protagonist appears to have engineered a world where he/she—this barbarism makes sense in this context—is its own first and final cause, there are still irreversible time events, "a thing either is, or isn't, now and forever, amen."[2] The same is true for the myriad "mind labyrinth" stories of French sf, like Michel Jeury's *Chronolysis*, where the protagonist enters what seems a "subjective eternity" at the moment of his death, a moment he seems condemned to relive over and over till the end of time. Throughout the narrative, this time traveler seeks ways to break this infernal circle and finally does so, emerging into linear time. True solipsisms belong to the type of story we might call the "quantum reality" or "many worlds" narrative. Examples are Gregory Benford's "Of Space-Time and the River," and Greg Egan's *Permutation City*, to be discussed.

Tales of the Loop: The Time Machine Model

One generally associates Wells's creation of the Time Machine as a supremely liberating feat: "A civilized man . . . can go up against gravitation in a balloon, and why should he not hope that ultimately he may be able to stop or accelerate his drift along the Time-Dimension, or even turn around and travel the other way. Long ago I had a vague inkling of a machine . . . that shall travel indifferently in any direction in Space and Time, as the driver determines."[3] Ironically, given the instant of departure and return fixed by Mrs. Watchett, the exercise of this freedom proves the means of affirming the fixity or "rigidity" of the temporal continuum. No one can escape from time, and perhaps this explains why Wells (setting aside the possibility of later calculations of a special relativity that was not yet formulated, which demonstrate that the Time Traveller could not have gotten back to his present from 800,000 years in the future) had to bring his Traveller back to the laboratory from which he began his odyssey.

For Paul Nahin, stories that represent "a time loop as a continual, cyclical process, with events repeating with every passage around the loop, with a consequent duplication of the time traveler 'each time around,' are based on error." Any point in spacetime where a world-line arbitrarily closes on itself, Nahin remarks, does not happen twice or n-times, but *once*: "With the four-dimensional block-universe concept, all world lines lie tenseless in spacetime and so the encounter happens just once in spacetime—the older version speaks the same words he heard (even if he has forgotten them) when his older set of memories formed. He has to or else the past would be changed."[4] The problem with such loops is that narrative itself, the act of telling the loop, cannot remain tenseless nor without declension. In theory we can say that what happens once cannot happen twice at the same spacetime locus or we violate the principle of non-simultaneity. We cannot say, however, that a narrator or protagonist, moving around this loop and by the logic of this movement, would be condemned to speak the same words, do the same things, as he did the previous time. For by the logic of narrative, there is a former time, even if it is the *same time*. Though the protagonist advances on a curved spacelike line, he or she still advances in sequential fashion. If *the* past cannot be changed, the protagonist's past, as he meets it coming around the loop, apparently can change, if through memory he can at least opt not to continue the loop. This form of tale works at the level of a sequency-simultaneity paradox. Its effect on the subject, who must live the loop in the conventional sequential spacetime of the narrative, is one of tragic fatality.

Robert Silverberg offers two striking examples of this closed-loop scenario. "Absolutely Inflexible" is the story, in the idiom of Heinlein's famous "By His Bootstraps," of an individual who breaks with the continuum only to isolate his "subsequent" existence in a closed cycle in which categories like "beginning" and "end" or "cause" and "effect" cease to have meaning.[5] They cease to have meaning because, when the cycle (as in Heinlein) closes on two "versions" of the same person facing each other, there is no one present to answer the questions asked. Silverberg's story is set in a future world where time travel is common and human disease all but eradicated. The task of "inflexible" Judge Mahler is to send all travelers from the disease-ridden past to a quarantine prison on the moon. In a bow to *The Time Machine*, visitors are frequently scientists exploring the future in hopes of finding a better world. Unlike Wells, however, time travel here is one-way only; not only is there no way back, but there is the unpleasant surprise of Mahler waiting in this otherwise utopian future. One day a traveler comes before Mahler who, surprisingly, does not struggle but in fact seems to know and accept him as "absolutely inflexible," his nickname. But this traveler, it appears, has a two-way machine. Mahler, who has come to detest his role as judge, sees the machine as a way to break the deadlock by sending time travelers back and gives in to the temptation to try it. Predictably, he goes to the contaminated past, returns to his time, and is taken in custody to be judged. He reasons he has landed somewhere in his own future, perhaps "shortly after his own death." But rather than finding a new judge in place, he finds himself. What was a past encounter with the two-way traveler will be for this "new" Mahler the start of another ("future") segment of travel, return, and encounter with self.

Yet at this point, the protagonist realizes, tenses, even identities, cease to have meaning: "But if he's Mahler, then *who am I?*" He suddenly sees the "insane cycle complete": "But how did the cycle start? Where did the two-way rig come from in the first place? He had gone to the past to bring it to the present, to take it to the past, to . . ." (108) This is the same dilemma Heinlein's Bob Wilson expresses as he becomes the Diktor he had encountered "earlier" in his time travels: "Which comes first, the hen or the egg? If God created the world, who created God? Who wrote the notebook? Who started the chain?"[6] Bob realizes this question cannot be solved from inside the loop ("he had about as much chance understanding such problems as a collie has of understanding how dog food gets into cans"). He sees correctly that "he was the *only* Diktor," that "*there never had been two notebooks.*" And yet, living as if this were not so, he engages actively, in typical Heinlein fashion, the "next time" around: "He had work to do. . . . Everyone makes plans to provide for their future. He was about to provide for his past" (86). Bob, in a sense, is trapped in his condition by a mind as selfish in its outlook as his physical situation is isolated in extended spacetime. But why is the sadder and wiser Mahler, at the end of his narrative, so fatalistic, so willing to accept the absolute inflexibility of this loop without trying to warn or persuade the other self? Nothing stops him from revolting against fate except the horror of the situation. But if he now knows he must go to the moon, why, short of some fatal sense of damnation or original sin, does he ask to have his face shown from his contamination suit and thus confront the new Mahler with the old? The flaw here lies not (as Nahin sees it) in the "science" of the situation but rather in the human character itself.

French sf has a grim penchant for engineering infernal loops of this sort. The fixity of temporal progression is tragically underscored in Chris Marker's 1963 film *La Jetée*. The story is of a boy who witnesses a man shot on the jetty at Orly Airport as he runs toward a woman. The boy grows up to experience the destruction of Paris in a third world war. In an underground camp this survivor is used by scientists in a time travel experiment. Because he is fixated on the childhood memory and the face of the woman on the jetty, he is sent to the past. Here one of the offshoots of his perfecting techniques of time travel is an impossible love affair with a young woman from the pre-holocaust era. He is suddenly yanked from the past and sent to the future where, reciting the lines of this "sophism," which is the time loop, he tells these humans that, because they have survived, they must give him the energy source to take back that will allow them to survive. Back in the present, he is visited by time travelers from the future, who allow him the choice: return with them or go back to the past, to be with his beloved. Choosing the latter, he is once again on the jetty at Orly, a morning before the war. Seeing his beloved, he begins to run toward her, then notices a man from camp, who shoots him. As he falls, he realizes that he, as a little boy, is in the crowd watching him. What we have is a spiral that can never be broken: the boy who watches will never know the man shot is himself until the end of his line, too late to warn or turn in a different direction. The love that, in so many sonnets, could suspend the course of time, is in fact the element that holds together this fatal concatenation of events: the "love" of this woman is both effect and cause of his time traveling, the power that brings him fatally back to the jetty when, in the one seeming moment of choice, he is offered escape in the future. But he must die, so that the boy can see him die and fixate on the woman's face that will bring the loop around over and over. It is through the endless suffering and death of this single individual that the links between past, present, and future in this universe are upheld. The time traveler is a Sisyphus, or modern, tragic Atlas, forced through eternity to hold up the entire world with his sole being, with impossible love found and lost.

La Jetée creates a complex interaction between two opposing senses of time—the one finite and linear (the human "life line"), the other infinitely manipulable, in which mind seeks to exceed or extend the limits of biological time. This latter is the time of Zeno rather than Heraclitus. Instead of flux and the "river" of time, we have the Eleatic sense of mind as the master of material motion—what Marker's narrator calls a "sophism," in the sense not merely of tautology, but of *false*, even *bad*, arguments, this time in favor of temporal extension. The interplay of these two versions of time plays out at the level of interplay between two distinct media—images and spoken words. On one hand, there are the words spoken by the voice-over, the conventional narration that tells the story of the protagonist in linear fashion and one time only—from jetty to jetty—despite the circular nature of this story. The images, in contrast, are almost entirely stills, single frames without motion, as in a "photo-novel," though their use in the context of a "moving picture" is paradoxical, where what gives the illusion of motion is a number of such single frames passing over a light source at twenty-four frames per second. Marker's effect is that of the "snapshot," generated by running a long sequence of the same image to create a counterillusion of immobility.

In terms of linear, sequential time flow, still photos are islands of time, which can be rearranged in any order, as we do in photo albums. When moved out of chronological order, they become miniature time machines. These photos, in turn, present objects we might not think of as time machines except in this context—various statues as works of art that (like the pretensions of Shakespeare's sonnets) claim to "immortalize" by plucking its subject from the stream of "devouring Time." In the photos of the film, however, we see that time has taken its toll on these frozen monuments—we see statues without heads, stones that replace lost heads, ironic images insofar as it is through acts of the head or reason that these art works—attempts to escape from time—were conceived and executed in the first place. In addition, we see stuffed animals, even tree sections turned sideways, whose rings are made to measure "layers" of time, turning its linear flow into concentric rings. But all these objects are themselves old, defaced by vandalism or graffiti, signs of time's "blunting."

The protagonist's own time travel is depicted as a game of rearranging snapshots. He is able to "travel" because he is fixated on the single scene on the jetty, itself frozen as a silent scream. By shuffling images, time is "reversed" in terms of chronology, of past and present. Yet almost at once, as the still images appear, we notice a countermovement in the camera movements that gradually seek to penetrate and erode their flat, still surface. The camera travels up a still, as with the Arc de Triomphe, to discover, in the same frame but initially hidden from view, part of the arch is missing. Fades and dissolves are increasingly used as means of transition between "past" and "present." The dissolving and reframing become more insistent, and as this happens we experience a time miracle, in which two figures from different time frames gradually come to occupy a single frame where, despite visual differences between clothes styles, they gradually accept each other's presence, impossible but increasingly desirable to both. The ultimate scene—a Pygmalion-like awakening of the still image—occurs at the center of the film. The viewer witnesses rapid dissolves and reframings of the woman's sleeping face. The effect is an increasing sense of quasi-movement that culminates in a moment of real moving-picture time, as the woman opens her eyes and engages our gaze, putting her still life out of time momentarily in sync with our sense of normal temporal flow.

Following this comes the great love scene, which takes place in the Parisian Museum of Natural History, among glass cases filled with stuffed beings ("des bêtes éternelles"). In some marvelously shot "instants of time," these two impossible lovers are captured in moments of miraculous rapport—as if, with the ancient poets, love conquers all, time and death included. This is the longest sequence with these two in same frames, but in the logic of the film (they too are museum specimens behind glass for the "scientists" who manipulate them), this "time machine" is also an artifice of cruelly finite duration. The protagonist is returned to the infernal loop, in which this moment of love is but a necessary link, an instant of "perfect adjustment" that permits the voyage to the future and in turn the traveler's flight back to the jetty, after which the protagonist, as he falls shot by the man from the camp from which he has fled, realizes that no one escapes from time. But escape from time posits its opposite—entrapment in time, where the drama we have witnessed proves to be an infernal loop that the protagonist must repeat endlessly (the boy that is there to watch sees the man fall, will fixate on the image . . .), enduring love and loss forever, as *necessary* condition for the order of this circular universe: he must suffer endlessly in order for it to be. It is as if this protagonist—an everyman with everyman's yearning to find impossible duration in time—were the scapegoat for humanity's general *hubris* in its desire through art and technology to extend or escape time. Yet there is the other way, the way of the narrative voice-over, of the single timeline and its acceptance of biological time and its limits. The voice tells its tragic story once. And in the one moment when the still photo comes to "life" and the sleeping woman engages the viewer's gaze, the story enters our sense of time and shares our limited destiny, yet a destiny where love can occur, and peaceful death as well.

Forking Paths: The Sound of Thunder Model

Time travel stories to the past, in the post-Einsteinian age at least, are almost universally marked by a sense that that past is inviolable ("what has happened, has happened"). Travelers to the past not only should not attempt to change it but cannot do so. In many instances, to do so results not in any change in *the* past, but in simply erasing oneself from that timeline (which of necessity is the reader's timeline, the historical line he/she knows). To writers like Larry Niven, a traveler who goes to the past and changes his timeline only embroils himself in self-destructive paradox. For if his actions in the past result in the creation of a new timeline, this traveler could not have been born in it. Worse, the time machine was not invented in that timeline, hence could not have brought him to the place where the new timeline is generated. The fictional principle governing this seems to be what Fritz Leiber's *The Big Time* calls "the Law of Conservation of Reality."[7]

Mark Twain's Hank Morgan, in *A Connecticut Yankee in King Arthur's Court*, is hit on the head in nineteenth-century America and wakes up in sixth-century England. By introducing his modern technology to that period, he should have radically altered the course of history as we know it. But this has not happened. Hank's story, which the reader gets both from the mouth of the protagonist himself and from a manuscript (itself of dubious antiquity), is framed by comments from an "editor" comfortably placed in a quite unchanged setting contemporary to Twain's readers. Indeed, the conservation of reality seems justified, for the reader cannot ascertain that Hank actually *was* in the past. The bulletholes he claims to have shot in the sixth-century armor hanging in the local museum could just as easily have been put there, the editor notes, by Cromwell's troops having target practice. What is more, Hank's means of getting back from the past is as just as questionable as his way of going there, for Merlin has purportedly put a spell on him, placed him in a cave with his manuscript, and let him sleep until he awakens in his original time. Might not the whole thing have been a dream or delusion? In light of Leiber's Law, it certainly seems so. The reader's reality, if he is remain comfortable, must not change.

If it does, then something like a nightmare occurs. The most famous tale of violation of the past and its consequences is Ray Bradbury's "A Sound of Thunder."[8] In this story, elaborate preparations are made so that time travelers can go on safari in the prehistoric past, face and kill monsters from this horrific past— dragons in their own technological "Eden"—and return without having made the least change in that past. Here the devices used to sanitize their visit are, themselves, dubious—time bands, reconnaissance to find animals ready to die natural deaths, after-hunt surgery to remove bullets. But technological accuracy is not the point here (it cannot be fully achieved, since people still were in the past). The barrier in this story is not physical, but rather a poetic reality, even a theological one: that of the primal mystery of the Fall. Before even signing up for the "time safari," Bradbury's protagonist Eckels has a vision where he hears a sound like "a gigantic bonfire burning all of time, all the years and all the parchment calendars" (89). To cause the least change in the course of time, most of all to seek as an individual the source of humanity's fallen condition and hope to rectify it in any way, is to hasten the general Apocalypse, the end of all time. "Step on a mouse and you crush the pyramids" (92) says the lyrical safari guide Travis. All these people seem poetically aware of the wages of violation but at the same time are fatally drawn to make it happen. The "butterfly effect" must occur, and a terrified Eckels steps off the time band as he faces Tyrannosaurus Rex and later discovers that he has crushed a butterfly (were there butterflies in the Jurassic period?). No time paradoxes can prevent this transgression. The reason given, for example, for why travelers going back and forth on a same timeline, leaving from and returning to a same spacetime instant, do not meet themselves is simply "Time stepped aside." Eckels returns, however, to a present that has changed, necessarily for the worse. And the final emphasis in the story is on his horror: "Not a little thing like *that*! Not a butterfly . . . an exquisite thing, a small thing that could upset balances and knock down a line of small dominoes" (98). This is, in other words, a replay of the Fall itself, but at a worse degree of evil.

One common consequence of time travel to the past, where again the ancestor is Bradbury's "butterfly effect," is the creation of alternate timelines or "histories." In such scenarios, travelers do not erase themselves from the reader's timeline, but actually do things that effect a sufficient level of interference with events, causing the timeline to split. This "chronoclasm" shunts the reader's familiar history to some dead-end track, replacing it with a different sequence of events. This would be the real result of murdering the real Mohammed or the real Hitler, two prime "targets" for time hunters in such stories. Yet even in tales where this seems possible, we still encounter a sense of the past that opposes its unyielding rigidity—what is done is done and cannot be any other way. An example where a proposed freedom to generate alternate past scenarios is rudely brought into line is John Wyndham's "Opposite Number."[9] Comfortably married Peter Ruddle meets a double of himself in the company of Jean, the woman he once loved but did not marry. They appear to have come from old Whetstone's room where Jean's scientist father had worked on building a time machine until he died, leaving his notes to remain untouched. Confronting them, Peter learns that they occupy a world where the time machine was brought to completion, and in doing so they discovered time was "something similar to quantum radiation." The result is the following: "So every 'instant' an atom of time splits. The two halves then continue upon different paths and encounter different influences as they diverge—but they don't diverge as constant units; each of them is splitting every instant. . . . The pattern of it is the radiating rib of a fan" (133). The couple explains that their time machine (a "transfer chamber") has allowed a lateral move from one rib of the fan to another, in this case a world in which they did not marry, exploit Whetstone's notes, and build the time machine.

For Niven's dilemma, that time travelers to another timeline would find that their time machine had not been invented in that timeline and hence would be stranded there, Wyndham offers a solution—but one that only enforces the inflexibility of time, the hegemony of the past as that which determines the course of future time. Whetstone's original theory of time sees the past as a "frozen sea": "The present was represented by the leading edge of the ice, gradually building up and advancing. Behind it was the solid ice that represented the past; in front the still fluid water represented the future. . . . About the solid stuff behind, the past, he thought you could probably do nothing; but he reckoned . . . you ought to be able to find a way of pushing out a little ahead of the main freezing line. . . . In other words, by going a little ahead you would create a bit of the future which would *have* to come true" (132). But if, as said, past and future are so rigidly determined, which way is our time traveling couple moving, and does it make a difference? The two timelines may seem parallel, but the temporal instant that determines them both (the rib of the fan) is that in which the time machine is created. It is a moment, in Wyndham's circular scenario, where time is frozen. If that moment lies in the past on the timeline of the traveling couple (it had to be created before they could cross lines), it is in the future on Peter's timeline. What is more, their appearance in Peter's timeline turns that line (their future) into an exact copy of their timeline—a "past" where Peter will marry Jean after all, and the time machine be built, which will carry them in turn back to other aberrant timelines, forcing these endlessly into the same conformity. The vicious circle is iron proof that the sequence of past events that constitutes time cannot be altered, even with a time machine, which in this case only serves to reinforce the fact that time is an advancing glacier.

In terms of alternate histories, the reader accepts living in another timeline only if he/she can have its own past restored in the end. Time out of joint must be set right, if only *in extremis*, and by punishing the impudent time traveler who first sought to change things by killing Napoleon or Hitler or some such act causing a bifurcation of history lines. Ward Moore's *Bring the Jubilee* is a good example. The world the reader enters on the first page is an alternate United States where the South won the Civil War.[10] The protagonist Hodge grows up in a world that is a parallel America in terms of technological advancement, though with different manners and culture. The first three-fourths of the narrative is a *bildungsroman*, detailing Hodge's formation in a society moving toward the invention of time travel. In 1953 (the year of the novel's publication) Hodge, now a historian, is drawn fatally to return in time to witness the battle at Gettysburg where the South won the war. When he does so his presence, predictably, disrupts the movement of Confederate forces, causing them to lose the battle and subsequently the war. Moreover, he inadvertently kills a grandfather—not his own, but the ancestor of the woman who, in his continuum, invented the time machine he used to come to the past. At this point he should have erased his presence in this past altogether. But, because he kills the grandfather *after* he has effectively delayed the Southern troops, the damage is already done, and he remains stuck in this timeline. Hodge is "orphaned," now a stranger in a strange land which, to the reader, is his/her familiar history restored. The story of this alternate America is now reduced, through a device familiar to readers since Twain, of a manuscript found in a barn in Pennsylvania circa 1953. We can then, as Wells's Time Traveller suggested of his own story, take it as a dream or a lie. Readers need only blink, because their history was there all the time, unchanged and unchangeable. The punishment for those who invent time machines and try to change the past is the total, unalterable isolation of the time travelers.

The Solipsism Model

The human mind and its activity can affect the way we measure the flow of time. Relativity involves how the position of an observer affects the measurement of spacetime events. But what do we make of the sort of intervention in the spacetime continuum that John Wheeler describes as "participation"? "May the universe in some strange sense be 'brought into being' by the participation of those who participate? . . . The vital act is the act of participation. 'Participator' is the incontrovertible new concept given by quantum mechanics. It strikes down the term 'observer' of classical theory, the man who stands safely behind the thick glass wall and watches what goes on without taking part."[11] The first two models proposed—the Time Machine and the Sound of Thunder models—might be termed "classical" in that they afford time travelers, moving behind the "thick glass wall" of their time machines, *knowledge* of the future and the past, though they cannot change the nature and direction of temporal progress, whether on a single or on forking paths. Gary Zukav, however, sees quantum mechanics as providing a different, solipsistic experience of time: "Quantum mechanics is based on the idea of minimal knowledge of future phenomena (we are limited to knowing probabilities) but it leads to the possibility that our reality is what we choose to make it." Zukav goes on to see, in the light of this "new" physics, our sense of temporal continuum as an "illusion": "The illusion of events 'developing' in time is due to our particular type of awareness which allows us to see only the narrow strips of the total spacetime picture one at a time."[12] But, of course, what then is the "total spacetime picture"? In Cartesian terms, is it "located" out there in the extended world or in the mind of the participator? The awareness that totality in this latter realm is an "illusion" clearly has to do with our finite sense, and their limited ability to process the various phenomena input into our brains. Our sense of time, to the extent this is understood, is the product of all the time this processing requires in order for our minds to sense that "something has happened."

Sf has recently begun to explore the possibilities of this solipsistic or quantum model of time displacement. An example is Greg Egan's *Permutation City*.[13] In the novel, Egan creates a world where virtual humans (VH) are constructed from living humans but are "run" on a worldwide linked computer system, a VH Paul. But under such conditions, where is the VH you? You are everywhere and nowhere. All forms of human perception are created, but when they are created, it is by the machine. Thus time/space becomes impossible for the virtual human to perceive, except in the manner the machine wishes it to be perceived: "Paul struggled to imagine the outside world on his own terms, but it was almost impossible. Not only was he scattered across the globe, but widely separate machines were simultaneously computing different moments of his subjective time frame" (132).

A series of simple counts from 1 to 10 is generated for the VH Paul in random order and given to him. But he counts in perfect order with no hesitation. The assembly for the VH Paul is generated perfectly, so again Paul cannot tell what was "normal": "But . . . if the pattern that is me could pick itself out from the other events taking place on this planet . . . why shouldn't the pattern we think of as 'the universe' assemble itself, find itself, in exactly the same way?" (134). This alteration of the virtual human thought pattern can be done easily and seamlessly by the VH mind. The VH Paul can sense new ideas and concepts. He is becoming more knowledgeable about the universe—which is his universe. The human who is controlling the experiment (*the djinn*) is the template of which the VH is a copy, is he not?

"You're a Copy in a virtual environment under computer control. . . . [the djinn explained] You haven't visited any other worlds, you haven't built yourself out of fragments of distant galaxies."

Paul laughed: "Your stupidity is surreal. . . . I've had a glimpse of the truth behind everything: space, time, the laws of physics. . . . a new Principle of Equivalence. . . . Relativity threw out absolute space and time—but. . . . We have to throw out absolute cause and effect!" (135–136)

Time here is simply how fast the outside world is perceived and how fast memories are constructed; the process can be totally under the control of the machine building the VH: Peer "was working with his favorite timber . . . but slowing himself down to a time frame in which the trees grew fast enough to meet his needs would mean leaving Kate far behind" (251). A virtual universe (but one that is simpler than ours) is built by Kate, but not totally built. She assembles the initial seeding of the built world with pseudo-bacteria, and from there they evolve, since their universe easily allows it, although taking billions of years as our universe has done. The initial seed of life becomes a sentient being, much like bees who begin a philosophical discussion among themselves concerning their place in the universe: "Somehow, they still would have found a way to assemble themselves [Lambertians] from the dust . . . if the internal logic of their experience would have been enough to bring them into existence—then there was no reason to believe that they would ever be forced to conclude that their universe required a creator" (295). Paul and Kate decide to see if the rest of the VH decide to come back to the city. How long would this take? Years, perhaps centuries. Their time machine is merely a simple control pad of the computer system that is building them continuously. They can move forward in time easily, by just slowing the normal progression of *their* own time frame. The description of what follows blends Wells's departing time machine experience and Mrs. Watchett with Poul Anderson's *Tau Zero*:

they set up the simple time machine. Slowdown one hundred. The puppets using the walkway accelerated into invisible streaks. Slowdown ten thousand. Night and day chugged by, then flashed, then flickered—slowdown one million—then merged . . . the arc of the sun's path slid up and down the sky with the City's mock season, ever faster, until it smeared into a dull glowing band. (326)

Conclusion

Commentators from Arthur C. Clarke to Hawking have remarked that, if time travel is possible, why have we not seen any time travelers? Two explanations are possible: Either time travel is impossible, or time travelers are more clever than we are and hide their presence. Our conclusion is this: because of the Grandfather Paradox (and the local consistency of time/space), backward time travel is impossible; the past is fixed and cannot be altered. But time travel is possible in a forward direction, even if only at one second per second; the future is a blank slate to be written on. Of course, significant forward time travel can be done only after a time machine has been invented, and since that has not yet occurred, we are not "visitable" and never will be. We are safe from visitors and interference from the future. Forward time travel by others in the galaxy may be possible if they have already invented time machines. But just as galactic space travelers have not yet visited us, their time travelers have not either. We are either unknown to them or too backward to be interesting.

This may seem facetious. However, lack of observation is not proof unto itself, and the absence of time travelers proves little about the possibility of traveling through time. We cannot yet say with certainty that time travel is impossible. But even if it is true, our ability to write about travel in time, and to place imagined human beings in new, different, often terrifying situations, is not a bit diminished by its impossibility.

Notes

1. Robert Silverberg, *Up the Line* (New York: Ballantine Books, 1969), 38.

2. Robert A. Heinlein, " 'All You Zombies—,' " in *6 x H: Stories by Heinlein* (New York: Pyramid Books, 1961), 136.

3. H. G. Wells, *The Time Machine* (1895; New York: Berkley Books, 1957), 6.

4. Paul J. Nahin, *Time Machines: Time Travel in Physics, Metaphysics and Science Fiction* [first edition] (New York: American Institute of Physics, 1993), 208.

5. Robert Silverberg, "Absolutely Inflexible," in Silverberg, *Needle in a Timestack* (New York: Ballantine Books, 1966), 94–108. A later page reference in the text is to this edition.

6. Robert A. Heinlein, "By His Bootstraps," in Heinlein, *The Menace from Earth*, (New York: Signet Books, 1962), 87. A later page reference in the text is to this edition.

7. Fritz Leiber, *The Big Time* (New York: Ace Books, 1961), 23.

8. Ray Bradbury, "A Sound of Thunder," in Bradbury, *The Golden Apples of the Sun* (New York: Bantam Books, 1954), 88–99. Later page references in the text are to this edition.

9. John Wyndham, "Opposite Number," in Wyndham, *The Seeds of Time* (London: Michael Joseph, 1956), 140–161. Later page references in the text are to this edition.

10. Ward Moore, *Bring the Jubilee* (New York: Farrar, Straus, & Young, 1953).

11. J. A. Wheeler, K. S. Thorne, and C. Misner, *Gravitation* (San Francisco: Freeman Publishers, 1983), 1273.

12. Gary Zukav, *The Dancing Wu Li Masters: An Overview of the New Physics* (New York: Bantam Books, 1979), 29, 220.

13. Greg Egan, *Permutation City* (New York: Harper Prism Books, 1994). Later page references in the text are to this edition.

3

Impossible Times: Some Temporal Labyrinths in Science Fiction

Richard Saint-Gelais*

Anticipation

Anticipation, historically and statistically, is so rooted in the repertory of science fiction that the two terms have become virtually synonymous for the reading public. While the consanguinity of imaginary travel narratives and science fiction can be clearly demonstrated, writers definitely crossed a threshold when they began situating their narratives not in distant lands, but in an as yet unexplored realm: the future. [1] We are thus obliged to forsake our familiarity with anticipation—at least for a moment—to appreciate the narrative mutation that it has engendered. With anticipation, fiction can no longer claim to dwell at the core of reality (or merely within its limits), but affirms itself for what it is: an extension into the imaginary. Gulliver's countries, however implausible, allow for a reading that plays the game, that pretends to believe, or in any case a skeptical reading necessarily based on fragile criteria such as the outlandishness of the narrative or the gradual saturation of anthropological and geographical knowledge. Anticipation is entirely different; from the outset, the narrative refuses to be governed by reality or by what has already come to pass. Confronted with narratives of anticipation, readers can no longer play the game—or, at the very least, they must play a game whose rules have changed.

We have become so accustomed to playing the game, to modulating our readings according to it, that we are no longer even aware of the rules. The game nevertheless retains a quality of strangeness that is thrown into relief on closer examination of certain texts. The first of these qualities of strangeness stems from the temporal and logical ambiguity of anticipation. On one hand—I'm not the first to comment on this—anticipation should not be confused with prediction. Prediction is a serious proposition, in the pragmatic sense of the term—serious not

*Translated from the French by Carolyn Perkes.

because of its content, which may prove inaccurate, but by virtue of the enunciation, which implies a commitment on the part of the enunciator, so that we may accuse futurologists of having erred in their portraits of what the future holds for us. Anticipation, in contrast, stems from the imaginary, not hypothesis. It calls for another kind of reading that does not merely rely on comparing fictional situations with real situations, a reading that takes into account other values in the text, one that does not merely seek to classify texts such as George Orwell's *Nineteen Eighty-Four* under the label of unrealized predictions. Hence the paradox to which we shall return: Anticipation, even one that is outmoded or belied by the real future, never stops being an anticipation.

On the other hand, despite its imaginary nature, anticipation is situated in linear—albeit, imaginary—time, delineated by the past and the present. It is not dissociated from reality, but attached to it by a thread, however tenuous: The imaginary futures of science fiction remain virtual continuations of the present. This is not without consequences for the status of fiction: If anticipation is perceived as an extrapolation based on the present moment of writing, we come to suppose that the fictional world can only refer to our own, the distinction being that it is perceived and described at an ulterior stage of development. The emphasis on the chronological gap thus coincides somewhat surreptitiously with the premise that would postulate an ontological continuity between reality and the imagined future. Ultimately, anticipation merely becomes a possible extension of reality—which brings us back, curiously, to a futurological concept of science fiction. Two examples illustrate this type of extension.

The first example is taken from Peter Fitting's critical reading of Suzette Haden Elgin's *Native Tongue*:

Another of the basic premises of *Native Tongue*, published in 1984, is that in 1991—a mere seven years later—an amendment to the U. S. Constitution will pass which makes women legally minors. This is preposterous. . . . I cannot believe that it would be any easier for a minority of bigots and fundamentalists to draft and pass such an overwhelming denial of women's basic rights in such a short space of time while remaining within the framework of the U.S. Constitution. This inconsistency undermines my ability to take the novel seriously. Such a misreading of the contemporary political situation makes me skeptical about the alternatives it offers.[2]

Fitting's argumentation is relatively complex. Writing in 1989, Fitting does not compare the future described in *Native Tongue* with the real present; he does not reproach Elgin for having formulated an anticipation that didn't "come true." Rather, his criticism is based on the unlikelihood that such a future, envisioned as of 1984 could ever come to pass in 1991. The temporal movement thus implies a projection into the past and then on the basis of this past, a second projection to the near future such as it might have been conceived of in 1984. (We might, however, wonder whether knowledge of the real future did not influence Fitting: of course, one could have declared *Native Tongue* to be implausible in 1984, but it was easier to do in 1989, when one knew, as Fitting did at the time of writing, that this future would not materialize.) Nevertheless, anticipation is being judged here in terms of its plausibility, the implicit argument being that a "good" anticipation must be located in the straight line of the present and deliver a "probable" future taking account that which the present allows us to foresee. This argument is only valid if one adopts an aesthetic that makes anticipation pure projection. One could instead approach *Native Tongue* not as factual veridicity but as a cautionary tale by stressing its argumentative value rather than its predictive validity. Just as one could have considered *Native Tongue*'s version of 1991 as an imaginary world valid in itself and not in terms of its conformity to either empirical or projected reality.

The second example is more surprising. Christopher Priest's *Indoctrinaire* tells the story of a journey in time undertaken by the character Wentik, who finds himself projected into the future. In his reading of a future essay entitled "Brazil—Concise Social History," Wentik learns of a series of interpolated events, more specifically a world war that would have taken place in 1979. At least that is what we read in the original edition of *Indoctrinaire*, published in 1971.[3] In the 1979 edition, however, a "minor" detail was changed: the world war described in "Brazil—Concise Social History" now takes place in 1989.[4] A curious detail, since by postponing the fatal deadline by ten years, the text seems to try to preserve if not the novel's predictive value, then at least the reader's capacity for belief. The changed date is all the more strange given the clearly speculative nature of Priest's novel which should make such considerations extraneous.

In a way, the republishing of Priest's novel seems intended to rescue it, at least temporarily, from the fate that usually befalls anticipations outmoded—and belied—by the real passage of time: the fate that abruptly transforms them from anticipation narratives to narratives about parallel worlds.[5] For instance, the fact that a World State did not emerge in 1965 can provide sufficient cause to consider H. G. Wells's *The Shape of Things to Come* as an involuntary case of a parallel universe narrative. Anticipation narratives thus have the curious ability to switch subgenres under the pressure of external events. This phenomenon, that the first science fiction writers did not perhaps anticipate, is now a common occurrence—to the point where one might wonder whether contemporary science fiction doesn't rely, consciously or not, on the passage of time to produce some disconcerting effects. From this perspective, the relationship between reality and anticipation appears in a new light. Reality is not only an external criterion for the evaluation of the accuracy of an anticipation, but an intrinsic component in the ontological games of science fiction, either because the date of writing must be kept in mind to maintain the novel's status as anticipation narrative or because anticipated futures inevitably end up appearing as futures of the past, futures that do not stem from a linear concept of time.[6]

One of the most spectacular illustrations of this phenomenon is found in Terry Gilliam's film *Brazil*, a disconcerting film that seems to plunge viewers into the future, thus an anticipation; yet the future that is proposed seems curiously nostalgic. There are computers, but with their cathode-ray screens and manual keyboards, they seem to originate from the imagination of an artist working in the 1930s or 1940s. Are we still talking about anticipation? Before answering, it would be useful to take a small detour around the idea of parallel past.

Uchronia

Anticipation is not science fiction's only temporal mode. Writers may locate their narratives in the near or distant future—at least with respect to the time of writing. A writer may also locate his or her narrative not as an extension of our temporal line but within another temporal line, a line that diverges from the path taken by our history. We are no longer in the realm of anticipation or the imagined future; we have entered the realm of uchronia, or the reinvented past.

The principle underlying each uchronia is the same: It proposes a fictional world that implies a history whose course has deviated from the course of real history. To do this, the uchronia must effectuate a bifurcation in the framework of real historical events at any given point deemed to be decisive: For instance, the outcome of a military conflict such as the Civil War, a successful (or failed) assassination attempt on a political leader, and so on. The principle is simple, but the outcome proves to be considerably disturbing. In any case it distinguishes uchronia from the more widely known forms of science fiction: imaginary travel narratives and anticipations. The latter, as Emmanuel Carrère notes, do not formally contradict our knowledge of the world: "there is sufficient room elsewhere (or in the future) to rule out any threat to the status quo between reality and the imaginary."[7] Things happen quite differently with uchronia, which produces a pronounced effect of interference between the real present and its altered version—between, for instance, the 1997 as we know it and the 1997 that might have followed a German victory in 1945. If uchronia has shock value, it is because it disrupts the "peaceful coexistence" ordinarily maintained between reality and the imaginary. With uchronia, the imaginary is not located in an obscure zone of reality (a distant land or an unrealized future era); the imaginary hits reality head-on, confronting us with an irrevocable shift from coexistence to open contradiction. What is important here is that this contradiction be readable. It should be remembered that all fiction triggers this kind of interference between reality and the imaginary: All fiction renders fictional characters having fictional adventures within a framework that appears to coincide with reality. But while problematic in principle, this insertion of the imaginary into a supposed reality is conventional enough to be neutralized by the reader; here the reader does not ask whether the novel's world has been fictionalized by the presence of fictional individuals. Uchronia disrupts this delicate balance: It is the entire fictional world that tips over into the imaginary.

Even so, it should be noted that uchronia is not a homogeneous realm, first because the writer's attitude may vary between nostalgia (for a state of affairs that the real course of history has interrupted) and fear (of a disturbing event that has not in fact occurred but that is developed by the narrative in a more or less masochistic manner). Uchronia thus overlaps with utopia and dystopia; It may also be located beyond these two genres when it explores historical alternatives in a humorous mode, neither valuing nor devaluating the historical possibilities. The reader's judgment is also a factor. The reader may, as Paul K. Alkon suggests in *Origins of Futuristic Fiction*, see uchronia as a rhetorical device: "Uchronias of alternate histories . . . may also be more or less explicitly intended as portraits of possible futures presented for convenience as though their distinctive features had already come into being."[8] Judgments about parallel history aside, uchronia may take a variety of distinctive textual forms. I will emphasize three such forms: imaginary historiography, novelistic uchronia, and uchronic artifacts.

Imaginary historiography probably constitutes the first form of uchronia. This form can be traced to such founding works as Louis Geoffroy's *Napoléon apocryphe*[9] and Charles Renouvier's *Uchronie*.[10] These works are distinct from the novel because they relate, as would a history book or manual, the events that bridge the gap between history as we know it to a parallel history. In Geoffroy's book, Napoleon never experienced military defeat and extended his empire over the entire world. In Renouvier's book, the Roman Empire did not adopt Christianity, which remained a marginal religion. These uchronias do not contain characters in the narrow sense; the actors are entire collectivities or known historical characters who are called upon to play roles that differ from the ones they actually played in real history, thereby emphasizing a sometimes spectacular gap between history and parallel history.

Today, novelistic uchronia is much more common than imaginary historiography. Well known examples include Philip K. Dick's *The Man in the High Castle*,[11] Keith Roberts's *Pavane*,[12] and William Gibson and Bruce Sterling's *The Difference Engine*.[13] Some mainstream novels also come to mind, such as the Russian writer Vassily Aksyonov's *The Island of Crimea*[14] or Kingsley Amis's *The Alteration*.[15] Novelistic uchronia can be distinguished from imaginary historiography in at least two ways. First, the characters in the uchronic novel are not the counterparts of great historical figures, but are entirely fictional; their actions do not necessarily have an important impact on the course of history. Second, the uchronic novel does not present the chain of events leading to the historical bifurcation in a didactic manner; instead, it is immediately located in a parallel setting that the reader must reconstruct little by little, with the help of more or less explicit allusions scattered throughout the text. The uchronic novel is therefore a narrative that presupposes—rather than exposing—a deviation from history; the deviation is not the object of the text, but a background against which a novelistic plot stands out, a plot that sometimes is not intrinsically science-fictional except for its insertion into a curiously unfamiliar world. This is the case in *The Man in the High Castle*, in which the otherness of the fictional world is gradually revealed, not through a detailed and explicit expose but rather through the dispersion of details throughout the text: the American Robert Childan has a conversation with a Japanese client, Mr. Tagomi, a painful conversation about respecting a "code" that is unknown to the reader; later on, Childan bows spontaneously when two other clients praise the quality of the items in his boutique. These and other clues, such as the mention of "Marin County, PSA" and of the last bomb to have fallen on San Francisco, are sufficient to allow readers to revise their frame of reference. But these clues are not adequate to recast the frame of reference that underlies the narrative. *The Man in the High Castle* is thus presented as a puzzle, a game of hide-and-seek between the narrative and the reader—or, from another perspective, a thin narrative thread drawn through a fictional world that is for the most part invisible, except when the narrative allows for brief and enigmatic glimpses.

At least, this would be the case if not for the cover blurbs telling readers that *The Man in the High Castle* is set in a world in which Japan and Germany emerged as the victors of the Second World War. We are all familiar with jacket blurbs that "sell the goods," that lay bare the underpinnings of the imagined fictional world before the reader begins reading and that abort the "encyclopedic suspense" created by many works of science fiction. This practice dispels the reader's legitimate claim to astonishment. What self-respecting detective-novel reader would tolerate a flyleaf that divulges the criminal's identity at the outset? Science fiction reading resembles detective-novel reading except that instead of seeking to reconstruct an isolated fact (a murder), the reader seeks an imaginary frame of reference. This reconstruction is affected—in fact, simplified, and in some cases short-circuited—by jacket blurbs that provide the answers from the start, even before the questions arise. In other words, books, as editorial devices, may contradict the text as an enigmatic device, as a mechanism that, especially in contemporary science fiction, abandons didacticism and situates itself in a context taken for granted and therefore all the more disorienting.

This brings us to the third type of uchronia: the uchronic artifact. This type of uchronia further amplifies the paradoxical treatment of fictional worlds, making them into obvious facts that aren't so obvious to the reader. Such artifacts do not describe parallel history in a didactic way, any more than they tell a story located in an altered history. Instead, they constitute sample texts that a parallel civilization might have produced—and that end up in the hands of real readers like you or me. What essays, what geographical maps, what newspaper stories would the inhabitants of such a parallel world read? Uchronic artifacts, mysterious objects passing from an imagined universe to another (ours), provide us with some indications. Let's take, for instance, "The Index" by J. G. Ballard[16] or *Les trois Rimbaud* (*The Three Rimbaud*) by Dominique Noguez.[17] The first text is a fragment of an autobiography destroyed under obscure circumstances, and about a disturbing character, Henry Rhodes Hamilton, who has come into contact with some of the important figures of the twentieth century—including Adolf Hitler, Ingrid Bergman, Dwight Eisenhower, and Lee Harvey Oswald—and who, as we might have guessed, has profoundly influenced the course of the twentieth century. But this is not our twentieth century; it is different (for example, there is an entry in the index devoted to Pope Hadrian IV) and it is fragmented, just as enigmatic as our own century would be for someone whose knowledge of it would be limited to a fragment of a biography about, say, Winston Churchill.

Les trois Rimbaud is presented as a literary biography like any other: Dominique Noguez describes the aesthetic evolution of the French poet, Arthur Rimbaud, until his death in 1936. This biography is not quite so trivial when we recall that in actual fact, Rimbaud did not die in 1936, but in 1891, so that the last forty years plunges us into a literary history that is both plausible and perfectly imaginary—a history that Noguez "traces back" with the help of imaginary documents: writers' homages, excerpts from criticism, and fragments of novels written by the parallel Rimbaud. The entire text takes the form of a conventional monograph except for one "detail": It deals with a fiction. Better yet, the book as such is a fiction: On the whole, it is as though we were reading a work written and published in another world. Noguez's astuteness also stems from imagining that the first part of Rimbaud's literary career—the only period that actually occurred—is, in the parallel universe of the book, a period that is nearly forgotten by the public; the work's task is to allow the imaginary public to discover the only facts that are known to us (and rightly so!). Hence the unusual reversal of perspective that observes the "real" Rimbaud (for us) in a uchronic light. Our universe ultimately becomes a variation of a parallel universe, thereby losing the ontological privilege of being the initial universe from which the fictional versions can be spun.

Pseudo-Anticipations

Both anticipation and novelistic uchronia have become, over the decades, familiar models for science fiction readers. The effects of such familiarity should not be underestimated: As anticipation and uchronia have become familiar, readers have developed a repertory of corresponding strategies. I think that such strategies explain, to a large extent, the general movement over a century that has caused science fiction to progressively abandon didacticism (the explicit description of the peculiar features of fictional worlds) in favor of discursive devices that presuppose and take for granted fictional worlds that readers must reconstruct throughout their readings of such narratives and that, in certain cases, remain inaccessible.

The evolution of the generic competence of science fiction readers has also fostered the emergence of increasingly audacious narrative formulas, particularly with respect to the treatment of temporality. I will focus on one of these formulas, what we could call pseudo-anticipation. The best way of describing it is with an example, the first that I have encountered: Philip K. Dick's *Ubik*.

At first, *Ubik* seems a standard anticipation: First published in 1969, the novel takes place in 1992. But even when we bracket out the differences between the novel's 1992 and the real 1992, *Ubik*, on close scrutiny, proves to be a rather unusual anticipation. Let's examine the following passage:

"If Runciter were alive," [Joe] said, "sitting out here in this lounge, everything would be okay. I know it but I don't know why. . . . Do you remember dentists?" he asked Al.

"I don't remember, but I know what they were."

"People's teeth used to decay."

"I realized that," Al said.

"My father told me what it used to feel like, waiting in a dentist's office. Every time the nurse opened the door you thought, it's happening. The thing I've been afraid of all my life."[18]

We might note that this excerpt presents the world that we know—a world where dentists are commonly known to exist—as a world that is now distant and almost enigmatic in the eyes of the characters. In other words, facts that are taken for granted by the reader—deteriorating teeth, dentists, and the fear they inspire—have, in this fictional world, become the object of indirect knowledge ("My father told me"), a knowledge that is about to be lost. What is fascinating here is that the usual relationship between the reader's frame of reference and the imagined world seems inverted. On one hand, the imaginary world is strange in the eyes of the reader—even though science fiction readers are accustomed to such strangeness—but, on the other hand, the reader's world has become strange to the characters. Dick thus throws into relief the fact that otherness does not only work in one direction; he also shows that the real world is only one frame of reference among others.

But things are not quite so simple. We have just seen that information that is familiar to us has become past knowledge for the characters. This fact is likely to confirm for us, indirectly, the reality of the world in which teeth deteriorate and where one has to go to the dentist. In addition, this world appears to the characters as a real world, although an elapsed one. The world of *Ubik* seems therefore to be a fictional extrapolation, but whose premise is the real world of 1969.

However, one question threatens to overturn this premise. The question is: When did the dentists disappear so as to be relegated to the fringe of the characters' memory? The reader asking this question could, as I did, do a little arithmetic. The story, as I have indicated, takes place in 1992; we must understand that dentists disappeared several decades earlier, since Al Hammond, an adult, does not remember them (we later learn that he is in his thirties). The disappearance of dentists can be dated to at least the end of the 1960s or, more likely, further back in the past. The novel, once again, was published in 1969. Taking all these factors into consideration, we must conclude that the past to which the characters allude does not correspond to the frame of reference of the reader—either the reader of 1969 or today's reader. The evoked past is just as fictional as the world of 1992 described in the novel. What first seemed a speculation based on real data is in fact an imaginary world derived from an equally imaginary past.

I would add that the interest of this excerpt stems from its very unobtrusiveness, which means that the reader has an initial tendency to consider his or her frame of reference as the point of departure for the science-fictional speculation before noticing that this point of departure must be revised. But the adjustment remains disquieting since the only information that we have about the 1960s in the novel is the fact that dentists had already disappeared. This is just enough evidence to let us imagine a past that may be quite different from the real past, a past about which we know nothing and is thus as fascinating as it is mysterious.

Ubik is obviously a peculiar case, but a peculiar case that suggests a general lesson: Dick's novel invites the reader to mistrust the reflex that causes us to anchor our anticipations in the real world, either in the past or the present as we know them, the reflex to suppose that speculation could only be rooted in the writer's reality. Moreover, *Ubik* is not an isolated example. Other texts deliberately set out to obscure the reader's reference points, to construct second-degree speculations, that is to say, anticipations themselves based on parallel settings-in other words, pseudo-anticipations. Thus, Alkon's *Origins of Futuristic Fiction* examines a now forgotten text, Jacques Guttin's novel *Épigone* (1659). *Épigone* is an anticipation, yet a very strange anticipation, for, as Alkon shows, "the 'future' in which *Épigone* lives is in effect a future that might follow from some other history rather than the one we have known in our world."[19] *Épigone* is a curiosity that has probably not influenced twentieth-century science fiction. Nevertheless, many examples of contemporary science fiction bear some resemblance to it in that they propose not only a future, but also a temporality that is obviously imaginary. One of the most interesting examples is the novel *1985*, by Hungarian writer György Dalos.

Like *Ubik*, Dalos's *1985* is at first glimpse an anticipation: The first edition, in German, appeared in 1982. But even at the time of publication, the anticipation could only have seemed impossible: In 1982, one could not have imagined that three years later the geopolitical situation described in the novel would actually come to pass. The novel's anticipation is therefore immediately read as a parallel history, even before reality invalidates it: It is therefore a pseudo-extrapolation.

Yet the situation is much more complex because *1985* calls for an intertextual reading: Of course it is a sequel to Orwell's *Nineteen Eighty-Four*, a novel whose status of anticipation is no longer the subject of any doubt.[20] Thus we have an extension both in terms of the content (astonishing enough in itself), referring to the Orwellian anticipation and in terms of the composition, a sort of pre-uchronia, that is, an anticipation compelled to slip (and on the brink of slipping) into uchronia.

The interest of this novel also stems from the fact that it demonstrates the fictional nature of anticipation. We have seen that anticipation is a fiction, but a limited fiction, which is based on a present and past identified with the present and the past moment of writing. In contrast, in the case of *1985*, the basis for the extrapolation is overtly fictional. The device is therefore more subtle than that of Anthony Burgess who, in his novel also entitled *1985*, attempts to "rectify" Orwell's anticipation by proposing a supposedly more plausible anticipation based on what "really" happened in the 1980s. Dalos, in contrast, constructs a sort of second-degree anticipation: a fictionalization about characters and situations that are in themselves fictional.

In fact, the temporal structure of Dalos's *1985* is more complicated because the novel is presented by a somewhat indiscrete "editor" who frames the text with his introduction and footnotes. As the novel progress, the footnotes become less and less academic and more and more autobiographical, relating the editor's difficulties with the authorities of his era. The editor is not writing in 1985 or 1982, but in 2035, fifty years after the novel's events. The chronicle of events is based on various archival documents dating from 1985—the editor's 1985, which is perfectly imaginary in our eyes. Through the editor's notes, we discover a new anticipation, even more distant in time, but one that is constructed, like the preceding ones, on an imaginary basis: The society of 2035 is nothing more than an extrapolation based on a fictional 1985, itself based on the 1984 imagined by Orwell in 1948.

We understand more clearly now why Terry Gilliam's *Brazil* is disconcerting: Like Dick in *Ubik*, like Guttin in *Épigone*, like Dalos in *1985*, Gilliam's film does not show us a future but a future of the past—a future that seems to come straight out of the imagination of an artist of the 1930s or 1940s—briefly, a pseudo-anticipation. These examples demonstrate that science fiction, while not turning its back on reality, has ultimately constructed a considerably extensive and complex field of fictional explorations, capable of evolving according to its own logic and thereby continually inventing and reinventing time.

Notes

1. Paul K. Alkon examines this crucial stage in his *Origins of Futuristic Fiction* (Athens: University of Georgia Press, 1987).

2. Peter Fitting, "The Turn from Utopia in Recent Feminist Fiction," in Libby Falk James and Sarah Webster Goodwin, editors, *Feminism, Utopia, and Narrative* (Knoxville: The University of Tennessee Press, 1990), 147.

3. Christopher Priest, *Indoctrinaire* (Richmond Hill, Ontario: Pocket Books, 1971), 112.

4. Priest, 116.

5. See Brian W. Aldiss's introduction to the 1965 edition of *Space, Time and Nathaniel* (London: Panther Books, 1979), 12.

6. Science fiction, of course, came to be aware of this phenomenon and, moreover, to integrate it recursively in its thematic repertory; thus, for instance, John Crowley's orthogonal time as described in his "Great Work of Time" in *Novelty* (Garden City, NY: Doubleday & Co., 1989), 63.

7. Emmanuel Carrère, *Le détroit de Behring: Introduction à l'uchronie* (Paris: P.O.L. éditeur, 1986). 8–9.

8. Alkon, 129.

9. Louis Geoffroy, *Napoléon apocryphe, 1812–1832: Histoire de la conquête du monde et de la monarchie universelle* (Paris: Tallandier, 1983). Originally published in 1836.

10. Charles Renouvier, *Uchronie (L'utopie dans l'histoire), esquisse historique apocryphe du développement de la civilisation européenne, tel qu'il n'a pas été, tel qu'il aurait pu être* (Paris: Fayard, 1988). Originally published in 1876.

11. Philip K. Dick, *The Man in the High Castle* (Toronto: Popular Library, 1964). Originally published in 1962.

12. Keith Roberts, *Pavane* (London: Panther, 1970). Originally published in 1968.

13. William Gibson and Bruce Sterling, *The Difference Engine* (New York: Bantam, 1992). Originally published in 1991.

14. Vassily Aksyonov, *The Island of Crimea* (London: Abacus, 1986). Translated from the Russian by Michael Henry Hein. Originally published in 1981.

15. Kingsley Amis, *The Alteration* (London: Penguin, 1988). Originally published in 1976.

16. J. G. Ballard, "The Index," in Ballard, *War Fever* (London: Collins, 1990), 171–176.

17. Dominique Noguez, *Les trois Rimbaud* (Paris: Minuit, 1986).

18. Philip K. Dick, *Ubik* (New York: Dell, 1970), 86–87. Originally published in 1969.

19. Alkon, 41.

20. At least, this is the accepted view. I have demonstrated that an attentive reading of the "Annex on Newspeak" allows one to infer that *Nineteen Eighty-Four* is in fact an historical novel published in the mid-twenty-first century. See my *L'empire du pseudo: Modernités de la science-fiction* (Quebec: Nota bene, 1999), 328–330, and Larry W. Caldwell's chapter in this volume.

4

The Jaws of the Intellect Grip the Flesh of Occurrence: Order in Time Travel

David Leiby

About halfway through Keith Laumer's *Dinosaur Beach* the two main characters attempt to sort through their horribly snarled timelines in the following manner:

> "So I did the only thing that occurred to me. I used the station facilities for a jump I hoped would put me back at Nexx Central. It didn't work. In the absence of a programmed target, I reverted back along my own timeline and ended ten years in my subjective past. A class-A paranomaly, breaking every regulation in the book."
>
> "Regulations don't cover our situation," she said. "You had no control over matters. You did what seemed best."
>
> "And blew a job that was successfully completed and encoded on the master timeplot ten years ago. One curious item in that connection is that the Karg I was supposed to take out—and didn't—was the same one I hit in Buffalo. Which implies that the Buffalo sequence followed from the second version rather than the original one."
>
> "Or what you're considering the alternate version. Maybe it isn't. Perhaps you doubling-back was assimilated as a viable element in the revised plot."[1]

Thus the protagonist, a time agent named Ravel, and Mellia Gayl, his companion throughout most of the harrowing adventures in the novel, analyze the tangled timelines that have stranded them at the time station known throughout the eons as "Dinosaur Beach." To this point in the story, Ravel, the time agent, has completed an assignment which required that he establish an alternate identity complete with an apartment and girlfriend, and that he track down and disable an entity derisively described as "Karg" because of its non-human, machine-like characteristics before the "Karg" can damage the timeline in twentieth-century Buffalo. Having successfully completed that mission, Ravel returns to the station at Dinosaur Beach for adjustment and reassignment. The adjustment includes having his memory of his just completed mission removed. Before Ravel accomplishes this, an enemy faction in the ongoing time war attacks the station at Dinosaur Beach, completely destroying the installation. Of course, Ravel is shunted off into time somewhere by his boss before the transmitters and the remainder of the station are leveled. Having found himself bereft of aid of any sort from the time service, he uses his personal energy to make a jump in time; unfortunately, this lands him in the midst of another mission that he had concluded ten years before. His next jump brings him back to Dinosaur Beach, but in a much later era, an era containing Mellia Gayl when the previously cited discussion occurred.

Attempting to analyze the structure of time is the usual occupation of the protagonist of a time travel story. In order to survive, protagonists must come to understand the physical laws of their fictional world. True, survival in one way or another is every protagonist's problem; however, the necessity of reaching an immediate understanding of certain physical laws is more likely to be the case in time travel than it is in traditional narratives. A protagonist in a narrative set in the mundane world can make certain assumptions about the nature of time, but a time traveler must figure out how his world works to survive from moment to moment. At some point in the narrative—as a rule, rather early—the protagonist discovers that the conception of time which governs his/her world is different from that which governs the mundane world. Is the conception of time in the world of the story linear, branching, parallel, or circular? Different geometric forms of time provide different problems for the protagonist to cope with. In the segment of *Dinosaur Beach* previously quoted, we have two main characters analyzing a plot—not the plot of the novel, of course. They are discussing Ravel's past as if it were part of a plot, a malleable plot at that. To sort these matters out, these agents who are a part of a massive timesweep effort must bear in mind the concept of various timelines coexisting. Moreover, Ravel and Mellia are trying to determine the ordering of events in each of these timelines.

If the main characters focus on the order of events in the story, readers will focus on the order of events. Thus, readers will be forced to focus on the activity of plotting, will be forced to draw on their knowledge (experience) of traditional literary conventions. Time travel narratives have metafictional characteristics inasmuch as they encourage readers to think about the construction of narrative. If we analyze these narratives with those characteristics in mind, we gain new perspectives on plot, the concept of flashback, and the convention of beginning a narrative *in media res*. In short, one reason readers are interested in time travel narratives is that the subject matter mirrors the experience of reading a narrative. It's not so much that these narratives are playful or melodramatic, or that "a circular causal structure may signalize a frivolous content."[2] They may be all or none of these. Rather, the act of reading such narratives may cause a reader to think about the process of making fiction.

Metafiction is a type of fiction that directs a reader's attention to the elements of fiction itself—plot, point of view, and so on. But time travel narratives differ from some usual notions about metafictional narratives. Patricia Waugh says that metafictional narratives "tend to be constructed on a principle of a fundamental and sustained opposition: the construction of a fictional illusion and the laying bare of that illusion. In other words, the lowest common denominator of metafiction is simultaneously to create a fiction and to make a statement about the creation of that fiction." She then claims that "contemporary metafictional writing is both a response and a contribution to an even more thoroughgoing sense that reality or history are provisional: no longer a world of eternal verities but a series of constructions, artifices, impermanent structures."[3]

Nevertheless, in general, time travel narratives differ significantly from the self-reflexive works of Robert Coover and Thomas Pynchon, for example. In *The Metafictional Muse*, Larry McCaffery characterizes some of the work of postmodern writers such as Robert Coover, Donald Barthelme, and William H. Gass as unlike

the kinds of social or psychological studies that dominated fictional tastes in America from 1930 to 1960. Not only did postmodern works tend to be more artificial but also they became more formally outrageous and darkly humorous. A kind of bleak, absurdist comedy permeates the epistemological skepticism of most of the contemporary authors; they tend to treat ironically the attempts of their characters to settle on secure systems and truths. As a result, we observe their characters continually seeking answers and assurances, creating their own systems, and then becoming imprisoned in them, finally claiming they can't go on in such a world and then going on anyway. At the same time we are usually aware that the writer's irony is also self-directed, that their own efforts to organize elements into a work of art are as arbitrary and tenuous as those of their characters.[4]

As a rule, time travel narratives are not formally outrageous—they rarely feature stream-of-consciousness techniques, sight poems, or two-page-long sentences—although they may be obviously artificial, that is, the narrator may speak directly to the reader or neglect to disguise the fact that his tale has been created of whole cloth, as it were. Nor do these time travel writers appear, as a group, to be skeptics who treat their characters' attempts to discover truth ironically. Characters in time travel narratives are continually seeking answers—particularly to questions concerning the structure of time in their worlds. Nevertheless, time travel narratives comment on the mechanics of narratives themselves. A writer need not intend to create fictions that comment on the nature of fiction to accomplish something of that same effect.

In nearly every time travel narrative the central issue is that of order, the protagonist's concern with order, and thus with plot. Hence the reader becomes unusually aware of the ordering activity the narrator of the story is engaged in. Seymour Chatman argues that "our minds inveterately seek structure, and they will provide it if necessary."[5] By being concerned with the ordering of events in a time travel narrative, by wondering what will transpire if and when two temporal manifestations of a character appear in the same scene, by speculating on the ability of a character to escape a time loop, and so on, a reader focuses on the construction of the plot just as a writer does. Thus the conversation between Ravel and Mellia in *Dinosaur Beach* mirrors the normal plotting concerns of both the writer and reader of traditional fiction.

We can better understand how readers cope with these stories laden with contradictions and anomalies by analyzing the element of fiction we call plot. In the opening pages of *Reading for the Plot: Design and Intention in Narrative*, Peter Brooks offers a useful definition of the term:

Plot . . . is hence an embracing concept for the design and intention of narrative, a structure for those meanings that are developed through temporal succession, or perhaps better: a structuring operation elicited by, and made necessary by, those meanings that develop through succession and time. A further analysis of the question is suggested here by a distinction made by the Russian Formalists, that between *facula* and *sjuzet*. *facula* is defined as the order of events referred to by the narrative, whereas *sjuzet* is the order of events presented in the narrative discourse. The distinction is one that takes on evident analytic force when one is talking about a Conrad or a Faulkner, whose dislocations of normal chronology are radical and significant, but it is no less important in thinking about apparently more straightforward narratives, since any narrative presents a selection and ordering of material. We must, however, recognize that the apparent priority of *facula* to *sjuzet* is in the nature of a mimetic illusion, in that *facula*—what really happened—is in fact a mental construction that the reader derives from the *sjuzet*, which is all that he ever directly knows. This differing status of the two terms by no means invalidates the distinction itself, which is central to our thinking about narrative and necessary to juxtapose two modes of order and in the juxtaposing to see how ordering takes place.[6]

Thus, readers of time travel narratives are encouraged to think of plot. The protagonist pondering the nature of time in his/her fictional world mirrors the writer reflecting on the structure of the plot in his narrative. In this particular characteristic, time travel narratives resemble detective narratives: The reader observes the protagonist working through the tangled web of events. Of course, a protagonist of a time travel narrative normally struggles with an analysis of a set of events that is as yet incomplete, whereas the protagonist of a detective story focuses on an event (usually a murder or a theft) that occurred before the first event presented by the narrator. Thus, the *facula* of a detective story does not change; although it may appear to change constantly as a reader works through the text, it's just because the proper order of events is not yet clear to the reader. However, the *facula* of a time travel narrative may very well be, or at least appear to be, incomplete at the time the narrator begins his tale. This mutability of the fabula invests the tale with a sense of incompleteness, a condition perhaps increasing the interest of a reader of such a narrative; a reader's attention focuses on the construction of the *facula* (the complete story that the actual narrative implies). Thus, each excursion, or even contemplated excursion, into the past in a time travel narrative reminds a reader that one of the mechanisms of narrative is the activity of plotting, the superimposition of one ordering process on another.

Moderns such as Faulkner also force readers to think about plot. Indeed, the very nature of narrative in *The Sound and the Fury* directs the reader's attention to the composition of the fabula, because the unusual form of the *sjuzet* compels the reader to attempt to clarify the sequence of events that the narrative implies. In the portion of the novel narrated by Benjy, the generating principle of the narrative is chance; that is, the chance remarks, sounds, and sights that Benjy hears and sees trigger journeys along oft-traveled streams of consciousness in Benjy's mind. However, Benjy does not appear to differentiate between recollection of events from his childhood and events in his present surroundings. Thus, a reader may want to speculate on the sequence of events from his childhood and events in his present surroundings, may want to speculate on the sequence of events in the *facula*, but he does so in order to understand the difference between Benjy's consciousness and Benjy's memory of the past. On the other hand, Benjy's brother Quentin, the narrator of the second segment of the novel, displays the ability to distinguish between past and present but not the ability to forget the past. In order to focus on the activity of plotting, the protagonist (and the reader) must conceive of a world having not only a past and present but also a future. Moreover, that very activity, that ordering process created by superimposition of one order on another, is precisely the activity the time travel writer draws attention to by presenting a protagonist about to travel into the past to alter the order of events referred to by the narrative.

In his analysis of Proust, *Narrative Discourse: An Essay in Method*, Gerard Genette concentrates on the three aspects of time that he considers most important in narrative: order, duration, and frequency.[7] The first of these categories, order, is indeed the most important in any analysis of plot in time travel narratives because the relations between events, namely, *before*, *simultaneous with*, and *after*, are the building blocks of all narrative; moreover, these relations assume an absolutely critical role in time travel stories largely because they determine cause and effect and thus dictate the chronology of unusual events in the story. Genette concentrates on listing the various story times and the order of their appearance in the narrative; however, the reader of a time travel narrative is typically concerned with the justification of the order of the various story times and the possibility of paradoxes arising because of the unusual ordering of events in the story. The reader of a time travel narrative is aware of the narrator's switch to an earlier portion of the *facula*, of the flashback, as we usually identify the technique; but the reader of a time travel narrative is also waiting for the narrator to introduce another story time (whether future or past), a time brought into the narrative because of the protagonist's movement in time or because of a paradox in the story—the sort of story time that could not be introduced by the narrator of a traditional story. This may engender the duplication or triplication of a character who has traveled into his own past, the preceding of cause by effect, and the creation of multiple timelines.

The ordering operation underpinning time travel narratives is carried on in a different manner and for different reasons than the same operation is carried on in traditional narratives. In many time travel narratives, the protagonist not only wants to change the past for one reason or another, but also thinks that he can do so. Now, changing the past does not alter the order of events presented in the narrative discourse, but such a change appears to alter the composition of the *facula*, the order of events referred to by the narrative. Altering the *facula* draws specific attention to the ordering process itself; that is, a reader observes the narrator making choices concerning which events to present, which events will make up the composition of the *sjuzet*. To examine this ordering operation and the mechanisms that distinguish time travel narratives from traditional narratives, we must define the two major ways in which we think of time. We can then investigate how to use those conceptions of time to understand narrative, to determine how the process of reading time travel narratives differs from the process of reading traditional narrative, and to elaborate on the unusual characteristics that result from these differences.

The A-Theory and B-Theory are names given to the dynamic and static concepts of time by J. M. E. McTaggart in his famous argument to demonstrate the unreality of time, an argument first published in 1908. McTaggart, Donald Williams, Willard van Orman Quine, and Bertrand Russell supported the B-Theory of time, the static concept of time, in which events are fixed and always have the same relations to all other events in the B-series of events. An event B2, for example, is always earlier than event B3 but always later than event B1. On the other hand, philosophers such as C. D. Broad and A. N. Prior argue for the A-theory, the dynamic concept of time. In this conception of time, events are either past, present, or future. One metaphor used to describe the A-theory is that of a person floating along a river at night in a small boat and playing a spotlight on various features along the bank. That which is illuminated by the spotlight is the now, that which is receding into the darkness is the past, and the future, which is in darkness, has yet to be illuminated. When human beings think in the mode of the A-series, they conceive of time in a "dynamic and tensed way, as being the very quintessence of flux and transiency."[8] Thus, events which are future become present and then past. The results of this process of temporal becoming appear in metaphors that utilize the image of time as a river. However, when we think in the mode of the B-series, we think of a static structure or order. The same events "which are continually changing in respect to their pastness, or futurity are laid out in a permanent order whose generating relation is that of 'earlier than' or 'later than' (or simultaneous with)."[9] This is the static or tenseless way of conceiving time, in which the history of the world is viewed in a God-like manner, all events being conceived as coexisting. Events can never change their position in the B-series. If an event M is ever earlier than an event N, then M is always earlier than N. The only change an event can undergo is a change in its A-determination. Thus, M was present but is now past, and N was future but is now present. Such change has been described as temporal becoming.

Consider, to clarify these two conceptions of time and their significance in narrative, the use of the A-Series and B-Series in H. G. Wells's *The Time Machine*. This passage is from an earlier version that appeared in William Henley's *New Review* between January and June 1895. In the first installment, the Time Traveller describes the fourth dimension:

To an omniscient observer there would be no forgotten past—no piece of time as it were that had dropped out of existence—and no blank future of things yet to be revealed. Perceiving all the present, an omniscient observer would likewise perceive all the past and all the inevitable future at the same time. Indeed, present and past and future would be without meaning to such an observer; he would always perceive exactly the same thing. He would see, as it were, a Rigid Universe filling space and time—a Universe in which things were always the same. He would see one sole unchanging series of cause and effect to-day and to-morrow and always. If "past" meant anything, it would mean looking in a certain direction; while "future" meant looking the opposite way.[10]

On the next page, Wells elaborates on this concept of time for the inhabitants of the world he has created: "From my point of view the human consciousness is an immaterial something falling through this rigid universe of four dimensions, from the direction we call 'past' to the direction we call 'future.' "[11] Note that events cannot change in relation to one another. Furthermore, in this version of the novel, the writer explicitly superimposes the A-Series on the B-Series; that is, the consciousness (a dynamic concept) "falls through" the Rigid Universe (a static structure).

But how can these two conceptions of time help us understand the process of reading a narrative? In a manner similar to that just mentioned, the reader's consciousness (an A-Series, a dynamic concept) moves over a text (a B-Series, a static concept) while experiencing a reading. Becoming conscious of the events that appear in the narrative, the reader builds a structure to accompany the text (the supposed story or series of events from which the narrative must have been drawn). A reader travels into the past by imitating the narrator. The dynamic conception of time illustrates the reader's consciousness as the reader moves through a text. The static conception of time, however, illustrates the construction in the reader's mind created by his understanding and experience of reading a narrative. Or perhaps, we may more usefully say, the static conception of time utilizes the reader's mental construction of the story behind the narrative—the entire sequence of events from which the narrator appears to have extracted the story, otherwise known as the *facula*. Whether writers employ them consciously or not, they utilize various combinations of these two conceptions of time to construct different types of narratives. Similarly, when a reader reads a time travel narrative, on one level he observes a time traveler moving over a static structure of time; moreover, this activity imitates a narrator illuminating events from the past in order to create a narrative, a narrator delving into his memory in order to relate his narrative, a narrator picking and choosing in retrospect from the structure of his memory, from a long, diminishing parade of events. In this manner, a reader of time travel narratives appears to be watching a reader in the act of reading.

Writers such as Fred Hoyle and Kurt Vonnegut, Jr. have used several methods to draw attention to these conceptions of time and, as a consequence, to the idea of plot. In *October the First Is Too Late*, Hoyle has the protagonist's friend, John Sinclair, a mathematician and chief advisor to the British Joint Chiefs of Staff, offer a detailed description of the sudden break up of time the world has undergone. That is, the time in England is now, presumably the early 1960s; suddenly the time in France is 1918, in North America about 1700, and so on. Sinclair begins to describe time by claiming that most of us are stuck with an absurd illusion:

"The idea of time as an ever-rolling stream. The thing which is supposed to bear all its sons away. There's one thing quite certain in this business: the idea of time as a steady progression from past to future is wrong. I know very well we feel this way about it subjectively. But we're the victims of a confidence trick. If there's one thing we can be sure about in physics it is that all times exist with equal reality. If you consider the motion of the earth around the sun, it is a spiral in four-dimensional space-time. There's absolutely no question of singling out a special point on the spiral and saying that particular point is the present position of the earth. Not so far as physics is concerned."

"But there is such a thing as the present. Without the ideas of the past, the present, and the future we could make no sense at all out of life. If you were aware of your whole life at once it would be like playing a sonata simply by pushing down all the notes on the keyboard. The essential thing about a sonata is the notes are played in turn, not all at once."[12]

Thereafter, Sinclair continues with a parable featuring a static structure of time in the form of a matrix of pigeonholes into which an imaginary postal clerk peers, each act of looking into a pigeonhole constituting a present moment. Since the clerk is not constrained to look into the pigeonholes in any particular order, the sequence of events (pigeonholes examined by the clerk) may be in some order other than ascending numerical order; indeed, they may be in any order. From the clerk's perspective, these observations of different pigeonholes, these realizations of various events, form a sequence which (for the clerk) has a past, a present, and a future. Thus, the clerk has an impression of time as an "ever-rolling stream." However, note the static nature of the pigeonholes in Sinclair's analogy: as a series of points exists in space, a series of events exists in time. Note also the apparent freedom the clerk has to follow any of a variety of sequences. But what causes the clerk to look into one pigeonhole and not another? And what is the effect of the clerk's choosing one sequence over another? In time travel narratives, the result of such a choice often means that a second universe comes into existence, a universe in which the protagonist chooses the second option.

In *Slaughterhouse-Five*, Vonnegut provides another occasion for a reader to think about the idea of order. Protagonist Billy Pilgrim, has come unstuck in time. Vonnegut uses the occasion of Billy's encounter with the Tralfamadorians to describe the nature of time more fully. The Tralfamadorians perceive time differently than human beings do, as one of them explains to Billy:

I am a Tralfamadorian, seeing all time as you might see a stretch of the Rocky Mountains. All time is all time. It does not change. It does not lend itself to warnings or explanations. It simply *is*. Take it moment by moment, and you find that we are all, as I've said before, bugs in amber.[13]

That is the ordering principle behind this narrative. The narrator may first describe an event from the timeline of one world and next describe an event from the timeline of a parallel universe. Thus, causation breaks down when Billy is suddenly transported from a golf course to the zoo on the planet named Tralfamadore. The narrator focuses first on one static line of events and then on another to construct the plot of his narrative. That is, the protagonist moves from one timeline to another. Thus the B-Series created by the events in which the protagonist is involved belongs to different timelines; but all of these events belong to the protagonist's personal timeline.

The narrator of Vonnegut's time travel narrative draws additional attention to the nature of time by dramatizing the protagonist's attempt to understand the nature of time on Tralfamadore:

Billy couldn't read Tralfamadorian, of course, but he could at least see how the books were laid out—in brief clumps of symbols separated by stars. Billy commented that the clumps must be telegrams.

"Exactly," said the voice.

"They are telegrams?"

"There are no telegrams on Tralfamadore. But you're right: each clump of symbols is a brief, urgent message—describing a situation, a scene. We Tralfamadorians read them all at once, not one after the other. There isn't any particular relationship between all the messages, except that the author has chosen them carefully, so that, when seen all at once, they produce an image of life that is beautiful and surprising and deep. There is no beginning, no middle, no end, no suspense, no moral, no causes, no effects. What we love in our books are the depths of many marvelous moments seen all at one time."[14]

Thus the narrator of *Slaughterhouse-Five* unobtrusively presents the analysis of the structure of time that informs the narrative. Since the present of the narrative skips from one sequence of events to another, completely different set of events for no apparent reason, there is, in a sense, no cause, no effect, no beginning, and no end. Each parallel universe exists alongside all the other universes that Billy inhabits as the narrative progresses.

Readers understand these stories fraught with loops into the past because they have been conditioned by previous reading experiences to understand sudden changes in the story time as both useful and acceptable devices for constructing narrative. Having encountered the protagonist in the opening pages, the reader is not concerned with the narrator's sudden focus on events from the protagonist's past, because the reader has been conditioned to expect such flashbacks. Since flashbacks eliminate a few voids in the protagonist's background, they help the reader understand, or imagine, how the protagonist will react to certain events and thus create interest by building tension. Knowing that the narrator will eventually return to pick up the thread of each subplot, the reader is content to hold in suspension the activities of characters in one subplot while the narrator describes the actions of the characters in another subplot. In *Slaughterhouse-Five* and *October the First Is Too Late* these phenomena assume different forms because the narrators's movements from timeline to timeline appear to consist of more than just loops into the past. In those cases the narrator appears to move from one parallel universe to another instead of just into the past.

Time travel narratives with a protagonist traveling into his own past mirror the activities of a narrator who presents events from a protagonist's past in an order different from the order which must obtain in the *facula* of the narrative. Thus, having introduced a protagonist in the opening scenes of a narrative, a narrator may suddenly begin describing events from that protagonist's distant past. A reader may desire to imitate the actions of a narrator in this regard. Just as a narrator presents events out of order—that is, he changes (or appears to change) the order of events, and, of course, the relations between events—readers may suppose that they too may alter time (relations between cause and effect) by traveling into the past and changing the order of events. Thus encouraged about the possibility of changing the past, readers may seek out narratives portraying travel into the past to vicariously experience the mutability of time.

Narratives about changing the past create a situation in which readers may view themselves as rereading a text. The process of rereading a text involves a reader's consciousness repeating a previous journey through the text. This process is similar to a character traveling into the past, revisiting some of the events that he experienced before. Similarly, readers in the process of rereading already know the order of events to be encountered, knows which events a narrator will present, because they have experienced these events before. Moreover, the experience is different upon rereading, in part because the pace of reading is likely to increase because readers know something of the order of events in the narrative. The sense of duration may seem different because readers experience the tension of bringing about the past. All of this only adds to the feeling that the reader is observing the creation of the narrative structure.

The idea of the mutability of time inevitably led to stories involving parallel time, circular time, and the breakdown of time, all of which paved the way for the moderns and postmoderns. Time travel writers actually experimented with techniques employed by the moderns and postmoderns; however, these writers did not foreground their techniques. Arguably, they were creating self-reflexive fiction without being aware of it. Thus, we may view time travel narratives as self-reflexive narratives that comment on the logic of all narratives by analogy: They provide a protagonist whose predicament mirrors that of the writer in the throes of building his plot. And even time travel stories that are ludic or melodramatic may create some of these metafictional effects. Branching time stories such as Gregory Benford's *Timescape* focus on the points in the plot where significant choices are made. Parallel time stories such as *Slaughterhouse-Five* comment on development of parallel subplots. Circular time stories mirror plots of revelation—postmodern narratives in which nothing new happens, in which events remain the same, in which in-depth revelation of character is the major thrust of the narrative—and Philip K. Dick's "A Little Something for Us Tempunauts" is a good example of this sort of story. Finally, linear time stories such as *Dinosaur Beach*, with their loops into the future and past to describe further the elements of the story, mirror the standard narrative technique of beginning *in media res*, which is after all where we, like the protagonist of *Dinosaur Beach*, must begin if we wish to unravel the snarled and tangled timelines, the narrative, before us.

Notes

1. Keith Laumer, *Dinosaur Beach* (New York: DAW Books, Inc., 1971), 67.
2. Stanislaw Lem, "The Time-Travel Story and Related Matters of Science-Fiction Structuring" in Lem, *Microworlds: Writings on Science Fiction and Fantasy* (San Diego: Harcourt Brace Jovanovich, 1984), 145.
3. Patricia Waugh, *Metafiction: The Theory and Practice of Self-Conscious Fiction* (London: Methuen, 1984), 6, 7.
4. Larry McCaffery, *The Metafictional Muse: The Works of Robert Coover, Donald Barthelme, and William H. Gass* (Pittsburgh: University of Pittsburgh Press, 1982), 14.
5. Seymour Chatman, *Story and Discourse: Narrative Structure in Fiction and Film* (Ithaca: Cornell University Press), 53.
6. Peter Brooks, *Reading for the Plot: Design and Intention in Narrative* (New York: Vintage Books, a Division of Random House, 1984), 12.
7. Gerard Genette, *Narrative Discourse: An Essay in Method* (Ithaca: Cornell University Press, 1980), 29.
8. Richard Gale, "Introduction" to chapters on "The Static Versus the Dynamic Temporal," in Gale, editor, *The Philosophy of Time: A Collection of Essays* (Atlantic Highlands, NJ: Humanities Press, 1968), 65–66.
9. Gale, 66.
10. Robert M. Philmus and David Y. Hughes, editors, *H. G. Wells: Early Writings in Science and Science Fiction* (Berkeley: University of California Press, 1975), 93.
11. Philmus and Hughes, 94.
12. Fred Hoyle, *October the First Is Too Late* (Greenwich, CT: Fawcett Crest, 1966), 64.
13. Kurt Vonnegut, Jr., *Slaughterhouse-Five* (New York: Dell Publishing Co., Inc., 1969), 85–86.
14. Vonnegut, 88.

5

"Backward, Turn Backward": Narratives of Reversed Time in Science Fiction

Andrew Sawyer

Backward, turn backward, O Time, in your flight,
Make me a child again just for tonight
Mother, come back from the echoless shore,
Take me again to your heart as of yore;
Kiss from my forehead the furrows of care,
Smooth the few silver threads out of my hair;
Over my slumbers your loving watch keep;
Rock me to sleep, mother, rock me to sleep.
          —Elizabeth Chase Akers, "Rock Me to Sleep, Mother"[1]

The importance of this sentimental nineteenth-century lyric lies in the wish that time could, for at least a single occasion, reverse itself. This is a simple enough wish: How many times, after an embarrassing gaffe or threatening encounter, have we wished we could turn back the clock and escape the dangerous present? Yet it depends upon a mental map of Time—what it actually is, how it operates—which is fairly recent, and certainly sophisticated. The terror of Christopher Marlowe's Faustus in the face of certain eternal damnation causes him to wish only that time would cease, or at least run slowly: "Lente, lente currite noctis equi" ("O horses of the night, run slow, run slow").[2] He is bound to time's arrow and its one direction. The voice in Akers's poem, however, apparently wishes for a reversal of the flow of time. That this process is possible in some theoretical form is something which has been increasingly debated. Science fiction allows us—in imaginary time, at least—to do this. Physicists and philosophers question the nature of time itself. As neither physicist nor philosopher I am, when discussing the question of time, entirely dependent on authority: More acute minds than mine have floundered in the swamp between the self-evident and the inexpressible. I will therefore going to skim over the mathematical and symbolic logics of time and focus on how these have been manipulated in storytelling. Here, I will look at a number of scenarios that offer not time travel as such but the reversal of the arrow of time, where future becomes past and past future. This conceit offers some bizarre images for our contemplation but it may also allow us to look with a different viewpoint at some of our cherished moral maps.

When I say that this view of time is "fairly recent" I am, of course, overlooking Plato's description of the unwinding of the universe in *The Statesman*:

[A]ll began to change in the reverse direction and grow younger and more tender of semblance. The white hair of the elderly began to grow black; the cheeks of the bearded to grow smooth, and one and all to return to the season of bloom they had left behind them. Young men's bodies grew smoother and smaller day by day and night by night till they reverted alike in mind and body to the likeness of a newborn infant, and then dwindled right away and were clean lost to sight.[3]

I also overlook William Blake's mystical poem "The Mental Traveller," which is echoed in two of the works discussed here, as well as St. Augustine's frequently-cited meditations[4] on time:

What, then, is time? I know well enough what it is, provided that nobody asks me, but if I am asked what it is and try to explain, I am baffled.[5]

Nevertheless the question of the "Arrow of Time" has certainly been given greater currency through the new views of time given by post-Einstein physics.

The arrow of time is a simple metaphor (coined by Sir Arthur Eddington in 1927) based upon our perception of time as possessing direction. Indeed, direction is perhaps the only quality we can discern: We can all sense that time is passing and that, to quote another passage constantly cited by writers on Time:

the Moving Finger writes; and having writ,
Moves on; nor all your Piety nor Wit
    Shall lure it back to cancel half a Line
Nor all your tears wash out a Word of it.[6]

A moment's thought, however, could persuade us that our perception may be faulty. We can also perceive that the sun and the stars are revolving around the Earth. The absolute time of Isaac Newton has been replaced in modern physics by Albert Einstein's relative time, in which we cannot say with certainty that two events separated by space occur at the "same" time. The "big bang" may lead to a "big crunch" in which matter rushes together and time itself collapses into a singularity from which the cycle starts again: not so much an Arrow as a Boomerang, or Ping-Pong Ball of Time, which returns to the beginning or endlessly oscillates between two states.

A diagram in John Gribbin's *In Search of Schrodinger's Cat* shows two apparently identical "Feynman diagrams"—representations along a space-time axis of the trajectory of subatomic particles.[7] In one, a gamma ray photon produces an electron/positron pair and the positron, in colliding with another electron, annihilates it to make another photon. In the other, a single electron interacts with two photons, moving for part of its journey backward in time. According to Gribbin, the two pictures are mathematically identical. In the sub-atomic realm, at least, time may not "flow" in a uniform fashion.

Time as a dimension—a spacelike dimension in the way described by Paul Davies in *About Time*—could be dependent on viewpoint (70–77). To say something happens "before" or "after" something is perhaps analogous to saying that an object is to the left of another. So, I place two objects in front of me—one to the left of the other. But an audience looking toward me will perceive it as to the right. Davies explains how "now" is relative (66, 67), how gravity affects the speed of time (87–89) and how time and space themselves may depend on the observer's stance. He also devotes a chapter to the question of moving backward in time. John Wheeler and Richard Feynman, following up the apparently time-symmetrical implications of Maxwell's equations describing the propagation of electromagnetic waves (Davies 198), suggested that an electromagnetic source emitted "advanced" waves into the past as well as "retarded waves" into the future. The arrow of time was due to secondary radiation generated by these advanced waves, which itself produced interference effects by which the retarded (forward) wave is strengthened and the advanced (backward) wave canceled out. In some circumstances, perhaps, retarded waves may not be completely canceled, a theory expanded in Gregory Benford's *Timescape*. Jack Cohen and Ian Stewart agree that the equations may allow time to be reversed, but suggest that their context in this universe forces them to act one way—and then indulge in a fantasy in which entities in a reversed-time universe observe how rivers are formed by water "devaporated" into the sea, forced up mountains until raindrops are spurted into waiting clouds, and how mature salmon absorb eggs and sperm, fight their way tail-first downstream to the sea to become young enough to journey upstream to be turned into eggs and sperm to be absorbed by the next generation, and then wonder why time couldn't run the other way "and wouldn't it be strange to live in a universe where rocks fall off cliffs, salmon lay eggs, and rivers run into the sea?"[8] That this is a mini-sf narrative in itself is unsurprising: Cohen and Stewart are well-known figures on the British sf scene and Cohen has provided biological and ecological scenarios for many sf writers.

The philosopher J. M. E. McTaggart, in 1908, provided a proof that time did not exist.[9] J. T. Fraser, in *Time: The Familiar Stranger*, identifies several types of time, ranging from "nootemporality" or what he describes as "the temporal reality of the mature human mind," to "Prototemporality": the undirected, noncontinuous time of elementary particles that we cannot pin down to location or instant. Electromagnetic radiation, travelling at the speed of light, necessarily exists in an "atemporal" state.[10] In *The Arrow of Time* Peter Coveney and Roger Highfield bring chaos and complexity and chemical clocks to the question: "Rather than maintaining that the arrow of time is an illusion, we must ask whether it is the time-symmetric 'fundamental' laws that are approximations or illusions."[11]

This continuous questioning has naturally led to fictional models. Not all these examples are to do with the reversal of time's arrow, but increasingly in fiction—and not only in science fiction—time is played with and the distinctions between future and past become less defined, more arbitrary.

H. G. Wells introduced *The Time Machine* with a philosophical discussion involving time as a fourth dimension in which movement is possible. However, he was predated by the American journalist and fictioneer Edward Page Mitchell, whose 1881 story "The Clock That Went Backward" was published in *The New York Sun*. Sam Moskowitz claims that Mitchell predated by seven years Wells's first use of a time machine (in "The Chronic Argonauts," published in the *Science Schools Journal*, 1888). In fact, time is reversed by what appears to be a magic clock which runs backward—essentially a fantasy device, although the explanation is certainly philosophical and arguably scientific:

Time is a condition, not an essential. Viewed from the Absolute, the sequence by which future follows present and present follows past is purely arbitrary. Yesterday, today, tomorrow; there is no reason in the nature of things why the order should not be tomorrow, today, yesterday.[12]

In *Sylvie and Bruno*—which with its sequel published four years later is a key text of pre-twentieth-century science fiction—Lewis Carroll imagines a scenario that has since become popular. It's something we can now access through reversing a film or video, but for Carroll it was an act of imagination largely inspired, no doubt, by his studies in the philosophy of mathematics and the topsy-turvy reversals he had previously created in *Alice in Wonderland* and, especially, *Through the Looking Glass* where we encountered the phenomenon in the backward-life of the White Queen, although there may be an element of the curious advice given to Tom, in Kingsley's *The Water Babies* by Mother Carey: "if you look forward, you will not see a step before you, and be certain to go wrong; but if you look behind you, and watch carefully whatever you have passed . . . then you will know what is coming next, as plainly as if you saw it in a looking-glass."[13] Again, the device that brings the perceptual change about in *Sylvie and Bruno* is nothing more than an enchanted timepiece. By manipulating the hands of the Professor's "Outlandish Watch," the narrator can "replay" events and by setting it in reverse he is able to observe a mother and her daughters unstitch their needlework before walking backward into a dining-room where they seat themselves at the dirty plates and fill them discreetly (like "cautiously conveying a cherry-stone from their lips to their plates") with mutton and potatoes:

what need to tell how the mutton was placed on the spit and slowly unroasted—how the potatoes were wrapped in their skins, and handed over to the gardener to be buried—how, when the mutton had at length attained to rawness, the fire, which had gradually changed from red-heat to a mere blaze, died down so suddenly that the cook had only just time to catch its last flicker on the end of a match—or how the maid, having taken the mutton off the spit, carried it (backwards, of course) out of the house, to meet the butcher, who was coming (also backwards) down the road.[14]

Even where the focus is not time travel as such, the flow of time is important. T. H. White's Merlin in *The Once and Future King* (1958) is another backward living figure. Dream-journeys are important in early utopian/dystopian fictions such as William Morris's *News from Nowhere* (1890) as methods of reaching the future that need to be examined. In W. H. Hodgson's *The Night Land* (1912) we visit the far future from the viewpoint of a narrator who is first encountered in a context which may be late medieval or Renaissance and whose consciousness is reincarnated in a mind epochs hence. The backward-looking of *The Night Land*—a deliberate motif of Hodgson's—derives partly from this structure but in large part from the echoes of Mallory, whose Arthurian romances are reflected in plot (pure knight rescues damsel in distress from giants and monsters) and language.[15] Olaf Stapledon's *Star Maker*, in its final burst of cosmos-creating "conceived many strange forms of time."[16] James Blish's "Common Time" (1953) looks at two sorts of time flowing at different rates, while his "Beep" (1954), in common with a number of other science fiction and near science fiction stories such as Fred Hoyle's *October the First Is Too Late* (1966) and J. B. Priestley's play *Time and the Conways* (1937) give us time as a fixed continuum within which consciousness is moving. The latter is explicitly indebted to J. W. Dunne's *An Experiment with Time* (1927), which is also referred to by J. Barrington Bayley in his *Collision with Chronos* (1977) where time is a moving wave of "now." In Bayley's novel, time travel shows the past as void of consciousness, the future as void of life, and an expedition into the past discovers that certain ruins are older in the past that than they are in the present. The explanation is that a wave of time is travelling from the future to the present, carrying with it an alien civilization on a collision course. We have not so much an Arrow of Time, nor even a Boomerang of Time, but a Concertina of Time in which both "ends" of future and past are rushing to collide in the middle. From the viewpoint of each civilization, the other is experiencing time backward. To continue these images, Ian Watson devises a catapult of Time as his "Very Slow Time Machine" reverses to spring forward.[17]

Other science fiction shows us the reversal of a single consciousness within the context of a "normal" flow of time. J. G. Ballard's "Mr. F. Is Mr. F." and F. Scott Fitzgerald's "The Curious Case of Benjamin Button" (1922) are both reversed biographies. "Button" begins with the birth of his character as an old man and watches him grow younger. We see the comic tribulations of an apparently mature man insisting that he is a teenager and an apparent teenager insisting that he is a brigadier-general in the U.S. army, leading back to the mindless idyll of infanthood. Ballard retells this scenario—dare I say reverses it?—in a more malevolent fashion as the picture of a marriage in which the manipulative wife actually becomes her husband's mother. As the Freemans prepare for their first child, the husband becomes aware that he is shrinking, growing younger; retaining his "adult" consciousness almost to the last minute when "Hating the naked hair that rasped across his face, he now felt clearly for the first time what he had for so long repressed. Before the end he cried out with joy and wonder."[18] Roger Zelazny's "Divine Madness" gives us a character whose seizures, brought upon by grief and epilepsy, cause him to experience time flowing backward, eventually replaying until he is given a second chance to live through the crucial event that he is able to undo. The life of the central character in Malcolm Ross's *The Man Who Lived Backward* (1950) is one of reacting to events whose cause he has yet to find out.[19] Each day, he wakes one day in the past. His knowledge of "historical" events such as the Portland shipwreck of 1898 does not give him the power to prevent them: Indeed, his attempts to dissuade passengers from boarding the ship only makes things worse. We read about, but never encounter directly, his romance with a woman whose life juxtaposes with his briefly as they "age" in different directions—a more prosaic incarnation of Blake's "Mental Traveller": "And she grows young as he grows old."

"That's the effect of living backwards," the White Queen says to Alice: "It always makes one a little giddy at first."[20] Narrative can play tricks with time. The classical structure is beginning, middle, end, but it is easy enough to imagine a fiction beginning at the end of the chronological flow of the characters's lives: Indeed the classical narrative flow—following Homer's use of the structure in *The Iliad*—finds a dramatic point near the climax of the chronology (in this case, of the Trojan War) and focuses in close detail on events leading up to that climax. More modernist texts reflect the problematic structures of time itself (or, if we are to follow Fraser, themselves). Faulkner's *The Sound and the Fury* (1931) reflects the lack of direction in the mental processes of the retarded Benjy, for whom sensory perception and memory seem to fuse in a continuous present. Works as disparate as James Joyce's *Finnegans Wake* (1939), E. R. Eddison's *The Worm Ouroboros* (1922), and Samuel R. Delany's *Dhalgren* (1975) are circular narratives in which the end leads us back to the beginning. George Turner has demonstrates with diagrams how Ursula K. Le Guin's *The Dispossessed* (1974) tells a double narrative: what happened after Shevek's journey to Urras and the events that led up to it.[21] Iain M. Banks's *Use of Weapons* (1990) is a typical example of a story told backward, in which the flow of the narrative leads to the moment of trauma that informs the events we have been reading about. (Banks's genius lies in the fact that no sooner have we absorbed this than we are given another "revelation" which reinterprets this moment of trauma.) Pure narrative structures, however, are not what I want to deal with.

Instead, I now want to look at three full-blown narratives of reverse-time. There are perhaps psychological reasons why a writer might find the reversal of Time's Arrow a seductive conceit—I say no more about Carroll who has had his every word psychoanalyzed—but more general anxieties also arise. What is the nature of this future which causes the very fabric of time to retreat in apparent horror? What is happening around the corner? But above all, what is the nature of writing a reverse-time narrative? Both writer and reader are engaged in something beyond the construction of a shared fictional reality, but are trying to engineer a shift in perspective while themselves using the very process of "beginning, middle, and end" to tell a story that reverses the process. This leads to particular compromises and contradictions.

The "backwards-time" scene in *Sylvie and Bruno* is a single episode in a narrative that explores a whole series of altered states of consciousness and in which an elderly narrator is forced to play second fiddle to a more virile suitor to the hand of the fair Lady Muriel. The reversed lives in "The Curious Case of Benjamin Button" and "Mr F. Is Mr. F." are fantastic oddities in which a single current of time is reversed in the context of the constant greater flow. Ballard's story, particularly, plays with chilling effectiveness on the basic Oedipal scenario, but both echo Elizabeth Akers's desire, even if Freeman's desire is fought against until the final orgasmic cry of "joy and wonder" while he is killed and conceived in the same act of ultimate cuckoldry. Zelazny's "Divine Madness" is the embodiment of the desire to turn back the clock and somehow change the past. But three novels in particular take us into worlds in which the scenarios suggested by the scientists and philosophers in my first section are given greater form by science fiction writers: Brian Aldiss, Philip K. Dick and—if we can admit him—Martin Amis.

In the mid 1960s two novels appeared in which Time's Arrow reversed. Dick's *Counter-Clock World* is a theological thriller set some time after (or, what we might perhaps rather say, "before") the Hobart effect, when time has begun to run backward. Aldiss's *An Age* (published in America as *Cryptozoic*) is a psychological time-travel novel set partly in the far past, partly in a dystopic future, and partly in the more recent past. The fact that humans traveling into the past are not entirely physically "there" creates a dream-like impression heightened by protagonist Bush's visions of a "phantom dark-haired woman" and the way he learns that the flow of time is not what we believe it to be.

Dick's novel is set entirely within the world of the "Hobart effect," in which time has somehow reversed. Corpses come to life within their graves and have to be dug up by rescue teams. Like Plato's men of the Age of Chronos, they grow younger. Lotta agonizes because she is growing ever more childish.[22] Ann Fisher seduces Sebastian Hermes, owner of the Flask of Hermes Vitarium by telling the story of how she applied to have a baby put inside her womb: "it's a marvellous feeling—you have no idea—how it feels to sense another creature, one whom you love, merging molecule by molecule with your own molecules" (49). People in this counter-clock world are nourished by "sogum" (inserted with ceramic tubes) and offended and embarrassed by eating and drinking. "Fe-ood!" is an obscenity and "Mouth-hole" an insult. The Library tracks down and eradicates the final texts of literary works, expunging the very idea of devices like the "swabble" upon which the librarian Appleford reflects post-erasure, trying to recall just what a "swabble" actually is (18).

The most powerful use of this notion is, however, in Dick's image of death reversed as a theologically potent experience. Each soul experiences its own resurrection and it is not the child but the full adult who emerges from unconsciousness "trailing clouds of glory." The plot—such as it is, and it is confused—revolves around the need of various parties to secure the "old-born" Thomas Peak, founder of a religious sect, who may recall his "post-death"/pre-Resurrected experiences. Apart from this, as we shall see, it is not one of Dick's most consistent or coherent novels. Reviewing it in 1969, Bruce Gillespie of *SF Commentary* called it "[a] bad novel with every chance of having been a good one."[23] The "Hobart effect" is itself a crude piece of obfuscation. It is a localized process. We learn that it is weaker on Mars (does this mean that time somewhere stands still?) and one of the characters uses a drug that cancels it out. What it is, what causes it and how it works is of no concern to the author. Nor is it a mere reversal of Time's Arrow. People who died before the Hobart Effect come to life again, but do not actually live their lives backward. In fact, the plot focuses precisely upon the change that this process causes. We have a social system, an economy based upon the counter-clock time-flow. History will be different now that time goes backward. If there is a problem grappling with the sequence of tenses there, it is the novel's most authentically Dickian legacy.

Aldiss's novel, on the other hand, is both more consistently visionary and more of a science fiction novel than is *Counter-Clock World*. Although it is a novel intimately about time, most of it is set in "normal" time. What happens is not reversal as such: simply that human consciousness reverses itself. In an act reminiscent of the optical illusion in which we can gaze at a picture and see first a candlestick, and then two faces, humanity has/will reverse(d) its perception of time. It is not that causes suddenly follow events. As Silverstein explains, this has always happened: "It is only our perception that has suddenly changed, is suddenly clear. What has always happened is that light has dashed from bodies into your gun; then you have pressed the button and had the intention to do so" (159). Why this sudden forgetting of the true nature of things? Because the vast Stapledonian universal consciousness that once was humanity has become too closely aware of its impending death and dissolution into the mindless mock-life among the rocks of the Cryptozoic. Time as we know it is the result of an act of collective amnesia. The reversal of the flow of time is an act of escape from something horrific around the corner—ironically this "something horrific" is nothing we do not already know.

The time travel that Bush engages in is a mental as much as a physical act. Time travelers do not make physical contact with the "real" world: Bush's observation of the horror of a working-class English life in 1930 is made colder by the fact that he cannot interact with it: he can only observe the mime-like actions he is powerless to affect. Bush's experiences and meditations offer counterpoint and foreshadowings (backshadowings?) of the final revelation. As early as page 20 a minor character is suggesting that the Devonian sea may be "the end of the world, not the beginning." Bush's own psycho-sexual fantasy plays its part in timelike reversals. He is first encountered "brooding about his mother" (11) and the dark-haired woman, anima-figure, who follows him about is revealed to be his granddaughter. The English family he observes acting out their own tragedy of incestuous fantasy and loveless sex is called Bush, while he is the object of an attempt at seduction by the younger woman who looks after (in more ways than one) his father. When "the very concept of timeflow is in the human consciousness, not in the external universe" (86), Bush's obsession with sex and his horror of incest is a psychological reversal which we must, if we wish, interpret in a counter-clock way. In this time-frame, the goal of all men must be to enter their mothers, whether they like the idea or not.[24] It is also perforce—and this Aldiss does not address (the role of Ann in the later chapters is to make the tea and add common-sense indignation while the men philosophize)—the goal of all women.

In 1992, Martin Amis published *Time's Arrow*, a novel that expands many of the ideas in the two just mentioned and uses the device of reverse-time to tell the complete biography of a German war criminal from death to birth. (Neither novel is among the works Amis makes reference to in his author's note, though Amis's knowledge of science fiction may well have stretched to them: indeed, Aldiss is convinced that Amis reviewed *An Age*—see his letter in *Extrapolation*, Fall, 1996.[25]) David Moyle, in the article in an earlier *Extrapolation* to which Aldiss takes exception, takes pains to avoid any reference to a science-fictional tradition that leads to Amis's story, choosing rather to attribute Amis's choosing of that particular device to something called "thematic requirement," thus creating in the heart of his otherwise perceptive essay a blank space.[26] (It is as if Amis's discovery of science fiction as a natural form of expressing what he needs to say about the world is in some ways qualitatively different from that of Aldiss, Dick, or a hundred other science fiction writers of whatever level of talent.)

Time's Arrow provides a brilliant solution to one of the fundamental problems of the reversed-time narrative: the fact that the reader's timeflow is opposed to that of the "world" of the story. Whether the novel is anything more than a philosophical conundrum is open to debate:

whole chapters of hyperkinetic Amis prose and clever postmodern bits come to seem a desperate waltz of distraction, smoke and mirrors to obscure the fact that uneventful decades told backwards are not really more interesting than their forwards version. Successive shocks of reversed bodily functions have a diminishing effect (and we are spared nothing, not even the preliminary to a good backwards puke as the protagonist pulls the toilet handle and "The bowl filled with its terrible surprises"). The sf reader begins to shuffle slightly, remembering perhaps that *Counter-Clock World* also had a plot going before the end of chapter one.[27]

Its novelty was certainly overestimated among certain reviewers unfamiliar with sf and an implied message that, viewed in a certain light, Auschwitz is a healing experience was too much for others to accept. Nevertheless, I will return briefly to these points later.

What is the nature of the reversed-time narrative? What are its attractions for a writer? I can identify three devices or "conceits" in which this imagery can be played with.

First, the physical conceit: This is the physical game the writer can play with the device of reversing time—the film being run backward through the projector. It is the oddity of walking backward, regurgitating food, seeing a collection of scattered china fragments scramble together into the form of a cup and leap upwards into one's hand. It is the images coming to the mind of the Cohen and Stewart passage cited earlier, the flow of time backward into the Big Crunch, the reversal of entropy and the Second Law of Thermodynamics. It is the basic science fictional idea, and like many science fictional ideas is beyond the capacity of many who conceive it. Once it extends beyond the bounds of a brief scene or speculation, the sf reader cannot help but ask: Yes, but how does it work? Can you have an effect without a preceding cause or does the flow of energy cause the cup to reassemble? Is time an illusion; are we misinterpreting reality when we think of time as a series of events preceding and following? Is not every event that ever happened or could happen somehow "real"?

Second, the "spiritual conceit": beyond the physical reversals, if death is the coming to consciousness of a corpse—the spontaneous generation of life from nonliving elements—does this have any implication about life after death. Conventional theology tells us that after death the spirit travels on: Is this process reversed? Dick, with the Anarch Peak, returning to life, tries to answer this question. Perhaps a major religious leader will know the answer. Does Peak recall what happened before death? The answer is ambiguous, but is linked with Sebastian Hermes's apparent dreams of what might be the presence of God. Peak is a messiah:

> "You were dead. . . . You died around twenty years ago." . . .
> "Then Alex Hobart was right," the Anarch said. "I had people who thought so; they expected me back." (58)

But he is a secular messiah: His experience is shared by everyone of his generation; "it has no religious significance; it's just a natural event, now." The end of the book gives us what appears to be a mass resurrection. The dead are knocking at their graves, but they are not transformed or transcendental.

An Age also possesses eschatological images, with the implications of the reversal showing us "the dead coming to life again—lying bleeding on the ground, perhaps and the blood sucking back into the veins, and then the chap getting up and walking away as if nothing had happened" (161). It is significant that the image which immediately follows is of Christ on the cross coming to life, the nails pulled from his hands, being taken down and given back to his disciples. Aldiss plays more creatively, even rhapsodically, on the theme of spontaneous generation:

> In the mouldering bones of the grave, organisation stirs; worms put flesh on to bones; something more and more like a human is built. . . . Human life bursts in upon the world in countless ways! Bodies rise again from the sea bed during storms and are washed back on to ships that also emerge from the waves. Before road accidents, you will see ambulances rush backwards with broken limbs that are strewn over the road to join themselves into a living being, jerking into a car that deconcertinas away from another car. (163)

God is identified as the universal intelligence that divided into individual fragments. From the future backward, the theological imagery is the same as from the past forward.[28]

Amis's use of this conceit is perhaps too mixed with the third to be distinguishable from it, but his device of seeing through reverse vision the Jews of the Holocaust incarnated and integrated into German society is only an expansion of his beginning in which the narrator incarnates (I am not sure whether we should say reincarnates) from Death. Amis's narrative voice offers us a number of problems: It is not that of the monster whom it inhabits, so we cannot say that this is a pure replay of the tape of a life. But it does have the effect of mediating between reader and the world the author creates, forming a bridge between the two currents of time. The narrator is aware that there is something unnatural about his situation, can perceive, in fact, that "It just seems to me that the film is running backwards." But while he shares general knowledge of his host's world, he does not have specific access to his host's thoughts (though he does to his dreams and emotions). "The other people, do they have someone else inside them, passenger or parasite, like me?"[29]

In the end, it might be precisely the difference between Amis and genre sf that he does not follow up this question, nor the hint implicit in the very fact of creating a reversed biography that when we die, we relive our lives backward.

Third, the "moral conceit": by looking at the physical nature of a life reversed, the moral questions of our mundane, "forward" lives are illuminated. Through comic or grotesque reversal, the everyday is satirized. Dick reverses, for example, the debate on abortion: "We must determine and agree on the precise moment at which the soul enters the corpse in the ground. Is it the moment when it is dug up? When its voice is first heard from below, asking for aid? When the first heart beat is recorded?" (103). He also reverses the sex act: The function of a man is purely to absorb the fertilizing sperm. Sometimes the comedy is clumsy: When we read the headline "DRUNKEN FATHER EATS OWN BABY" (104) we are unsure quite where to focus the nature of the offense—eating of any description is, remember, an obscenity. Sometimes it is subtle, as when Hermes wishes he could take back a misjudged remark: "If I could reverse just that one segment of time" (81).

Aldiss resolves Bush's sexuality in the revelation that the true flow of time is backward:

"In the past [that is, the future] you don't have any ban against incest, do you, Wygelia?"

. . .

"No. Nor do we have incest, since we all return anyway to our parents." (178)

But it is Amis who explores most closely the fact that in reversing cause and effect we are also reversing morality. The narrator speaks of the actions of Tod Friendly (the final pseudonym of his host, a bilingual pun: Tod = "Death"): taking toys from children and money from church collection plates (23). His profession, medicine, is not a matter of healing, but of destruction, torture—"a three year old girl whose hips we have decided to destroy" (91). Auschwitz, that twentieth-century center of horror, is where, in this cosmos, "the world is going to start making sense" (124). Is this a justification of the Holocaust, an argument that we only have to look at things the "right" way? No, I would argue that this looking-glass morality causes us to examine our own preconceptions and prejudices. If we can see Auschwitz as something healing and holy, perhaps there lies some equally horrific moral abyss behind those aspects of our lives we are more obviously smug and self-congratulatory about.

In the end, this moral opposition is perhaps too obvious. Evil is banal looked at forward or backward, and our Nazi doctor is seen, whichever way we examine him, as a monster. By creating a reverse biography Amis highlights the light and shadow in everyday lives and creates an ironic commentary on precisely what pattern we perceive. Nevertheless, I return to the motto of Lewis Carroll's *Sylvie and Bruno Concluded*: "Evil is Live backwards."[30]

There are still difficulties in creating a reversed-time narrative. Ideally, of course, it should be narrated backward. How are we, who live forward, truly to experience a consciousness which lives backward? Is—as Cohen and Stewart and Aldiss suggest, a reversed-time consciousness unaware that it is existing in reversed-time? Would we notice any real difference if both our consciousness and timeflow went into reverse? Dick has characters greeting each other with "Goodbye" and finishing conversations with "Hello," but while cigarettes are unsmoked and people get younger other physical processes seem to follow the "normal" pattern and even those speechtags contradict their locations in discourse. One may say "Goodbye" to denote the beginning of a conversation but what follows the word is the beginning of the next conversation working its way through to the end, not its end through which we progress to the beginning. Bullets go from gun to wound, not, as the patterns is described in *An Age*, the reverse: "You're asking me to believe that from now on a beam of lasered light could shoot out of some wretch's body and into my light-gun when I press the button" (159). Aldiss sets his reverse-time consciousness, transcendentally, offstage, underlying the paradox by referring to how Wygelia (the Dark Woman) has to learn to speak backward. Amis partly solves the problem by having a "normal" narrative consciousness trapped in the protagonist's mind, observing and understanding the flow of time. Finally, however, there is only one way to tell a reverse-time story, and to illustrate it I would need to deliver this chapter orally, record it, and place a cassette in the volume that would play my words backward. Perhaps, this would be too heavy-handed a joke. Instead, I will just recall Frederic Brown's "The End":[31]

Pushing a button as he spoke, he said, "This should make time run backward run time make should this, said he, spoke he as button a pushing.

. . . END THE

Notes

1. Elizabeth Chase Akers, "Rock Me to Sleep, Mother," in George Gesner, editor, *Anthology of American Poetry* (New York: Avenel Books, 1983), 711. Poem originally published in 1859.

2. Christopher Marlowe, *Doctor Faustus*, in Fredson Bowers, editor, *Christopher Marlowe: The Complete Works, Volume 2* (Cambridge: Cambridge University Press, 1973), 225.

3. Plato, *The Statesman*, in *The Sophist and The Statesman*, translated by A. E. Taylor (London: Thomas Nelson and Sons, 1961), 177.

4. See Jonathan Westphal and Carl Levenson, editors, *Time* (Indianapolis: Hackett Publishing Company, 1993), which includes a different translation of his chapter on time along with Wittgenstein's response. Philip K. Dick's *Counter-Clock World* uses quotations from St. Augustine and other Church fathers as epigraphs, and he is also cited in Brian W. Aldiss's *An Age* (London: Sphere, 1969), 151–152, and Paul Davies, *About Time* (London: Viking, 1995), 17. Later page references to Aldiss and Davies in the text are to these editions.

5. St. Augustine, *Confessions*, edited by R. S. Pine-Coffin (Harmondsworth: Penguin, 1977), 264.

6. Edward Fitzgerald, "The Rubaiyat of Omar Khayyam," in A. J. Arberry, editor, *The Rubaiyat of Omar Khayyam and Other Persian Poems: An Anthology of Verse Translations* (London: Dent, 1976), 27.

7. John Gribbin, *In Search of Schrodinger's Cat* (London: Black Swan, 1991), 186.

8. Jack Cohen and Ian Stewart, *The Collapse of Chaos* (London: Penguin, 1994), 261–262.

9. J. M. E. McTaggart, "The Unreality of Time," in Westphal and Levenson, 94–111.

10. J. T. Fraser, *Time: The Familiar Stranger* (Redmond, Wash.: Tempus Books, 1987).

11. Peter Coveney and Roger Highfield, *The Arrow of Time* (London: Flamingo, 1991), 295–296.

12. Edward Page Mitchell, "The Clock That Went Backward," in Mitchell, *The Crystal Man* (Garden City, NY: Doubleday, 1973), 79.

13. Charles Kingsley, *The Water Babies* (1836; London: Macmillan, 1890), 274. I am grateful to K. V. Bailey for drawing my attention to this quotation.

14. Lewis Carroll, *Sylvie and Bruno*, 1889, in Carroll, *The Complete Illustrated Works of Lewis Carroll* (London: Chancellor Press, 1987), 414–415.

15. The much-criticized "unreadable" prose of *The Night Land* makes more sense when read as a deliberate archaism reflecting the coincidence of past and future.

16. Olaf Stapledon, *Star Maker* (1937; London: Penguin, 1988), 251.

17. But none of these coinages are as delightful as Terry Pratchett's own explicit "Trousers of Time" in *Johnny and the Bomb* to describe how time travel into the past creates a "new" future that forks from the "old" one.

18. J. G. Ballard, "Mr F. Is Mr F.," in Ballard, *The Disaster Area* (London: Panther, 1969), 120.

19. I am grateful to Cherith Baldry for drawing my attention to this book and loaning me a copy.

20. Lewis Carroll, *Alice through the Looking Glass*, in Martin Gardner, editor, *The Annotated Alice* (London: Anthony Blond, 1960), 247.

21. George Turner, "Paradigm and Pattern: Form and Meaning in *The Dispossessed*," *SF Commentary*, 41/42:4 (February, 1975), 65–74.

22. Philip K. Dick, *Counter-Clock World* (1967; London: Sphere, 1968), 49. Later page references in the text are to this edition.

23. Bruce R. Gillespie, "Contradictions," *SF Commentary*, 4 (1969), 76.

24. See Brian Griffin and David Wingrove, *Apertures: A Study of the Writings of Brian W. Aldiss* (Westport, Conn.: Greenwood Press, 1984), 120.

25. Brian W. Aldiss, Letter, *Extrapolation*, 37:3 (Fall, 1996), 272–273.

26. David Moyle, "Beyond the Black Hole: The Emergence of Science Fiction Themes in the Recent Work of Martin Amis," *Extrapolation*, 36 (Winter, 1995), 305–315.

27. Dave Langford, "Highballs!," in Langford, *The Silence of the Langford* (Framingham, Mass.: New England Science Fiction Association Press, 1996), 266.

28. See also James Blish's poem "A Memory of Creation" (in Blish, *With All of Love: Selected Poems*, edited by Keith Allen Daniels [San Francisco: Anamnesis Press, 1995], 25), which in 28 words traces the created universe from Godhood and back in a manner reminiscent of both this Aldiss passage and *Star Maker*.

29. Martin Amis, *Time's Arrow* (London: Penguin, 1992), 16. Later page references in the text are to this edition.

30. Lewis Carroll, *Sylvie and Bruno Concluded*, 1893, in Carroll, *The Complete Illustrated Works of Lewis Carroll* (London: Chancellor Press, 1987), 435–641.

31. Fredric Brown, "The End," in Brown, *The Best Short Stories of Fredric Brown* (London: New English Library, 1982), 447.

Part II

Timescapes

6

Beyond the Endtime Terminus: Allegories of Coalescence in Far-Future Science Fiction

Kirk Hampton and Carol MacKay

What happens when science fiction stories postulate time travel into the future, especially the far-distant future? After exploring answers to this question at some length in literal time travel tales, we developed the concept of an extended family of stories, which included not only the effects of time travel through time machines and suspended animation, but also through visitations from the future and confrontations with incredibly advanced technologies. These and other members of the extended family seem to exhibit the same qualities as actual future-time-travel stories. We coined the term "timezap" to express the accelerated future shock that occurs when humans encounter the future by any of these means. For us, the most striking quality of forward-moving time travel is the disintegration—not only of the time-travelers, but of their environment, even of the fictional medium itself. In a genre often considered superficial and perhaps a mite short on style and characterization, this leap into literary psychodrama comes as a surprise. In addition, these journeys to the end of time bristle with motifs and stylistic qualities atypical of science fiction in general, as if progressive time travel tended to warp the medium into something other than itself.[1] We concluded that time travel exerts a kind of pressure on this already dissociated genre to deconstruct itself. As if in an effort to reconstruct their faltering world, "timezap" stories frequently graft symbols or images onto one another. That is, one set of meanings is superimposed on another in a metaphorical fashion. This grafting helps to explain the unusual motifs associated with timezaps—motifs that convey both psychological dissociation and the bizarre future world which the time traveler enters.

Unlike time travel to the past, moving into the future seems to weaken or negate the human will. Progressive time travel is either an involuntary experience in the first place or else proves to be more than the time-traveler bargained for. The hero of H. G. Wells's *The Time Machine*, for example, only inadvertently travels forward to the twilight of the Earth.[2] And in many of Michael Moorcock's stories, human beings reaching the end of time are trapped there and made into playthings of the

Immortals. Even those who deliberately send themselves forward seem to get in over their heads, like the hero of Larry Niven's novel *A World Out of Time* (1976). Niven's cryogenically frozen and revived protagonist awakens to a hostile society very much the opposite of what he hoped for, and which he feels compelled to escape as quickly as possible—by means of another timezap.

I. The Lightshow

The first unmistakable sign that forward-moving time-travelers are being ripped apart by their experience is what we call the dissociative lightshow—an event that disrupts all sense of cohesion and narrative sequence and symbolically conveys the psychic vivisection of a human mind. Both Stanley Kubrick's film and Arthur C. Clarke's novelization of *2001: A Space Odyssey* present intense renditions of this phenomenon. (Although Astronaut Bowman is not technically traveling to the future, his encounter with a supernally advanced alien race brings the scene into the extended family of timezap tales.) In the novel, Clarke employs a sudden flurry of conditional ideation, achieving a turmoil of consciousness that is the equivalent of the film's brilliant visual disorientation: "And still the far end of the shaft came no closer. It was almost as if the walls were moving with him, carrying him to his unknown destination. Or perhaps he was really motionless, and space was moving past him."[3]

Dissociative lightshows bring out some of science fiction's fanciest rhetoric, evoking all manner of linguistic games and figurative language, even reaching toward the negation of thought altogether. For example, Stanislaw Lem's novel *Return from the Stars* plunges its protagonist, a space-traveler timezapped by the Lorentz-FitzGerald contraction,[4] into a baffling sensory carnival:

> A wave of pedestrians caught me up; jostled, I moved forward in the crowd. It took a moment for me really to see the size of the hall. But was it all one hall? No walls: a glittering white "high-held" explosion of unbelievable wings; between them, columns, made not of any substance but of dizzying motion. Rushing upward, enormous fountains of a liquid denser than water, illuminated from inside by colored floodlights? No—vertical tunnels of glass through which a succession of blurred vehicles raced upward? Now I was completely at a loss.[5]

Yet other versions of the lightshow try to go beyond Lem's rendition of sensory overload, employing all the powers of language to invoke the mental disintegration that seems an inherent part of progressive time travel. Authors in this normally straightforward genre may even turn metafictional when time travel occurs. In this respect, the stylish Moorcock kicks out all the stops in *The End of All Songs*, highlighting language, form, and artifice to create the dissociative verbal lightshow *par excellence*:

Something huge and heavy and alive moved towards them, passed through them, it seemed, and was gone. Heat and cold became extreme—and seemed one. Hundreds of colours came and went, but were pale, washed out, rainy. There was dampness in the air he breathed; little tremors and pain ran through him, but were past almost before his brain could signal their presence. Booming, echoing sounds—slow sounds, deep and sluggish—blossomed in his ear. . . . [E]very movement took infinity to consider and perform, and he appeared to weigh tons, as though his mass spread through miles of space and years of time. . . . Words piped at him; all the words of his life.[6]

Authors stretch their rhetoric to its limits in the lightshow, striving to express an incomprehensible degree of psychological disorientation. Moorcock's rhetorical timezap resembles many others in its tendency to combine sensory gigantism with negation of the senses, to evoke an event both intensely physical and transcendent, at once immensely significant and mind-boggling.

Interestingly enough, the opening sequence of Isaac Asimov's classic novel of time travel, *The End of Eternity*, actually manifests a sort of anti-lightshow:

The kettle [the time machine] did not move.
Harlan did not expect it to. . . . Yet the spaces between the rods had melted into a gray blankness which was solid to the touch, yet nonetheless immaterial for all that. And there *was* the little stir in his stomach, the faint (psychosomatic?) touch of dizziness, that told him that all the kettle contained, including himself, was rushing upwhen through Eternity.[7]

Here we witness how Asimov confounds the senses through contradiction: the grayness is solid yet immaterial; the movement is swift yet imperceptible. Observe, too, the dissociative distrust of the senses implied in the word "psychosomatic." Similarly, Clifford D. Simak's *Highway of Eternity* expresses forward movement in time through anti-images: "He pushed [the control]. Darkness clamped in on them, a darkness that brought instant disorientation—as if they had been divorced from all reality. There was no sense of movement—no sense of anything."[8] Even more succinctly, Edmund Cooper's *Deadly Image* opens with a metaphor embodying both sensory experience and the cryogenic time-traveler's separation from that experience: "in a remote twilight of consciousness, memories burned like minute candles."[9]

Ultimately, language itself is foregrounded—sometimes to the point of deliberate incoherence—in the all-out effort to send us reeling forward in time. Our favorite example is the opening sentence of Frederik Pohl's tongue-in-cheek story "The Day of the Boomer Dukes" (1956), written in a far-future lingo: "*Paptaste udderly, semped sempsemp dezhavoo, qued schmerz.*"[10]

Powerful, upwelling emotions emerge in all these dissociative lightshows, but the feelings thus evoked usually appear and disappear with mechanical abruptness. In fact, these neat emotional expungements seem rather tonic in their effect. The protagonist of Gordon Eklund's *Serving in Time*, for example, struggles with intense yet impalpable emotions as he travels toward the future, but then quickly recovers:

He was about to tell Horatio that he couldn't go through with it when his chair began to vibrate. . . . He started to scream but hastily checked that urge. . . . As horrible as it was, the timevoid did not extend indefinitely. He told himself this, silently, again and again.

Then, suddenly, there was nothing around him.

And he did scream.

But nothing came out.

Then he knew he was on his way and, abruptly, without logical reason, relaxed and allowed the stream of time to sweep him effortlessly and inexorably forward.[11]

Eklund's version of the timezap underscores what is implied in all our examples—the repressed emotions that rise up in this rough-and-tumble cleansing of the psyche.

II. Microcosms

After the lightshow has died down, and those obtrusive emotions have been cleansed, the time-traveler enters a dizzying world of microcosms, in which the larger is paradoxically contained within the smaller. These magic containers are often some form of memory bank—like the beep in James Blish's story "Beep" (1954), in which each message of an instantaneous communication device is found to contain all the messages ever sent, or ever to be sent, by the time-spanning device. Other timezap stories posit literal miniaturized worlds, as in Donald A. Wollheim's *Edge of Time* (1958) or Theodore Sturgeon's story "Microcosmic God" (1941). There are also many science fiction stories featuring gifts or visitors from the future, and these inverted timezaps seem to contain a great deal of compacted, destructive energy. The opening of the film *Timecop* (1994), for example, features a nineteenth-century scene in which a thief from our own day pulls out two laser-sighted Uzis and opens fire on a stagecoach bearing a shipment of gold.

These beings or items from the future tend to hide their destructive potential in a cloak of deceptive ambiguity. The unfortunate recipients of these manifestations believe they stand to gain some sort of wonderful power, but all the while they are experiencing disguised timezaps, ultimately finding themselves dissociated and overpowered, just as they would be in travel to the future. The retro visitors act as time-spanning Trojan horses. For example, in C. M. Kornbluth's story "The Little Black Bag" (1950), a present-day doctor receives a medical kit from the future—and sure enough, the apparent boon leads to his grisly demise. Moreover, the destructive power of visitors from the future is often masked by the appearance that they are conveying crucial information, but the precise quality of the message remains ambiguous or two-edged. Gregory Benford's *Timescape* (1981) features a cryptic tachyon message, its nature and veracity left uncertain to the very end. As if to underscore the puzzling ambiguity of visitations from the future, there are in fact two subtypes of these stories, which might be called the "false timezap" and "time con" tales, respectively. In both accounts, the future seems to pay a visit, but its legitimacy is thrown into doubt.

False timezap stories characteristically present the deceit as a form of brainwashing. In the Star Trek novel *Timetrap* (1988) by David Dvorkian, Klingons convince Captain Kirk he's been zapped 100 years ahead, and in an episode of the television series *Star Trek: The Next Generation*, Commander Riker is similarly duped. In time-con tales, visits from the future, whether real or not, are part of a confidence game, and opposed reality systems reflect like mirrors, producing a bewilderment appropriate to the comedic themes of deception and ambiguity. In these time swindles, language and artifice are strongly foregrounded, and there is a great deal of razzle-dazzle to the plot. Kornbluth's story "Time Bum" (1958) hoodwinks the reader right along with the con-man protagonist, who is tricked by another trickster from the future, and is then put on trial for impersonating a timecop. And Fritz Leiber's "Time Fighter" (1957) manages to bilk the reader through its series of both bewildering and comedic convolutions.

III. The Superimposing of Symbol Systems

The predominant logic of future time travel entails the superimposing of one cognitive system onto another, in metaphoric or symbolic fashion. Niven's *A World Out of Time* posits a method of time travel that functions both literally and symbolically as this kind of superimposition: The cryogenically frozen protagonist's thought patterns and memories are copied like software onto the freshly erased brain of a healthy man.[12] This technique evokes eerie near-recognition, off-parallels, and archaisms to achieve effects ranging from the subliminal to the archetypal. At its most subtle, it produces the uncanny psychological effect known as *presque vu* ("almost seen," a cousin to *déjà vu*), a feeling of inexplicable familiarity or near-understanding. This inchoate feeling is both fearful and alluring to forward-moving time-travelers. The sense that some unknown element has been superimposed upon one's current perceptions has its analogue in the resurgence of dissociated thoughts and feelings.

Notably, the mysterious psychic allure of the living machine V'ger irresistibly draws Spock in *Star Trek: The Motion Picture* (1979); Dr. Morbius belatedly perceives the hideous form his repressed emotions have taken in the film *Forbidden Planet* (1956); and the astronaut in Clarke's *2001* encounters a strangely familiar scene as he watches television in an alien "hotel" room:

He continued to wander across the spectrum [of the TV programs], and suddenly recognized a familiar scene. Here was this very suite, now occupied by a celebrated actor who was furiously denouncing an unfaithful mistress. Bowman looked with a shock of recognition upon the living room he had just left—and when the [television] camera followed the indignant couple [he was watching] toward [their] bedroom, he involuntarily looked toward [his own] door to see if anyone was entering. (214)

This experience of the almost-seen sometimes hardens into the fearful or grotesque, as in stories about nearly meeting oneself in time. Other authors create slapstick, skewed-parallel images, like Moorcock's ship, the "Queen Elizabeth," in *The Hollow Lands*, which is described as being shaped like the Queen herself, lying face-down in the water and firing "tuxedos" from its breasts.[13]

As one ventures further forward in time, the created worlds sound increasingly mythological—an effect often accentuated by a deliberately archaic style. For example, *Forbidden Planet* is based on Shakespeare's *The Tempest*—itself strongly mythological in character—while the names used in the film have what might be called a Greco-Roman timbre: Altair, Morbius, Bellerophon. Even the hapless heroes of the film *Bill and Ted's Excellent Adventure* (1989) become templates for an entire future civilization. And Moorcock creates a vivid world of emblematic names in his "Endtime" stories—names like "Tall Laughter" and "Scar-faced Brooder" in *The Time Dweller* (1969), "Werther de Goethe" and "The Iron Orchid" in his *Dancers at the End of Time* trilogy (1972–1976). The disintegrative effect of timezaps seems almost invariably to lead to a powerful, compensatory urge on the part of science fiction authors to reintegrate, to intensify their allegorization. In this respect, we can observe a creative projection toward something like metamythology, in which whole symbol systems or portions of them are superimposed on one another. Roger Zelazny carries this tendency to the nth degree in *Lord of Light* (1967), in which human characters advanced toward the end of time take on the powers and personae of the Hindu pantheon.

As if guided by a creative instinct inherent to the genre, science fiction authors evoke a deliberate sundering—even a cleansing—of the would-be visitor to the future. As noted earlier, the most significant aspect of this process is the appearance of powerful, primal emotions. In a genre generally filled with plucky adventurers and stiff-lipped military types, the time-travelers are flooded with terror, rage, and madness itself. For Wells's Time Traveller, the "unpleasant sensations" of undertaking time travel soon give way to "hysterical exhilaration" and confusion; finally, he reports of his first protracted journey, "[W]ith a kind of madness growing upon me, I flung myself into futurity" (31). Even a mere brush with the future can induce discomfiting emotions. Seeing a woman from the future on their experimental television set, the protagonists of Ray Cummings's *The Shadow Girl* experience "a vague, uneasy sense of fear."[14] And one of the earliest victims of timezap—Buck Rogers himself, in Philip Francis Nowlan's *Armageddon 2419 A.D.*—struggles for mental balance after he awakens from a long period of suspended animation: "There were times when I felt that I was on the verge of insanity."[15]

The powerful emotions in these time voyages are more than just panic attacks. Authors often indicate that the purging of such feelings is a necessary procedure of movement into the future. Note the example of Poul Anderson's *The Corridors of Time*, whose timezapped hero is greeted by a reassuringly parental couple named John and Mary. With what the author calls "a mother's compassion," the woman announces, "We healed you, soma and psyche, while you slept."[16] That this may be a necessary procedure is also brought out in Clarke's *2001*, when the protagonist is emotionally cleansed by the supercivilization which is zapping him: "The springs of memory were being tapped. . . . [A]ll the emotions he had ever felt . . . were racing past, more and more swiftly. His life was unreeling like a tape recorder playing back at ever-increasing speed" (216). Moreover, the rampant emotionality of time travel helps to explain the prevalence of self-appointed timecops, dominating an entire subgenre of time travel stories. In works such as *Timecop*, *The End of Eternity*, *Serving in Time*, "The Day of the Boomer Dukes," and *The End of All Songs* (with its "Guild of Temporal Adventurers"), one specialized group tries to impose a meaningful structure on time itself.

The prevalence of timecop stories emphasizes some of the moral overtones that crop up in these psychodramas. The application of ethical or moral considerations to the fabric of a story is another example of the grafting of one system of thought (or values) upon another. The resultant psychological allegory takes on the form of a karmic cleansing. The heroes and heroines find themselves judged by unknown forces much greater than themselves. It is significant that the super-advanced character "Q" in *Star Trek: The Next Generation* and later series makes his initial appearance literally as a judge, complete with traditional British robes and wig, intent on deciding whether or not the sinful human race should be eradicated. And at the conclusion of *The End of Eternity*, the hero realizes his lifelong career of meddling with history as the worst sort of psychological and ethical disarray:

> He had never looked [the nature of his life] clearly in the face, until, suddenly, now.
> And he saw [his career as an Eternal] with great clarity as a sink of deepening psychoses, a writhing pit of abnormal motivation, a mass of desperate lives torn brutally out of context. (191)

It seems, too, that emotionality and the moral considerations that characterize future time travel are sometimes ironically inverted, as with Moorcock's end-of-timers, who pointedly have neither real feelings nor ethical considerations, and are often desperate for genuine emotions they can never feel. In the prologue to *An Alien Heat*, Moorcock observes, "Most of the old emotions had atrophied, meant little to them."[17] Perhaps the emotional purging of time travel has taken its toll on these characters. The result is a true *fin de cosmos*, not just a *fin de monde*—a terrible ennui and hunger for what cannot be. If the end of time holds out the promise of a cleansing spiritual process, that process can clearly be short-circuited—a fact evidenced by quite a number of decadent, wimpy worlds of the future (from that of Wells's Eloi to the devitalized civilizations of John Brunner's novel *The 100th Millennium* [1959] or John Boorman's film *Zardoz* [1973]).

IV. Mock Transcendence

As we've seen, a timezap is an extremely high-energy affair, warping the characters, the reader, and even the medium itself in its intensity.[18] With time travel forward and its related incidents, science fiction takes on either a great portentousness or a dissolute irony—depending on whether or not protagonists meet the challenge of integrating the fragments of their dissociated minds. At the end of the timezap, this genre based on the rational extrapolation of science turns suddenly into a stylized allegory dealing with repressed emotions. The structure of the allegory and momentum of the stories appear to promise the coalescence of the portions of one's scattered psyche. Yet the outcome of these symbolic adventures is at best an ambiguous mock transcendence, with the boundaries of the self distinctly maintained despite everything.

In Charles Sheffield's far-future novella "At the Eschaton," for example, the emotional tone appears thoroughly positive at endpoint. The hero's long-lost wife says, "You'll have me for as long as there is time," and the reunited couple are said to be "facing an infinite future."[19] But the author shuffles the rhetorical cards at the end, so that ironic undercuttings muddy the climactic scene. There is, after all, no more time for them to share. In addition, she tells him to make a wish, then forbids him to tell her what it is, "or it won't come true!" The hero then says that he *can't* make the wish, because it *has* come true. Within this spate of logical negations, we read that the two are heading *away* "from the hellfire of ultimate convergence" and that ahead of them lies "the last question, birth canal or final extinction" (348). So the novella flip-flops right off the edge of time.

Another tale about the virtual end of time, Greg Bear's "Judgment Engine," falls explicitly short of transcendence. This story involves digitalized super-intelligences existing at the end of time who reconstitute the personalities of a married couple from the distant past. Husband and wife are brought forward in a desperate effort to coalesce the warring factions of this mind-blowingly distant future. In Bear's story, too, we recognize a massive struggle for transcendence, but all the human couple can do when they reappear is continue their bickering. The hero notes sadly the "enormous triviality" of their exertion to come together, and the story ends in isolation, as the narrator faces "the Between," and the story trails off in an unpunctuated, Wakean fragment.[20]

In our extended family of timezap stories, *2001* and *Star Trek: The Motion Picture* exemplify an apparently transcendent extreme. Like "At the Eschaton," they proffer an optimistic, almost religious tone at their conclusions. Yet like Sheffield's tale, these works can posit only a sort of oxymoronic pseudo-transcendence in which the separated parts remain discrete. The closing passage of Clarke's novel has a distinctly unresolved and menacing quality, as the cosmic baby considers what to do with his new plaything, Earth. In *Star Trek: The Motion Picture*, Spock's final observation makes clear that the ostensibly transcended V'ger is doomed to carry an unending load of human emotional baggage.

V. Controlled Repression in Science Fiction

Why do these stories so tenaciously avoid the merging of opposites which their own imagery implies? We reply with a theory about science fiction as a whole. Science fiction embraces a central cautionary myth that postulates a need for controlled emotional repression. As a genre, science fiction prescribes this arduous maintenance of one's emotional shape as requisite for human fulfillment, survival, and progress. Such archetypes as Victor Frankenstein and Henry Jekyll—along with the countless mad scientists who have followed in their wake—act out harrowing, metaphoric tales about the dangers of losing control of one's carefully repressed emotions. The pop-culture phenomenon *Star Trek*—with its countless filmic and textual variations, parodies, mutations, and spinoffs—is an extended meditation on this theme. In the original series, Captain Kirk recurrently battles various forms of pain and ecstasy that might make him lose his emotional shape, while his arduous struggle is highlighted by the figures of the overly repressed Spock and the ill-controlled Dr. McCoy. Another television series in the Star Trek family, *Star Trek: Deep Space Nine*, continues this thematic tradition in the character of Odo, the polymorphous alien who visibly struggles to retain both his emotional composure and his physical shape.

Science fiction heroes and heroines indeed are struggling to maintain their shape, with the body as often as not symbolizing the psyche. We speculate that science fiction's overarching attachment to images of technology is part of its thematic attachment to images of control. Certainly outer space is appropriate both literally and symbolically for the enactment of this myth, with its shape-retaining (and isolating) spacesuits and spaceships, and with controls and gauges embodying the need for constant internal surveillance.[21] As we examine this motif in its incarnations throughout the field, we can uncover science fiction's spectrum of control, from excessive repression on one extreme (exemplified by a legion of emotionless aliens, such as the ant-like Borg of *Star Trek: The Next Generation* and the phenomenon of wimpy civilizations) to utter loss of control on the other (seen in the figures of mad scientists, rampant monsters, and insane superbeings of every stripe). In the middle are the ever-grinning heroes and heroines, as frequently as not military or scientific types, keenly aware of the need for both the passions which drive humanity and the requisite dissociative containment of those very passions.[22]

The works we have studied embody this prevailing theme. Perhaps the most appropriate scene among them is the moment in *2001* when Bowman is locked out of his spacepod and must brave the vacuum of space without his helmet. The act literally threatens his physical integrity even as it symbolizes his need to confront his inner fears. He can then systematically dismantle the insane computer HAL, who with ironic humor symbolizes the uncontrolled id.

In sum, progressive time travel holds forth the seductive but terrifying possibility of losing one's individuality altogether. Confronting the end of the world, Wells's prototypical Time Traveller feels "a terrible dread of lying helpless in that remote and awful twilight [which] sustained me while I clambered upon the saddle" (131). In this context, the "remote and awful twilight" stands for transcendence as seen through the eyes of fear, and the saddle of the time machine represents a re-attainment of control, with its concomitant price tag of perpetual dissociation.[23] As far as science fiction is concerned, time travel into the future is irresistibly fascinating, but it may prove to be terminally therapeutic—and thus the coalescence toward which such stories move is avoided, or else becomes an amplified view of the divided human psyche, with its perennial subdivisions writ large. Science fiction authors since Wells have played with the rousing rhetoric and the imagery, but have either fled or finessed the more profound symbolic possibilities of journeys to the end of time.

Notes

1. The inherent difficulty of far-future tales was hinted at by Brian Stableford. Prior to publication of Gregory Benford's *Far Futures* anthology (1995), Stableford noted Harry Harrison's inability to produce a companion volume to his near-future anthology, *The Year 2000* (1970), to be entitled *The Year 2,000,000*, apparently because the editor had received "insufficient suitable submissions" for his planned text. Stableford proceeds to observe, "The theme does not lend itself readily to conventional plot and character development." See his entry under "Far Future" in *The Encyclopedia of Science Fiction*, edited by John Clute and Peter Nicholls (New York: St. Martin's Press, 1993), 416.

2. H. G. Wells, *The Time Machine* (1895, rev. 1924; New York: Berkley, 1957); later page references in the text are to this edition. The novel, originally drafted as "The Chronic Argonauts" in 1888, was serialized as *The Time Traveller's Story* in *The National Observer* in 1894 before the author published it under its present title in 1895. Wells revised the novel in 1924 for the Atlantic Edition, reducing the number of chapters from sixteen to fourteen and removing their titles; since most publications follow this version, we have elected to cite a readily available paperback for purposes of quoting from the novel. In the 1895 edition, the journey to this netherworld is entitled "The Further Vision," as shown in the critical edition of the 1895 version: *The Time Machine: An Invention*, edited by Leon Stover (Jefferson, NC: McFarland, 1996). In the 1924 edition and thereafter, the chapter designation is "XI." All versions of this episode open with the words, "I have already told you of the sickness and confusion that comes with time travelling," and conclude with the final quotation we discuss at the end of our chapter.

3. Arthur C. Clarke, *2001: A Space Odyssey* (New York: Signet, 1968), 196. Later page references in the text are to this edition.

4. The term refers to the slowing of subjective time at speeds approaching that of light. This concept was independently postulated at the turn of the twentieth century by two scientists, British physicist George Francis FitzGerald and Dutch theorist Henrik Antoon Lorentz.

5. Stanislaw Lem, *Return from the Stars*, translated by Barbara Marszal and Frank Simpson (1961; New York: Avon, 1982), 7–8.

6. Michael Moorcock, *The End of All Songs*, Volume 3 of *Dancers at the End of Time* (New York: Harper & Row, 1976), 43.

7. Isaac Asimov, *The End of Eternity* (1955; New York: Lancer, 1963), 7. A later page reference in the text is to this edition.

8. Clifford D. Simak, *Highway of Eternity* (1986; New York: Ballantine, 1988), 25.

9. Edmund Cooper, *Deadly Image* (New York: Ballantine, 1958), xx.

10. Frederik Pohl, "The Day of the Boomer Dukes," in Pohl, *Tomorrow Times Seven* (1956; New York: Ballantine, 1959), 55. For other efforts—at once lighthearted and serious—to dramatize historical and future language change, see two of L. Sprague de Camp's early contributions to *Astounding Science Fiction*, namely his first published story, "The Isolinguals" (1937), and his classic essay, "Language for Time-Travelers" (1938), both cited in this volume's bibliography.

11. Gordon Eklund, *Serving in Time* (Don Mills, Ont.: Laser Books, 1975), 57.

12. Larry Niven, *A World Out of Time* (New York: Holt, Rinehart & Winston, 1976), 3.

13. Michael Moorcock, *The Hollow Lands*, Volume 2 of *The Dancers at the End of Time* (New York: Harper & Row, 1974), 16.

14. Ray Cummings, *The Shadow Girl* (New York: Ace, 1962), 5.

15. Philip Francis Nowlan, *Armageddon 2419 A.D.* (1928; New York: Ace, 1962), 12.

16. Poul Anderson, *The Corridors of Time* (1965; New York: Berkley Books, 1978), 130.

17. Michael Moorcock, *An Alien Heat*, Volume 1 of *Dancers at the End of Time* (New York: Harper & Row, 1972), xx.

18. John Gribbin emphasizes the psychological nature of this warping: "There is indeed far more to the Universe (or universes) than our physical senses and physical sciences can reveal, and what we see as reality may indeed be largely subjective, conditioned by our preconceived ideas and those of the society in which we live." He goes on to opine, "Timewarps exist. *Control* of timewarps (and spacewarps), however, is something to be sought not with the aid of mechanical devices, but through the improved understanding of the human mind, the nature of the unconscious, and their interactions with what we think of as the physical world" (Gribbin, *Timewarps* [New York: Delacorte Press, 1979], 187).

19. Charles Sheffield, "At the Eschaton," in Gregory Benford, editor, *Far Futures* (New York: Tor, 1995), 348. A later page reference in the text is to this edition.

20. Greg Bear, "Judgment Engine," in Benford, editor, *Far Futures*, 51, 55.

21. The self-evident necessity of these things on the literal level is augmented by an equally appropriate symbolic significance. When the literal and symbolic so neatly coincide, the result makes for potent allegory.

22. In the film *The Day the Earth Stood Still* (1951), we encounter an especially refined allegory of dissociation. The alien Klaatu travels with a menacing robot named Gort who is at once his double and a split-off segment of his personality; Gort's function is to contain the constantly threatening destructive tendencies of the various races in the interplanetary confederation which Earth is being pressured to join. While designed to keep a lid on bad behavior, Gort is himself a repository of dormant destructive power of genocidal magnitude, a walking figure of repression and rage.

23. It has been reported that director George Pal filmed this scene for his 1960 production of *The Time Machine* but that the studio deemed it too bleak for inclusion in the final cut. Speculation among film and science fiction buffs about its possible existence runs rampant, for the prospect of recovering such a key visualization for this classic tale remains tantalizing.

7

Time and Some Mysteries of Mind

Susan Stratton

The nature of time has been a source of fascination throughout the twentieth century. From Einstein's Special Theory of Relativity of 1905, which abolished absolute time, and his General Theory (1915), which described the movement of bodies in terms of the curvature of space time and predicted slower time near a massive body, through quantum theory's not-yet-widely accepted implications about instantaneous communication and infinitely multiple universes, science has challenged our traditional notions of objective, linear time and causality.[1] Fred Alan Wolf summarizes: "Perhaps the greatest mystery of all time is 'time.' There has never been an adequate definition, a clear metaphor, or even a good physical picture of what time is. . . . In quantum mechanics time is not even an observable." Wolf then recalls a Zen parable that suggests that consciousness is the real site of time, that time is not "out there" but "in here":

One windy day two monks were arguing about a flapping banner. The first said, "I say the banner is moving, not the wind." The second said, "I say the wind is moving, not the banner." A third monk passed by and said, "The wind is not moving. The banner is not moving. Your minds are moving."[2]

Science fiction has embraced the fascination with time, from H. G. Wells's *The Time Machine*, which predated Einstein, through Jack Williamson's *The Legion of Time*, Isaac Asimov's *The End of Eternity*, Robert A. Heinlein's " 'All You Zombies—,' " and Poul Anderson's *The Guardians of Time*, to Gregory Benford's *Timescape* and Connie Willis's "Fire Watch" and *Lincoln's Dreams*, not to mention a huge list of others that cover the whole spectrum of sf.

Also evident in twentieth-century sf is a fascination with paranormal psychic abilities, or psi. Science has been less interested in psi, so investigation has been confined to the scientific fringe of parapsychology. Here influential explorations of precognition, the psi ability most obviously associated with time, have included: J. W. Dunne's 1927 study of precognitive dreams that indicated a link to one's own future consciousness; J. B. Rhine's work on predictions of how cards would fall after being shuffled; statistical studies of passengers' avoidance of trains and ships that were headed for serious accidents;[3] studies of subjective factors in accurate predictions;[4] and studies of precognitive dreaming at Maimonides Medical Center in New York.[5] Despite all this work, we remain deadlocked over whether precognition is well supported by the evidence and may even be ordinary[6] or whether it is unacceptably inconsistent with entrenched convictions about causality and rationality. This makes it fruitful territory for sf, and writers who portray psi abilities have frequently related the mysteries of mind to the mysteries of time. In so doing, they have kept parapsychology linked with theoretical physics and kept the minds of the curious open to a relationship between science's temporal mysteries and the parapsychological mysteries of psi. Sf writers who explore the twin mysteries of time and mind repeatedly invoke the discourses of both science and mysticism.

In 1930 Olaf Stapledon published the first science-fictional connection between psi and Einsteinian relativity. The "Introduction" to *Last and First Men* establishes the striking narrative premise: "This book has two authors. . . . The brain that conceives and writes these sentences lives in the time of Einstein. Yet I, the true inspirer of this book . . . I who influence that primitive being's conception, inhabit an age which, for Einstein, lies in the very remote future."[7] The twentieth-century writer cannot distinguish the product of his own imagination from information transmitted telepathically across time and space. Stapledon asserted that he needed the radical device to "embody the possibility that there may be more in time's nature than is revealed to us" (10). His fascination with the nature of time underlies his depiction of psi.

Stapledon wrote when Einstein's non-linear view of space-time was beginning to catch on. Einstein's fame lent credibility to the sort of speculation about the nature of time that Stapledon found in Dunne's *An Experiment with Time*, published in 1927.[8] Dunne devotes a few knowledgeable pages to Einsteinian relativity in this book about his own precognitive dreams and the experiments he designed to yield an understanding of their nature. Dunne's empirical investigation combined with logical derivation from commonplace notions of time yields a theory of time that allows the consciousness to range through an "eternal" configuration of time in dimensions other than the one we are most familiar with. Stapledon went far beyond Dunne's assertion that communication with one's own future mind is possible and indeed commonplace. Neither Dunne nor Stapledon drew significantly on Einstein, but their references to Einstein lent legitimacy to their further speculations about the nature of time.

Stapledon's wonderful Fifth Men are much occupied by temporal research. They develop telepathic contact with past minds to the point that "every individual could at will project his vision into any locality of space-time which he desired to inspect" (181) through a compatible mind living in the past (231). Stapledon's metaphorical approximation of the means by which this is accomplished has aspects of both mysticism and science: it is a "partial awakening, as it were, into eternity, and into inspection of a minute tract of space-time through some temporal mind in the past, as though through an optical instrument." Stapledon keeps the scientific discourse dominant by emphasizing the limits of the physical capacity of a brain to assimilate the knowledge obtainable in this way (181).

The Sixteenth Men mirror the Fifth in their acquisition of this ability to range through time telepathically, but they still have not mastered time. The two intellectual problems that inspire the Sixteenth Men to create an order of intelligence higher than their own are "the mystery of time and the mystery of mind's relation to the world" (212). Both are central to Stapledon's conjectures about psi. He depicts time as having an eternal dimension, so that the mind of the future can contact the past without effectively changing anything. The Eighteenth Men have been "profoundly affected" by their experience of past minds, and they have also contributed to the "thought and action" of the past (239). Indeed, some very singular past minds—Jesus, Socrates, and Buddha are named—seem to have been influenced by someone beyond the Eighteenth Men, perhaps a Cosmic Mind that awakens in an even more remote future (240).

Stapledon tops Einstein's General Theory of Relativity. While Einstein accounts for gravitation in terms of the nature of spacetime, the Sixteenth Men tackle "the mystery of mind's relation to the world" and discover a relationship between mind and gravity. It is the gravitational effects of mental and spiritual development that enable the Eighteenth Men to detect remote intelligence with appropriate instruments. It was the "spiritual development" of the Fifth Men, it turns out, that caused the moon to spiral into Earth, ending human life there (230).

Stapledon's far-future narrator wishes to convey "not only the vastness of time and space, but also the vast diversity of mind's possible modes" (15). The final psi breakthrough of the Eighteenth Men is partly the result of research by group-minds that link ninety-six different types of individual mentalities telepathically to create a higher order of mind. The breakthrough is the occasional experience of the race mind by an individual. "The system of radiation which embraces the whole planet, and includes the million million brains of the race, becomes the physical basis of a racial self" (225). The experience encompasses all the time and space experienced by any of the brains and thus yields insight into the nature of time and space. The knowledge gained through this experience, the greatest triumph of eons of scientific progress, yet is related to our own mystical and creative insights: "Every human being, of whatever species, may occasionally glimpse some fragment or aspect of existence ... which normally he cannot see" (227). Stapledon uses all that fictional advanced intellect to support the insights of our mystics into the essential here/now of all the reaches of time and space.

The dramatic growth of Einstein's reputation during the 1920s meant that Stapledon could reintroduce what was a commonplace of mysticism with some scientific support from Einstein's spacetime. Stapledon's application of Einstein's thought to the concept of telepathy yielded precognition and retrocognition explained as telepathy across time.

Though quantum theory was taking root at the time Stapledon wrote *Last and*

First Men, it was another thirty years before it showed up clearly in a science fiction account of psi abilities. James Blish's novel, variously titled *ESPer* and *Jack of Eagles*, was the first to explain psi in terms of quantum physics. The language, the imagery, and the attempt on the part of the protagonist Danny Caiden to learn to understand his odd talents are all scientific. Danny's tour of all possible leads to understanding his psi abilities takes him to an occultist/medium, a university parapsychologist, the Fortean Society, and the Psychic Research Society. The medium is a fake and the PRS bunch are vicious power seekers, but the value of the parapsychologist Todd, with his equipment and his theories, is clear. David Ketterer reports in *Imprisoned in a Tesseract* that much of Blish's expansion of "Let the Finder Beware" "beefs up Danny's research [and Todd's role] and serves to put the theme of extraordinary psychic powers on an even more scientifically convincing basis."[9]

Blish's imagery and theory both derive from quantum theory. The imagery comes first, in descriptions of what Danny experiences when his psi kicks in. There are "a thousand billion tiny things" "whirling" or "spinning" in his brain.[10] The first explicit reference to quantum theory does not come until more than halfway through the book (123), but there is a much earlier mention of real-life parapsychologist Rhine's most recent book asserting that the accuracy of ESP increases with an increase in the number of things it handles (75), which reinforces the notion that quantum physics would be a likely place to seek a psi theory.

Although one could draw on quantum theory without particular attention to time, time is central to Blish's theorizing about psi, as it must be when precognition comes into play. Like Stapledon, Blish drew on *An Experiment with Time* (61, 77, 89). Blish adopts Dunne's theory that one's own past, present, and future are all accessible to one's consciousness.

Blish labors to connect Dunne's empirical observations about time to quantum theory. He starts with the assumption that psi powers use an otherwise unoccupied part of the brain and conjectures that this "unused part of the human brain might not share the one-way view of time that the gray matter is used to. The so-called 'arrow of time,' which points forward only, is a sort of myth that we grow up with" in our culture (88). This myth limits the cortical activity of the gray matter but not the psi activity of the brain. "Actually, all events—past, present, and future—exist together. They don't just flash into being in some mythical present. . . . They only seem to because the observer's consciousness is moving among them and hits them only one at a time" (88).

Predestination is explicitly denied; rather, Blish exploits the many-universe angle of quantum theory. Danny offers as a useful image Dunne's idea of an infinite series of overlapping event-levels, each keyed to some decision point. In an approximation of quantum theory discourse, parapsychologist Todd links the infinite series to what he calls "Heisenberg's 'probability packets'" (89). Todd works to express psi activity in mathematical terms, using as a starting point what he calls "the already well-known Blackett-Dirac formula" (122). The label links the name of a founder of quantum theory, Paul Dirac, to what I gather is a fictional parapsychologist's name. The plot removes Todd as a useful ally, leaving Danny to make a forced leap from scientifically careful work to a recognition inspired by general semantics that the quantum-value of Planck's constant isn't constant at all with reference to the infinite series of event-levels but varies at a constant rate from frame to frame (123–124).

This most mathematical portion of Blish's text is linked to the solution of a problem involving a mechanical device designed to keep a psi guy confined to one frame like the rest of us, so what one might regard as the most fantastic part of the story—this key hunk of hardware, which Danny alters to increase his psi abilities instead of limiting them—is most directly associated with quantum theory. Danny's powers extend across the whole range of psi abilities, from precognition, clairvoyance, and telepathy to the psychokinesis with which he wields objects and catapults himself from one place or reality frame to another. Though events get more and more fantastic as the plot progresses, Blish carefully grounds them in a quantum approach to the mystery of time.

The revolutions in twentieth-century scientific thought about the nature of the universe had a significant impact on science fiction depictions of psychic powers in general and precognition in particular. At the same time, a persistent factor in science fiction precognition is the mystical thought that is often associated with Eastern religions but is in fact found in the writings of mystics from all religious traditions.

Ursula K. Le Guin's *The Left Hand of Darkness*, in its presentation of the Foretellers of Gethen, reflects the impact of Eastern religions on American culture in the 1960s. Le Guin does not allude to contemporary physics in her depiction of precognition. Practitioners of the Handdara religion practice the "discipline of Presence, which is a kind of trance . . . involving self-loss (self-augmentation?) through extreme sensual receptiveness and awareness," the opposite of most techniques of mysticism, protagonist Ai notes, but probably "a mystical discipline, tending toward the experience of Immanence."[11]

The Handdarata Foretellers can accurately answer a question about what is to come. The answers sometimes have the ambiguity that has traditionally been a feature of prophecy, but there is no Uncertainty Principle at work; a precise question produces a precise answer (62). Unlike traditional prophets, these work as a group of nine who perform a variety of roles in a complex of interacting human nervous systems. They are powered by sexual energies, removed from the ordinary time by schizophrenics, focused on reality by practitioners of Presence, and directed by the clear intelligence of the Weaver, who connects the energies of the others into a self-augmenting pattern that climaxes in an overwhelming moment of brightly burning certainty (64–67).

The answer to Ai's precisely phrased question about whether Gethen will be in five years a member of the Ekumen is unambiguously "yes," and Ai, who came into the experience with all the skepticism of a rational man, is "aware of the quality of that answer, not so much a prophecy as an observation" (68). The Gethenian myth of the eye of Meshe is obviously connected with this experience of Ai's with the

Foretelling group. Meshe is said to have been a Weaver in a group that was forced to respond to the impossible question, "What is the meaning of life?" The effort destroyed other group members but enabled the Weaver Meshe to see All. In the discourse of mysticism, "Meshe is the center of Time. . . . And in the Center there is no time past and no time to come" (155). "The life of every man is in the Center of Time, for all were seen in the Seeing of Meshe, and are in his Eye. . . . Our doing is his Seeing: our being his Knowing" (156). The Weaver in a Foretelling group experiences a momentary access to this Center of Time where "Nothing is unseen" (155).

Ai believes that Foretelling may be the single most important thing that Gethen has to offer the other worlds of the Ekumen (238). Ai represents a scientific-rational culture, but he takes seriously the nonlinear, acausal time that has been largely dismissed by the scientific tradition of our culture. Although precognition is described in *The Left Hand of Darkness* entirely in the discourse of mysticism, Ai's response to it suggests Le Guin's desire to unite rationalist and mystical traditions. Her later *The Dispossessed* is a complementary expression of the same impulse, in which the discourse is entirely scientific, although its Simultaneity Theory is a formulation of mystical time.

Other classic sf texts that have drawn on the same nonlinear concept of time using discourse that is more mythological-mystical than scientific include Arthur C. Clarke's *Childhood's End* (1953) and Frank Herbert's *Dune* (1965). Clarke's stunning revelation that human mythology about the devil dating back millennia is actually grounded in the future association of the Overlords with the end of the human race is not theorized beyond the assertion that the Overmind encompasses a multitude of consciousnesses from across space and time, and it has somehow been tapped by human minds. This is pure Stapledon. Herbert's protagonist Paul has prescient powers that are associated as much with the mysticism of ancient religious practice as with anything scientific, though in describing Paul's visions of the future Herbert invokes a hint of quantum theory in allusions to probabilities, and there is one explicit reference in Paul's recognition that in the operation of his prescience "a kind of Heisenberg indeterminacy intervened: the expenditure of energy that revealed what he saw, changed what he saw."[12]

Close links between the new physics and the ancient mystical tradition have been repeatedly pointed out since the mid-1970s in nonfiction such as Fritjof Capra's *The Tao of Physics* (1975), Gary Zukav's *The Dancing Wu Li Masters* (1979) and Michael Talbot's *Mysticism and the New Physics* (1981). In *About Time: Einstein's Unfinished Revolution* (1990), Paul Davies observes that "Quantum cosmology has abolished time as surely as the mystic's altered state of consciousness [has]. For a typical quantum state in this theory, time is simply meaningless." He adds, "The crucial property of quantum physics is that cause and effect aren't rigidly linked, as they are in classical, commonsense physics. There is indeterminism, which means that some events 'just occur'—spontaneously."[13] But Einstein was notoriously opposed to this notion that "God plays dice." There is room is the exploration of intersections between science and mysticism for the possibility that mind operates in those quantum events that are currently thought of as random.

Although the label "New Age" is suspect because of some of its enthusiasts' disregard of rationality, what I take to be its essence is of utmost importance. New Age thinkers examine the intersection between consciousness and the world that has during the Age of Science been understood to be "outside" of us. In *Mysticism and the New Physics*, Talbot contemplates retrocausality: "A strange door is opened if the past must be seen as the new physics suggests." Talbot asks, "If conscious systems affect the Brownian motion of particles regardless of their spatio-temporal location, what limits should we place on our ability to interact with the past?"[14] Einstein pondered unexplained connectedness between quantum particles and decided, "One can escape from [the conclusion that quantum theory is incomplete] only by either assuming that the measurement of *S1* (telepathically) changes the real situation of *S2* or by denying independent real situations as such to things which are spatially separated from each other. Both alternatives appear to me entirely unacceptable."[15]

What defines New Age thinkers, including some physicists, is that they don't find these alternatives unacceptable. Telepathy is possible. All things are linked in a manner that disregards space and time. J. S. Bell's theorem, developed from pondering the same phenomena that threw Einstein, is (summarized by Peter Nicholls) "that any two particles that have once been in contact continue to influence each other no matter how far apart they move, [at least] until one of them interacts or is observed."[16] As Amit and Maggie Goswami point out in *The Cosmic Dancers: Exploring the Physics of Science Fiction*, "The question Bell's theorem enables us to ask is: if electrons can communicate at a distance without a space-time signal, can we?" They then conjecture, "Perhaps this is where the psychological evidence for nonlinearity originates," since "only through ourselves are we connected to the hidden dimension [in which such communication occurs], which would help to account for phenomena like telepathy and precognition."[17]

F. David Peat demonstrates that the New Thinkers embrace both the findings of science and the knowledge of past civilizations that has been disregarded by science in its focused path to knowledge. The index to Peat's *Synchronicity: The Bridge Between Matter and Mind* shows equal attention to physicists Heisenberg and David Bohm on one hand and to psychologist Carl Jung and bone oracles on the other. "Time does not consist of a single order of succession," Peat concludes, "but of a whole spectrum of orders of which eternity and the mathematical order of succession, or flowing stream, are just two particular aspects. Consciousness itself is not bound within any single one of these orders."[18] In Western society, the mechanical "time order, and the notion of progress that goes along with it, is considered to be self-evident so that the earlier eternal and timeful orders are taken to be illusions, or religious fictions for the weak-minded" (232). Similarly, he continues, today "the noise of the self blocks out the movement of the more flexible orders of consciousness and the interconnections of the individual to society and nature. . . . Whole areas of consciousness are lost to direct awareness" (234). While whole societies—like groups of primitive hunters—used to be commonly able to open up those areas of consciousness, we now find that "only in exceptional cases" do the floodgates of consciousness open to "the transformation in which the self is freed from the limited order of time" (235). This assumption that our minds *can* transcend linear time is exploited by many writers of what might be termed "psience fiction."

Many sf writers now use psi without theorizing it; it has become as conventional as faster-than-light speeds, as natural as folds in spacetime, no longer mysterious and awesome as it was when the mysteries of time and mind were invoked by writers to give a story significance. Many others won't touch psi, considering it irrational, unscientific, and thus outside the proper domain of sf. But the mysteries remain, and the need for theorizing remains. As scientific investigation and philosophical contemplation of the results continue to open new lines of thought, possibilities continue to unfold for sf about intersections between theories of time and theories of mind.

Notes

1. For discussions of Einstein's innovative concepts of time, see Stephen W. Hawking, *A Brief History of Time: From the Big Bang to Black Holes* (Toronto: Bantam, 1988), 20–22.

2. Fred Alan Wolf, *Star Wave: Mind, Consciousness, and Quantum Physics* (New York: Collier Books, 1984), 19.

3. Stuart Holroyd, *Psi and the Consciousness Explosion* (London: Bodley Head, 1977), 94.

4. Alfred Douglas, *Extra-Sensory Powers: A Century of Psychical Research* (Woodstock, NY: Overlook, 1977), 338, 355.

5. Montague Ullman, Stanley Krippner, and Alan Vaughan, *DreamTelepathy: Experiments in Nocturnal ESP* (Baltimore: Penguin, 1973), *passim*.

6. See J. W. Dunne, *An Experiment with Time* (London: A. & C. Black Ltd., 1927), 60; Holroyd, 87; and Lawrence Le Shan, *The Science of the Paranormal: The Last Frontier* (Wellingborough, UK: Aquarian Press, 1987), 11.

7. Olaf Stapledon, *Last and First Men*, in Stapledon, *Last and First Men and Star Maker* (1930; New York: Dover, 1968), 9. Later page references in the text are to this edition.

8. The connection between Dunne and Stapledon is discussed in Brian Stableford, *The Scientific Romance in Britain, 1890–1950* (New York: St. Martin's Press, 1985).

9. David Ketterer, *Imprisoned in a Tesseract: The Life and Work of James Blish* (Kent, Ohio: Kent State University Press, 1987), 49.

10. James Blish, *Jack of Eagles* (1952; New York: Avon, 1958), 48, 48, 53. Later page references in the text are to this edition.

11. Ursula K. Le Guin, *The Left Hand of Darkness* (New York: Ace, 1969), 59. Later page references in the text are to this edition.

12. Frank Herbert, *Dune* (1965; New York: Ace, 1990), 296.

13. Paul Davies, *About Time: Einstein's Unfinished Revolution* (New York: Simon & Schuster, 1995), 180–181, 188.

14. Michael Talbot, *Mysticism and the New Physics* (New York: Bantam, 1981), 108–

109.

15. Albert Einstein, "Autobiographical Notes," translated by Paul Arthur Schlipp, in *Albert Einstein: Philosopher-Scientist*, edited by Paul Arthur Schlipp (1949; New York: Tudor Publishing Company, 1951), 85.

16. Peter Nicholls, *The Science in Science Fiction* (New York: Alfred A. Knopf, 1983), 101.

17. Amit and Maggie Goswami, *The Cosmic Dancers: Exploring the Physics of Science Fiction* (New York: Harper & Row, 1983), 259.

18. F. David Peat, *Synchronicity: The Bridge between Matter and Mind* (Toronto: Bantam, 1987), 228–229. Later page references in the text are to this edition.

8

Jews in Time: Alternate Histories and Futures in Space. . . . And Who Was That Bearded, Yarmulkeh'd Old Man?

Susan Kray

Jews in science fiction and fantasy are connected with two aspects of time, manifested in alternate histories and stories of the future.[1] Alternate histories are tinged by wishful thinking that historical disasters had not occurred; stories of the future are suffused with questions regarding Jewish continuity (cultural), survival (physical), and identity (ethnic). These two kinds of stories echo the two most frequently articulated concerns of today's American Jewish community: survival of past disasters (particularly the Holocaust) and "continuity" (of religious practice and ethnic identity) in the future. I argue that a disproportionate number of sf/fantasy stories with Jewish characters or themes hinge on these two temporal perspectives; in both cases, Jewish characters have a special, limited, and limiting relationship to time, so that other perspectives are neglected.

For the most part, the Jewish characters, like other ethnic characters, are deracinated walk-ons, ethnic in name only and present merely for the sake of nominal diversity. A few appear as a pathetic remnant of a once-viable people. Many are refugees who have outlived their moment in history. When a Jew appears, he (usually "he") is often a sort of last Mosaic Mohican, like Benjamin in Walter M. Miller, Jr.'s *A Canticle for Leibowitz* or Sol Weintraub of Dan Simmons's *Hyperion*, hanging on as a quaint relic or object lesson. Thus, science fiction and fantasy, supposedly the literature of possibilities, often implies or even states that Jews, as Jews, are isolated remnants adrift in time—that time has turned on them and expelled them.

Therefore, Jews in Future Time do not forge viable spiritual/ religious/cultural forms. Nor do Jews in alternate histories, even those characterized by wishful thinking about Jewish survival. Jewish women, whom Jewish myth holds to be the conduits for Jewish religious continuity, are hardly in evidence, and certainly not as protagonists, with the exception of Shira in Marge Piercy's *He, She and It* (which was not marketed as science fiction). Other female Jewish characters include Sol's daughter Rachel in *Hyperion*, who "grows" backward to infancy; the Jewish housewife/refugee in Harry Turtledove's "Balance" series, who is a minor character; the grown daughters in Jane Yolen's *Briar Rose*; and the "little Jewish girls" I found in 1992 magazine stories.[2] None, however, are involved in forming— or even participating in—the religious and spiritual life of the Jewish community. Judging by science fiction, the future, it seems, has little use for Jews and almost none for Jewish women.

In fantasy and science fiction, Jewish communities seem unable to evolve or to formulate and pursue visions. Alternate histories dwell largely on fantasy fixes for the Holocaust and other disasters. They emphasize the ways in which real-life Jews have been confronted by attempts to delete them from history, that is, from time. Stories of the future are even more bleak. As one character in Simmons's *Hyperion* describes it, the only Jewish communities left are "nonvital, picturesque . . . tourist-oriented."[3] There is just the one old Jewish man of the novel. Similarly, in *A Canticle for Leibowitz*, Dom Paulo, a Christian priest of the thirty-eighth century encountering an old Jewish man, reflects that "The Jewish community was thinly scattered in these times. . . . Such an old Israelite might wander for years without encountering others of his people. Perhaps in his loneliness he had acquired the silent conviction that he was *the last*, the one, the only."[4] This seems an odd situation for science fiction, frequently characterized as this "literature of possibilities," of other landscapes, of the "next question," of inquiries into what will happen "if this goes on." Jewish themes in science fiction seem suited to Isaac Asimov's familiar definition of science fiction as a sobering activity from which the real world constitutes an escape. In a word, visions of Jews in Time often lack chutzpah. Future Jews in space are the rag-tail remnant of Alan Dershowitz's "vanishing Jew."

One reason for the scarcity of Jews and the invisibility of Judaism is that science fiction cannot relate to religion as a positive force. It does not understand how religion can exist in "creative tension" with modern life, scientific inquiry, and technological achievement. Usually it does not even *seek* to understand. Unlike the American masses, science fiction stories may be simply (even simplistically) anti-religion. Science fiction may even use religion to signify vicious, destructive ignorance and reaction, represented by raving preachers or insular, inbred communities rife with stupidity and mean-spiritedness. Religion is treated as deviant. Jewish characters may emerge as super-deviants, since their ethnicity is uniquely (and deviantly) defined by a religion, in a genre where religion itself is deviant.

Moreover, most science fiction takes place in an American universe—a generic American universe. This universe may ostensibly be post-American, posing as universalist and reinforcing that image with demographically diverse characters. Still, most humans in the stories are not only American, they are generic, white Protestant Americans of North European descent, usually male. In other words, they conform to the demographics of characters in most fiction, film, and television. Characters who have "ethnic" names or look Asian or African still act, talk, think, and feel much like generic white Protestant male Americans. So do many aliens, maybe with a few quirks to keep them from being too completely human. Jews who are recognizably Jewish defy this norm.

Interestingly, authors at times seek to defuse this deviation from the norm by making Jews comic or tragic. As classmates at Clarion West told me in the late 1980s, "Your character shouldn't be Jewish unless there is a specific reason why he/she has to be Jewish," a demand not made regarding African or Mexican characters. (It is an amusing reminder of the residency permits that the Czarist government required of Jews residing in Moscow. The demand is: Justify "your" presence among "us.")

Considering how many important science fiction and fantasy authors have been Jews,[5] it is remarkably difficult to track down stories with Jewish themes or Jewish characters.[6] It is even more difficult to find Jewishness in sf/fantasy films than in print fiction. There is Edward G. Robinson's Sol Roth in *Soylent Green* (based on the Jewish character in Harry Harrison's *Make Room! Make Room!*), Jeff Goldblum's David Levinson and Judd Hirsch's Julius Levinson in *Independence Day*, and possibly Sam Jaffe's character in *The Day the Earth Stood Still*. Lester D. Friedman identifies "a licentious Jewish vampire" in *The Fearless Vampire Killers* (1967); "the conflict between a Jewish schnook and the Gentile world that oppresses him" in both *The Little Shop of Horrors* (1960) and *A Bucket of Blood* (1959); and the "obstinate Jewish couple who reject immortality" in *Cocoon* (1985).[7] All these characters show patterns consistent with what I have found for print fiction.

Even in print fiction, Jewish characters and themes tend to be buried deep in a novel. Their subplots begin obscurely or relatively late in the book, where only persistent readers will stumble on them. For example, the first chapter of *A Canticle for Leibowitz* features a nameless old man called a "pilgrim"; nameless still, "the old wanderer" turns up again on page 96, but disappears on page 97. On page 114 he is identified for the first time as "the old Jew." We must read to page 143 before we learn that his name is Benjamin Eleazar bar Yehoshua.

In addition to dividing into alternate histories and future stories, these narratives divide along other lines: Some are written with a Jewish sensibility and others are non-Jewish stories which happen to contain Jewish characters. Both categories place Jews in interesting relationships to time.

Jewish-Oriented Stories

Many Jewish-oriented stories have as a main theme the interface between Jewish communities in peril and the Christian European communities imperiling them. Examples include Jack Dann's "Jumping the Road" (1992), Grania Davis's "Tree of Life, Book of Death" (1992), Lisa Goldstein's *The Red Magician* (1982), and the "Balance" series (1990s). The subtext is that Jewish communities have a natural future, but others try to interfere with it. Some stories turn on questions of Jewish identity within that future, implying that a vital question of future Jewish life is, "Is this [green or blue] [scaly or tentacled] alien really Jewish?" (Dann) or, "Would you want your [human] Jewish daughter to marry one?" (as in stories by William Tenn and Phyllis Gotlieb).

The Jewish stories focus largely on two issues: Isolated Jews of the future struggle with issues of Jewish cultural continuity while Jews in alternate histories struggle for physical survival. However, such science fiction often works against the grain of Jewish tradition, replacing the Jewish collective fantasy of women as the torchbearers and sources of wisdom and mediation with the individual American male Jew's fantasy of one male as the last Jewish hold-out in a Gentile universe. Thus, Jews frequently come from a past that dooms them; as men without women, they apparently have no collective future. This lack of a future is presented as natural and inevitable; nobody is going to do anything about it. In this way, some Jewish stories resemble some non-Jewish stories, which regularly assume that Jews have no natural future (an assumption that renders any Jewish character an anomaly).

Hence there are "Wandering Jew" stories (with venerable antecedents in Christian popular literature), with a lonely Jewish immortal man wandering through eternity without Jewish companionship or any relationship to a Jewish community or heritage. In addition, many non-Jewish stories use minor Jewish characters or offstage Jewish characters merely to personalize references to the Holocaust. For example, in David J. Strumfels's "Never Forget" (1992), about a little girl who is part chimpanzee and part human, the title invokes the Holocaust and other crimes of terror against Jews and, in one sentence only, a character refers to the Holocaust and notes that his grandfather "was a Jew."[8] The Jewish grandfather is invoked only to link discrimination to the Holocaust. In such cases, the author refers to someone Jewish only to evoke an image of victimhood that has nothing to do with Jewishness. (One might make an analogy to the man who claims he understands vulnerability because he has a "feminine side"—which has nothing to do with understanding the lives or judgments of actual women.) "Jewishness" is adduced in passing, reduced to a signifier of victimhood in the mind of a non-Jew.

Time and Real-Life Jews

If Jewish themes and characters cluster in alternate histories and stories set in the future, the reasons are not hard to find. In "real-life," Jewish cultures—considered across 3000 years of time and several continents—embody a tension between repeated threats of expulsions, expropriations, massacre, and genocide on one hand and a sense of destiny on the other. Moreover, the sense of past and future as being "here and now" is a constant theme in Jewish cultures through the ages. The instruction to "never forget" the past is balanced by the faith in "*Am Olam*," the sense of the Jews as an "eternal people." According to many, "never forgetting" the past is precisely what enables Jews to have an infinite future.

Hence, Jews have been called a "time-bound" (as opposed to space-defined) people that feels itself to be unified across vast distances of time, as well as space. Each Jewish woman, man, and child is supposed to regard him/herself as though he/she had stood at Sinai when the Jewish people accepted the Torah.[9] Indeed, a fantasy element in Jewish lore about Exodus claims that at Sinai, along with all Jewish men and women of the time, all the unborn souls of their descendants-to-be also assembled. Since normative Judaism considers converts to be adopted into the Jewish people (they acquire Abraham and Sara as their ancestors), all Jews[10] of every time are direct participants in that formative moment of history. Thus the popular Jewish feeling for time is that the Jewish community consists of all Jews everywhere and "everywhen," so to speak. The Ashkenazic[11] practice of naming a child after a deceased relative embeds the sense of continuity—the "chain of generations"—in everyday life.[12]

True, for individual Jews trying to get along in daily life, cultural memory can constitute a difficulty as well as a resource. Yet, the Jewish obsession with time persists. Jews, who (like women of all groups) are often regarded as external to history, feel they are defined by history; they commonly take a proprietary, intimate view of even the most ancient Jewish history—and of an assumed future in which new generations of Jews will arrive as full citizens who were already "there" at Sinai 3,200 years ago. It is logical that Israelis seem as obsessed by the archaeology of their country as Russians are by chess or Americans by baseball.[13]

God's Cosmic Time

The traditional Jewish concept of time is sophisticated enough to encompass paradox: "Everything [to the end of time] is foreseen [by God], yet you have the authority to make your own decisions."[14] God's ability to predict does not preclude a human's ability to determine. The time paradox that generates many plot complications in science fiction was long ago addressed by Judaism, for the scholar quoted in "Avot" declares that God resolved the paradox by accommodating human free will. It is consistent with the Jewish view of God that He would say, "I know exactly what you're going to do, but go ahead anyway and surprise me!" God Himself embodies paradox.

Another way of looking at it is that God's role evolves with time; humans must take over God's tasks. God is the nurturing parent whose children must grow up to take responsibility. Consistent with this theological view is the Jewish concept of Tikkun Olam, repair-and-maintenance of the world; humans must help God complete the world's creation by infusing it with social justice and compassion. Creation is ongoing, but is now in human hands. A bit of this concept finds its way into science fiction, with Jewish characters who try, or who think they should try, to "repair the world"—as in Dann's "Jumping the Road."

Everyday Time

The rule of time enters at the daily level as well. Jewish life is regulated by the lunar calendar. The key sanctifying observances of Jewish life are related to cycles of nature, especially the sun: One prays three times a day and observes cycles of the moon (Sabbaths and New Moons[15]), three Jewish New Years all celebrating natural events,[16] and a harvest holiday, Succoth. The cycles of living beings are important also. Traditional married couples observe the menstrual cycle to determine the proper times to have or avoid sex. Almost none of this "everyday" time finds its way into science fiction or fantasy depictions of Jews.

Christian-Based Stories: Eternal Youth and Human Sacrifice

Yet the Christian theme of the Wandering Jew occurs so frequently as to merit an anthology of its own: *Tales of the Wandering Jew*, edited by Brian Stableford. The theme first surfaced in written form in 1223 in Latin and featured a Jewish character under an eternal curse, although Stableford reasonably questions whether living an eternally young life until Jesus returns to Earth is really a curse.[17] (The "curse" is the character's "punishment" for mocking Jesus at his execution.) At another level, this "Wandering Jew" reflects the Christian view of "the Jews" as one people, always and everywhere the same, doomed to homeless wandering among other nations as punishment for not being Christians.

Hence, many ostensibly Jewish characters faithfully reflect the traditional Christian trope of the "Wandering Jew," creating an entire subgenre of non-Jewish "Wandering Jew" plots and subplots. Examples occur in *A Canticle for Leibowitz* (though some interpret the Jewish wanderer there as the Jewish prophet Elijah), Charles Maturin's *Melmoth the Wanderer*, Susan Shwartz's *The Grail of Hearts*, and perhaps Simmons's *Hyperion* and *The Fall of Hyperion*. The Jewish wanderer in the Christian story is a mythological figure whose wandering reflects his theological status in Christianity as the Misguided, Defeated Other.

So, an ostensibly Jewish character is deployed by a Christian sensibility to fill a role in a Christian myth with anti-Judaic overtones and roots in Christian history and theology. Authors sometimes make the Christian roots explicit, though the "Wandering Jew" is not necessarily part of the theology of any church. While this myth is unrelated to Judaism, it is deeply related to time, as it emphasizes the permanence of the Jew's exile, even more than the space traversed in wanderings. He is serving time ("until Jesus shall return"), not merely drifting through space.

In Jewish stories, the displaced Jew is more likely a refugee dispossessed of home and/or family by Nazis, Inquisitors, or other persecutors. One does not so much wander as flee from terrorism. Consider the flippancy and paradox of Mike Resnick's 1991 story about a *Jewish* "Wandering Jew" and the paradox of the title of Dann's anthology *Wandering Stars*, with stories that are Jewish, not Christian, in sensibility. The reference to "wandering" is whimsical, not theological; for

Jewish authors, a "Wandering Jew" can be a figure who makes a positive claim, however restrained or ironic, to a future for Jews and Judaism.

Some Christian-based stories use Jewish figures to signify doom or human sacrifice, the latter often female, like the character in James Morrow's *Only Begotten Daughter* or Rachel in *Hyperion*. Sometimes the Jew is a helper who is compassionate because he has been persecuted—another example of Jew as signifier of victimhood, but here a victim who helps others escape victimhood. Infrequently, stories present malicious Jews, like the unpleasant "Rose the Nose, Jewboy extraordinaire," the only Jewish character in Orson Scott Card's *Ender's Game* or Mark Birnbaum, a Hollywood agent's Orthodox, murderously avaricious, Jewish trainee in Phillip C. Jennings's "The Vortex": "Andrea had nothing against Jews, but this new sidekick was so thoroughly Jewish; nose, beanie and whiny New York accent." After destroying Andrea, Birnbaum says, "This way . . . my boss will get fifteen percent richer."[18]

In general, non-Jewish stories may be distinguished in that their Jewish characters exist in isolation without any visible Jewish family, religious practices, or community. Jewishness means nothing to such characters; for them, it does not exist. They see the world through secular or Christian eyes. "Wandering Jews" tell Christian stories related to Jesus, not Jewish stories related to Jewish people or spirituality. They accept roles—villain, reformed villain, or victim—but have no inner Jewish life. Indeed, aside from Christian or victim themes, few have any inner life at all.

More nuanced depictions are rare. Sometimes a subtle author like Simmons makes it hard to tell whether a Jewish or Christian sensibility is the best interpretation. With his wife dead and daughter regressing through time, Sol is another isolated old Jewish man without a future. Such old men occur in both Christian and Jewish stories. On one hand, Sol is a Jew with a rich inner life—too rich, for his dreams are haunted and he agonizes about religion. He in effect argues with God, a very Jewish activity that Abraham and Moses engaged in. (One European rabbi even sued God; he convened a *Bet Din*, a rabbinical court, and brought charges against God for inadequately protecting his people from violent European Christians.) On the other hand, Sol's arguments depend on a Christian premise: that the Abraham-Isaac story is about human sacrifice (Christians even call the story "The Sacrifice of Isaac"). For Jews, the story is the *Akedah*, "the Binding of Isaac," for the point is that no sacrifice takes place. The story is about the *end* of human sacrifice—about *not* sacrificing. Further, Sol lives in a future universe with only "nonvital" Jewish communities and is on a pilgrimage because the inhuman "Shrike" transformed his adult daughter Rachel into an infant—suggesting Christian themes of the sacrificed child.

Jewish-Based Stories

Stories with a predominantly Jewish sensibility roughly divide into three groups:

humor, alternate histories, and future Jews in Space. Jewish refugees and lone survivors are found in all three groups.

The humor often relies on the ostensible contrast between Jewishness and heroism or the supposed incompatibility of Jewishness and technological capability. Many have observed this theme with respect to the neurotic, buffoonish television/movie Jew, like Joel Fleischman of *Northern Exposure*, who is afraid of trees. As indicated, in two of the three science fiction films Friedman identifies, the Jew is a neurotic "schnook." These buffoon stories, however, do not focus on issues of time, which seem reserved for serious stories. This is partly because time is a preoccupation mainly of alternate histories, often with Holocaust themes that are inherently serious, as are other alternate-history themes such as the Expulsion from Inquisition Spain or the Myth of Ritual Murder, also known as Blood Libel.[19] The latter often forms a backdrop for golem stories, for in recent centuries golems (based on a creature in Talmudic myth) are usually seen as counter-terrorism devices in pogroms inspired by the Blood Libel. But I focus here on "serious" Jewish themes, not humorous subgenres, and on written science fiction and fantasy, not film.

Jews in Alternate Histories

In "serious" print stories, we confront two principal aspects of time: alternate-history pasts and Jews-in-Space futures. The alternate histories generally entail science-fictional uses of European history, focusing on traumatic historical events such as the Expulsion from Spain in 1492, as in Esther M. Friesner's "Such a Deal" (1992), or Blood Libel pogroms and the Golem story that arose from them.[20] Alternate histories are most often Holocaust stories. Whether dealing with the Expulsion, the Holocaust, or blood libel pogroms, alternate histories largely fall into two categories: (1) science fiction stories in which the Holocaust, Expulsion, or other disaster was prevented or halted mid-way; and (2) fantasy stories in which a Jew, usually a girl, miraculously escapes. The best and biggest example of the science fiction alternate history is the Jewish subplot in Turtledove's "Balance" series, his alternate history World War II epic.

As noted, in Jewish stories, a Jew away from home is more likely a refugee, not a wanderer. The difference is that the refugee was forced out of a perfectly acceptable home by evildoers. The refugee cherishes or mourns his/her family and wants to find a secure new home as quickly as possible. Examples include the characters in Goldstein's *The Red Magician* and Turtledove's "Balance" series. The ultimate, underlying reason that authors choose to make the Jewish character homeless is rooted, not in Jewish history or theology, but in Christian history and theology that are always beyond the scope of the story. The story (like most real-life American Jews) knows nothing of Christian theology and therefore cares nothing about it.

Jews of the Future

For the most part, Jews are missing from the future. Jewish territory is missing or displaced: Piercy locates a Jewish town in a future North America; stories by Robert Silverberg, Tenn, Dann, and others place small, isolated Jewish communities on other planets. Often Israel has been flooded or bombed out of existence— regrettably not an implausible image, considering what a tiny splinter of land it now occupies. Further, if the Jew in Space or Earth's future is typically a refugee, that refugee is often a lonely old man quaintly clinging to ancient traditions for no particular reason and reeling from culture shock. More humorously, an old couple causes culture shock; Avram Davidson's elderly couple in "The Golem" gallantly and naively refuses to be intimidated by a malevolent android ("When you talk to my wife, talk respectable, you hear?") with plans of world conquest, turning it into a household servant like the Golem of Prague in the Jewish folk story.[21]

Young Jews, if any, tend to be flippant and religiously ignorant.[22] Jewish aliens tend to the old man model. Jewish history (as in the "Balance" novels) is largely Holocaust or Inquisition history. In other works, the reader finds much in the way of parody, Jews-as-jokes, and victimhood, but, with few exceptions, little of joy or triumph or spiritual sustenance.

Hence, the future stories typically take place in that ostensibly generic, post-American but really middle-American Protestant universe of much space fiction. Characters may have any racial, ethnic or national *origin*, but diverse cultural *influences* are not much in evidence. "Religion" seems to mean fundamentalist Protestantism, and its influence is regularly seen as baleful or vicious. Judaism is not attacked as consistently in these stories. Attack is hardly necessary, since the stories hardly imagine Judaism as a religion, let alone envision its survival in the future. Judaism and Jews have little home in the past, either. The young girls in *The Red Magician* and *Briar Rose* are plucked out of real time into fantasy time so they can escape the Holocaust.

Hence, stories distort history and the aging process in bizarre ways. "Living backward" turns up a few times. Isaac Bashevis Singer's "Jachid and Jechida" are a male and female demon who live backward in time until they arrive in the womb to be born to mortal women. When we meet Gemma, the magically rescued girl of *Briar Rose*, she is an old woman mentally living in the past. In *Hyperion*, an aged Sol carries his regressed daughter, the archaeologist Rachel, as a newborn infant, trying to prevent her from becoming a fetus and dying. Sol, the one Jewish character besides Rachel, is also the only one in the novel explicitly described in the blurb copy as having difficulties with time. His story relates to not one, but three kinds of time signifiers: archaeology, time travel, and regression—no, four, for he is also the only character who is called an "old man." The cast of characters on the first page of the book describes

THE SCHOLAR—Sol Weintraub led a quiet life until his daughter went to Hyperion on an archaeological expedition . . . where the Shrike touched her and sent her reeling backward in time.[23]

Piercy's *He, She and It* (1991) tells its story on two time tracks, bouncing back and forth between the main plot set in a future America and a Golem subplot set in sixteenth-century Prague. Harlan Ellison's Matty Simon, in "Go Toward the Light" (1996), is a time-traveling man called a "fugitive," after the word "fugit" in the Latin phrase "tempus fugit," meaning "time flies." In Matthew Wells's "The Auschwitz Circus" (1996), Nora and Louis get to defy time in a museum that allows them to "go back" into history and (in simulation) shoot Hitler before he can murder the European Jews.

All in all, a high proportion of Jewish-oriented stories twist, double, reverse, or otherwise defy time, often (though not always) to rescue fictional characters from the Holocaust. The bottom line is frequently Jewish continuity, that is, survival, and survival *as Jews*. What that means in religious and ethnic terms is hardly defined, but then, the real-life American Jewish community, currently embroiled in turmoil over "Jewish continuity," has hardly defined what "continuity" means, either.

Difficulties with time are also reflected in the age and family status of Jewish characters. They are characters whose time is past. For both Jewish and non-Jewish authors, Jewish characters are often older men, sometimes *really* old men. But old or young, male Jewish characters typically have no family. Without Jewish women and children, these Jewish men lack a Jewish future (partly because in Jewish law, children follow the mother's religion).

Or they have a family, but *what* a family! They still lack a Jewish future, for they have non-Jewish children—children born to non-Jewish mothers—slated to murder humanity (the sons in W. M. Schockley's "A Father's Gift" [1992]); or they have a child with no mother at all (and thus not the child of a Jewish mother and not Jewish) who is destined to die for humanity (*Only Begotten Daughter*); or they have a Jewish daughter regressing to infancy whom an alien entity proposes to sacrifice for humanity (*Hyperion*). Or the Jewish character has Jewish children, such as those being raised in hiding in a Nazi-dominated alternate future (Turtledove, "In the Presence of Mine Enemies" [1992]) or a Jewish son being raised in an alternate history Europe in which Jews, having welcomed invading aliens as liberators from the Nazis, are accused of being alien-collaborators (the "Balance" series). Or the Jewish child is a distraught granddaughter to whom her Jewish grandfather appears as a ghost after having been murdered in the Holocaust (Goldstein's "Alfred" [1992]).

Jewish characters, it seems, are allowed no unproblematic posterity; every aspect of their participation in family life is problematical. The Jews of science fiction and fantasy also lack community; they are remnants of a community, not members of one. One would be hard put to identify a vital, evolving Jewish society in science fiction or fantasy. Perhaps the town of Tikvah—Hebrew for "Hope"—in *He, She and It* qualifies, assuming it survives corporate massacre attempts.

The Jew as refugee is a persistent image, even where that image is irrelevant to the story. Ellison's "timedrifter," Simon, a Jewish "chronocircumnavigator," is due to his occupation—not his religion—"euphemistically called a 'fugitive' " by the "one hundred and sixty-three Gentile techno-freaks and computer jockeys" with whom he and one other Jew work.[24]

Limited Jewish contexts—small families, references to history—appear occasionally, though almost always under threat in World War II contexts, as in *The Red Magician* and the "Balance" series. Matt Wartell's vampire novel *Blood of Our Children* is said to be set in the Jewish section of Lodz, Poland, with a richly described Jewish context. *He, She and It*, depicting a whole Jewish post-American town, uses the Golem legend and its real-life historical context, the Blood Libel pogroms of Europe, as a parallel story line, while the main story is anchored in the Jewish heroine's family life in a Jewish community. Some Jewish women (in Piercy and Turtledove) are in lasting, positive love relationships (unlike female Jewish characters on prime-time television[25]).

Most often, Jewish society is nothing but a vague memory when the story begins. Sometimes Israel has been destroyed and Jewish refugees are transplanted to hostile turf on Earth or elsewhere. In Simmons's *Hyperion*, all this is true, and Sol, moreover, denounces Judaism because he thinks it is founded on Abraham's willingness to sacrifice his son.

To put it whimsically and to overstate my case, science fiction authors seem bent on killing off their fictional Jewish communities and cultures in ways in which nobody seems to want to kill off the Chinese, French, or Indians. They seem equally bent on obliterating Jewish spirituality—or are simply ignorant of it. They fail to depict such spiritual practices as Sabbath, Kashrut (keeping kosher), prayer, study, or Tsedakah (the concept that giving to the needy is not voluntary "charity" but mandated "justice"), to name only a few.

Themes Not Developed, Stories Not Told

It is particularly interesting to focus on the things not stated. Jews as well as Christians portray Jewish characters and themes in very limited ways. From a list of possible Jewish science fiction and fantasy themes, one can easily pinpoint those few on which authors actually draw. We can then propose some alternative scenarios.

Recent scholarship has brought to light the diversity of Jewish communities in history. We read about Jewish monastics, both male and female (as recorded by Philo Judaeus),[26] women who headed synagogues,[27] numerous new perspectives on Jewish women of authority during biblical times, and the opinion of at least one respected authority that Jews could not have invaded Canaan because nobody invaded Canaan during the relevant eras and anyway, the Jews were clearly local, homegrown Canaanites who used Canaanite technology and agricultural methods from the start.[28] (We also note that the Bible calls the Hebrew language *leshon C'naan*, "Canaanite.") The probability is that beleaguered, colonized Jews of Persian and Roman times created a myth of immigration displacing their origin to prestigious ancient empires.

Many Jews, Orthodox and otherwise, have optimistic visions for Jewish development; Blu Greenberg, a well-known Orthodox feminist, defies current Orthodox leadership by foreseeing female Orthodox rabbis in the near future.[29] A 1997 conference in New York drew hundreds of Orthodox Jewish feminists seeking to develop their spiritual lives as both feminists and observant Jews. Some have created a welcoming ceremony (*simhat bat*) for infant girls that parallels the *bris* ceremony for infant boys. Many Orthodox as well as non-Orthodox girls now celebrate Bat Mitzvahs in Torah-reading ceremonies. Many American cantors and rabbis in non-Orthodox denominations are women and many of both sexes and all movements are young. Rabbi-couples and pregnant rabbis are fairly common.

Science fiction, however, lags far behind reality, with dull, constricted, nerveless visions of what constitutes a Jewish community and tiresome, quaint visions of what Jewish women and men can do. Rabbis and Jewish scholars are men, usually old men, in fact, solitary old men. Women can be secular scholars, like Rachel in *Hyperion* and a few of Turtledove's characters, but they cannot be scholars of Judaism. Science fiction and fantasy have no cantors of either sex or any species, no religious schools, no Sunday School teachers, no preachers, no welcoming-of-Sabbath or close-of-Sabbath ceremonies, no families or schoolmates singing blessings after meals. Aside from a few stories about conversions of aliens or intermarriage with aliens, nobody negotiates and renegotiates religious practices in alien surroundings. Not only are Jewish communities in *Hyperion* "nonvital"; one is hard put to find *any* such communities in fantasy or science fiction. The proportion of Jewish characters living in such communities is vanishingly small.

Alternative Scenarios

Jewish tradition yields many themes that could generate Jewish fantasy and science fiction but are vastly underexploited. A tiny sample of such themes includes the "thirty-six saints" whose virtue sustains the world;[30] Lilith stories; a wealth of other demon stories; the Talmudic concept of the golem as a kind of ephemeral performance art—like Tibetan sand paintings—intended as worship of the Creator (one creates the golem but does not use it for work or any purpose and destroys it within a day or so); the prophet Elijah as an immortal, saintly, wandering miracle worker; the Jewish concept of a messianic era of social justice and universal compassion; and Dybbukim, spirits of the dead that possess a living person until some vow is fulfilled (these do appear, rarely), to name a few.

Other Jewish traditions include that of arguing with God, as Abraham did; the historical relation of the Jewish people to their worship of the Goddess Asherah and their Canaanite origins; the relationship between God and Satan—which is completely different from that conceived by Christianity; Cabalistic themes about seeing to the end of the world, mystical union with the deity, and Kfitsat ha-Derekh, instantaneous travel by flying (Dann used an aspect of this concept in "Jumping the Road"); the ability of Cabalistic rabbis to project their images vast distances; and one of my favorites, the notion that pious, deceased Jews go "rolling" underground from their graves in the Diaspora to a more fulfilling resting place in the Holy Land. Many of these ideas are hundreds of years old; others are thousands of years old. Science fiction writers, feel free to help yourselves.

Judaism is a religion of time and seasons. What happens to the Sabbath and the rest of the lunar calendar on planets with no moons, or five, or in artificial environments? What new meanings will Passover have on alien planets? What meanings will develop on a vital, culturally alive Jewish planet? What about those converted aliens? What impact do Sabbaths, Passovers and the Ten Commandments have on alien society, maybe even on alien evolution?

In real life, Jewish history is far from over. Science fiction writers are only beginning to catch up with real life, but their best is yet to come.

Notes

1. The research behind this chapter was sponsored in part by the American Association of University Women.

2. Susan Kray, "Narrative Uses of Little Jewish Girls in Science Fiction and Fantasy Stories: Mediating Between Civilization and Its Own Savagery," in Gary Westfahl and George Slusser, editors, *Nursery Realms: Children in the Worlds of Science Fiction, Fantasy, and Horror* (Athens, GA: University of Georgia Press, 1999), 29–47.

3. Dan Simmons, *Hyperion* (1989; New York: Bantam Books, 1990), 252.

4. Walter M. Miller, Jr., *A Canticle for Leibowitz* (1959; New York: Bantam Books, 1961), 140–141.

5. A few examples include Isaac Asimov, Robert Silverberg, Harlan Ellison, Barry N. Malzberg, Avram Davidson, William Tenn (Phillip Klass), Judith Merril, Jack Dann, Esther Friesner, Lisa Goldstein, and Harry Turtledove.

6. In my research, I have received assistance from the listservs of the International Association for the Fantastic in the Arts and the Jewish Community Bulletin Board of America Online; Mike Resnick, who provided a bibliography of his own relevant stories; and a website, www.sfsite.com/~silverag/jewishsf.html, with a somewhat ragged bibliography of Jewish science fiction.

7. Lester D. Friedman, *The Jewish Image in American Film: Seventy Years of Hollywood's Vision of Jewish Characters and Themes* (Secaucus, NJ: Citadel Press, 1987), 173, 249.

8. David J. Strumfels, "Never Forget," *Analog Science Fiction/Science Fact*, 112 (February, 1992), 136.

9. According to "Midrash Parshat Yitro," the Midrash for the Torah passage in Exodus that begins with the story of Jethro. Midrash is the collective term for a creative, evolving body of stories, many of them fanciful, or even science fictional. The Golem theme, for example, goes back to about the third century C.E.

10. A category spanning 3,000 years and numerous countries on the major continents, with many "Judaisms" and many Jewish languages, including Hebrew, Jewish Aramaic, Ladino (Judeo-Spanish), Judeo-Arabic, and Yiddish (Judeo-German).

11. Ashkenazic Jews are descended from settlers of Northern, Central, and Eastern Europe. The term comes from the Hebrew "Ashkenaz," meaning "Germany." Yiddish, a Germanic language, was the unifying language of this community. Other Jewish communities, with their own languages (Judaeo-Spanish, Judaeo-Arabic, etc.) are found

throughout the Middle East, India, and Hispanic countries.

12. Sephardim (Jews from Spanish-speaking and Middle Eastern countries, to oversimplify) accomplish the same thing in their practice of naming a child after a grandparent.

13. See Chapter 10 of Neil Asher Silberman, *Between Past and Present: Archaeology, Ideology, and Nationalism in the Modern Middle East* (New York: Doubleday, 1989).

14. *Pirkei Avot*, verse 3:19, in R. Herford Travers, editor, *Pirke Aboth—The Ethics of the Talmud: Sayings of the Fathers* (New York: Schocken Books, 1962), 88. Text originally redacted by Rabbi Yehuda HaNasi, c. 600 A.D.

15. Every new moon was in ancient tradition a women's holiday somewhat like an extra Sabbath; many modern Jewish women are reviving the observance. See Susan Weidman Schneider, *Jewish and Female: A Guide and Sourcebook for Today's Jewish Woman* (New York: Simon and Schuster, 1985), and E. J. Kessler, "Why Blu Greenberg Waxes Optimistic on Orthodoxy, Feminism, and the Future," *Forward*, February 7, 1997, 1–2.

16. One, in the lunar month Tishrei (around September-October), commemorates the "birthday" of the world; one, in January or February, is the New Year of Trees (Jewish Arbor Day, 15th of the lunar month Shevat); and one, in Spring, just before Passover, marks lambing time (in the lunar month Nissan).

17. Brian Stableford, editor, *Tales of the Wandering Jew* (Sawtry, Cambridgeshire: Dedalus, 1989), 3.

18. Philip C. Jennings, "The Vortex," *Amazing Stories*, 67 (July, 1992), 11, 13.

19. A Christian myth claims that Jews murder a Christian child at Passover and use the blood in Jewish rituals. Accusations of ritual murder inspired terrorism against Jews in European countries resulting in torture, looting, and burnings. This myth is still circulated in some countries, though not officially approved by churches. The Golem of Prague was, the legend goes, created to defend the Jewish neighborhood against terrorism related to accusations of ritual murder.

20. In its more recent form, a rabbi created the Golem to protect Jews against terrorists. The fantasy figure of a golem had roots in ancient Jewish literature, as traced in David Honigsberg, "Rava's Golem," *Journal of the Fantastic in the Arts*, 7:2–3 (1995), 137–145, and has recently been a recurrent theme in fantasy/science fiction. To this figure, many trace Frankenstein's creature and such media characters as Superman and the Hulk.

21. Avram Davidson, "The Golem," in Jack Dann, editor, *Wandering Stars: an Anthology of Jewish Fantasy and Science Fiction* (New York: Harper & Row, 1974), 46.

22. Like some but not all Jewish youth today, during a period of resurgent Jewish education. But such flippancy and/or ignorance may have been even more prevalent when many classic and neo-classic SF-era Jewish writers—like Asimov, Ellison, Silverberg, Davidson, and Tenn—grew up. For example, Asimov (in *Gold* and *I, Asimov*) wrote that he knew nothing about Judaism and was an atheist. Ellison publically stated that he was brought up in ignorance of Judaism and knows little about it. Ellison has written (at least) three Jewish short stories, Asimov (at least) one—about a man who is last of his Jewish line.

23. Blurb on first (unnumbered) page of the paperback edition of *Hyperion* cited earlier.

24. Harlan Ellison, "Go Toward the Light," *The Magazine of Fantasy and Science Fiction*, 90 (January, 1996), 124.

25. See Susan Kray, "Orientalization of an 'Almost White' Woman: A Multidisciplinary Approach to the Interlocking Effects of Race, Class, Gender and Ethnicity in American Mass Media," in Angharad Valdivia, editor, *Feminism, Multiculturalism, and the Media: Global Diversities* (Newbury Park, CA: Sage, 1995), 221–243. The topic of prime-time female Jewish characters not having love relationships is on page 237.

26. See Ross S. Kraemer, "Monastic Jewish Women in Greco-Roman Egypt: Philo Judaeus on the Therapeutrides," *Signs*, 14, No. 2 (1989), 342–370.

27. See Bernadette J. Brooten, *Women Leaders in the Ancient Synagogue: Inscriptional Evidence and Background Issues* (Atlanta: Scholars Press, 1982).

28. William G. Dever, personal communication, 1995.

29. See Kessler, and Blu Greenberg, *On Women and Judaism: A View From Tradition* (Philadelphia: Jewish Publication Society Of America, 1981).

30. They are not, as one reader assumed, a "cabal" of the elite, ruling the world; they are separate, anonymous, poor, and powerless people whose virtue is not known, even to themselves; but it is for the sake of their inconspicuous goodness and humility that God allows this evil-infested world to continue to exist.

9

The Desire to Control Time
in *Doraemon* and Japanese Culture

Jefferson M. Peters

The rich and delightful treatment of time in the longest-running and most popular Japanese children's manga series, Fujio F. Fujiko's *Doraemon*, reveals interesting insights into Japanese culture. It is difficult to convey the vast popularity of *Doraemon* in Japan and the deep emotional hold it exerts over Japanese people. In Japan *Doraemon* in its many media is ubiquitous. From the beginning in 1970 to his death at age sixty-two on September 23, 1996, Fujio F. Fujiko wrote over 8,500 pages for 824 *Doraemon* short stories that appeared in a monthly anthology manga magazine (*CoroCoro*) with a circulation of over 750,000. The monthly stories were collected in forty-five paperback books, all of which remain in print and have sold over 100,000,000 copies. Then there are the top-rated Friday night TV cartoons, eighteen hit animated movies, TV commercials, and myriad products ranging from fish sausage to underwear that earn tens of millions of dollars each year.

Because *Doraemon* has flourished since the 1970s, nowadays parents who grew up on it take their children to *Doraemon* movies and buy them *Doraemon* calendars, clocks, candy, and clothes. I have repeatedly asked my Japanese freshman English majors in a survey, "If you could be friends with any fictional character, whom would you choose?" Each time well over half of them choose Doraemon; in April 2000, forty-eight of seventy-five did so. A forty-three-year-old Japanese former colleague at Kagoshima University keeps all forty-five paperbacks in his office. In Tokyo there are separate screenings of the movies for children and adults, and *Doraemon* manga produced by fans of all ages are big-sellers at manga conventions. When *Doraemon* won the first Tezuka Osamu Cultural Award in 1997, Frederik Schodt said, "*Doraemon* is more than a manga. It has become a quasi-eternal symbol of children's culture"[1]—specifically, a timeless symbol of friendship, dreams, and the future in the present.

Of the many *Doraemon* products, I will focus here on the manga, for they are the origin and heart of the phenomenon. "All the Way from the Country of the Future,"[2] the first story in the series, establishes the premise of *Doraemon*. Ten-year-old Nobita is lying around during new year's holiday imagining a nice new year, when a voice from his desk says, "Nothing good will happen." Doraemon, a rotund cat robot, pops out of Nobita's desk drawer and continues: "Until the day you die, nothing good will happen for you." Then a boy who looks like Nobita (except for lighter hair and futuristic clothes) climbs out of his desk drawer, calls him "grandfather," and tells him, "You're no good at sports, studying, or even paper-scissors-rock." The boy, Sewashi, is the grandson of Nobita's grandson. Sewashi and Doraemon have come to the present from the twenty-second century via a time machine whose exit and entrance are in Nobita's desk drawer. Sewashi and Doraemon proceed to show Nobita an album filled with photos from Nobita's miserable future: marriage to the neighborhood bully's overweight sister (instead of the cute girl he likes), six children, and financial ruin. Nobita despairs, but Sewashi and Doraemon tell him that he can change his destiny. Indeed, Sewashi has assigned Doraemon the task of helping Nobita improve himself and hence both his future and the present of his financially challenged descendants.

A typical story begins with Nobita being humiliated at school by his stern teacher, at play by the neighborhood bully and rich boy, or at home by his scary mother, and then whining until Doraemon reluctantly pulls a futuristic gadget out of his fourth dimension stomach pouch to help Nobita solve his problems and get what he wants. According to Fujiko, one reason for *Doraemon*'s popularity is that it belongs to "the 'wish fulfillment' genre of manga."[3] All the stories frankly depict the desires of children (and often of adults). *Doraemon*, however, is at least as much about wish-denial as about wish-fulfillment. Doraemon is an inferior model robot capable of gross errors. Nobita's wishes are simply and happily granted far less often than they are thwarted after an initial promise of fulfillment or granted with disastrous complications. Typically, due to carelessness, selfishness, and short-sightedness, Nobita misuses the wonderful tool and causes a snafu that may or may not be cleaned up by the story's end. While some stories are juvenile gags involving crude slapstick or urine humor, many rank with the best children's literature by being both comical and ethical and having rich thematic and stylistic textures.

Doraemon stories explore every conceivable children's desire, but the most common is *the desire to control time*. In the manga there are two main images of time. First, there is the bright, waking, rigid time of human institutions like school and office, represented by everyday clocks. Chief among these is the clock dominating the highest point of the severe, right-angled facade of Nobita's elementary school. This clock symbolizes the scheduled tyranny over Nobita of school, homework, and chores. It always appears in clear, bright sunlight and is always depicted the same way—so you can tell what time it is.

Behind this human-structured time lies the fluid time of the fourth dimension, represented by a set of curvy, dark, dream-like, womb-like caverns and tunnels lined with Dali-esque soft clocks. The exact time is unknowable. Whenever Nobita and Doraemon travel through it on the Time Machine, the fourth dimension changes in appearance, often according to the pair's emotional state. As Nobita and Doraemon head back in time to give medicine to a friend's favorite dog in "Pero! Come Back to Life" (3: 182–191; 1974), the hands of the soft clocks are hearts. This fourth dimension with its soft clocks protects and liberates Nobita from the world of the hard school clock.

The most commonly occurring twenty-second-century tools in *Doraemon* are those that enable Nobita to manipulate time to get what he wants. Here is a selective list of these devices:

A Time-Television that shows the past or future
A Time Cloth that ages or rejuvenates any object or being
A Time Warp Reel that makes short cuts in time
A Stop Watch that freezes time
A Mad Watch that makes time run faster or slower
A Change-the-Day-Calendar that changes the date in your house
A set of Canned Seasons that makes the opened season can come to your house
A Continuing Spray that, when applied to a picture, shows what happens next
A Future Universe Encyclopedia that summarizes your entire life
A Course Maker that shows the future result of each direction you think of taking
A Vending Time Machine that sells products from any time in the past or future
A Time Hole that shows anything in the past and enables you to pull it into the present
A Live Your Life Over Machine that allows you to live a life better the second time around

The time tool Nobita uses most often, however, is the Time Machine. Any time he wants to time travel, Nobita hops into his desk drawer, lands on the spiffy machine, sets the destination date dials, and takes off through the dark fourth dimension to a hole giving access to the bright world of actual time at any point in the past, present, or future.

Fujiko explains neither the scientific theory nor the applied technology that makes possible the Time Machine and the other tools. *Doraemon* remains blissfully free from the Western science fiction necessities of plausibility. The devices seem to spring into existence out of Doraemon's pocket pouch and Nobita's wishes. Mark Schilling even writes that "Doraemon's gizmos are less possible future technologies than magic lamps that fulfill every conceivable wish."[4] Yet *Doraemon* is science fiction. Doraemon represents a friendly and familiar future, and his "gizmos" are not "magic lamps" but products of advanced technology that would astonish nobody in their own future world. Doraemon is a twenty-second-century *robot* who uses a time *machine*.

Doraemon is, to be sure, more fantastic than most works of Western science fiction concerning time manipulation. Unlike *Doraemon*, the "hard" subgenre of science fiction, for example, features scrupulous explanations via scientific language for its fantastic technology. Gregory Benford's classic *Timescape* concerns an effort to transmit a message via tachyons back in time from 1998 to 1962 to warn scientists of the 1960s about the overuse of "chlorinated hydrocarbons"[5] and so to prevent the environmental disaster that has ravaged the 1990s. With copious technical detail observing current (as of his novel's publication) scientific theory, Benford explains how tachyons might be manipulated into sending a message across time. Compared to this "highly restricted form of time travel"[6] that can send only messages into the past, time manipulation in

Doraemon is remarkably free.

Doraemon, however, is not a pure wish-fulfillment fantasy depicting complete escape from time. As noted, often he does not get what he wants, and some stories feature gadgets like the Timer Wrist-Watch that keep you right on schedule. Other stories, like "Shadow Hunting" (1: 112–123; 1974), show the disastrous results of ignoring time limits. In this story, Nobita is lazy and would rather not pull weeds on a hot day, so Doraemon cuts the boy's shadow from his body and puts it to work. He tells Nobita that he must re-attach his shadow within thirty minutes. Nobita of course ignores the warning and sends the shadow on various errands. Doraemon returns and panics because after thirty minutes away from Nobita's body, the shadow may assert its own desire to replace Nobita. After much mayhem Doraemon has the shadow of Nobita's mother reattach the naughty shadow to Nobita in the nick of time.

Sometimes in the *Doraemon* universe there are also limits to how much the past and future may be changed. In "Time-Knot Hole" (36: 79–87; 1986), Nobita walks around the neighborhood looking through a hole in a small board at the future or the past. When he sees himself later that afternoon being attacked by an angry dog in the vacant lot he resolves not to go there; but every action he takes inevitably leads him toward the vacant lot and the dog. Here the future cannot be changed at all.

Nobita often uses time control gadgets to satisfy selfish desires for money, prestige, revenge, free time, escape from homework, and so on. Such time manipulation almost always leads to more sticky problems for Nobita than before he used the tools, or leaves him in the same position he was in before he manipulated time. To persuade his parents not to hire a private tutor to improve his grades in "I'm My Own Teacher" (3: 147–155; 1974), Nobita promises to study harder on his own. Then he time travels into the future to recruit his junior high school self, assuming that his future self will be glad to do his "easy" elementary school homework. But Nobita's junior high school self has other plans: He's going to force Nobita to work harder so that his own grades in junior high school will be better. Thus Nobita gets a severe tutor anyway! And suddenly out of the time machine pops his high school self, who has come back to bully junior high Nobita into trying harder and to stop wasting time bothering elementary school Nobita. The two older Nobitas head back to their futures, leaving Nobita to his homework. "No matter what age I become," Nobita says, "I'm no good at homework."

In stories where Nobita seeks to control time for selfless goals, conversely, the time gadgets usually work as they should. When Nobita controls time to do good deeds, he receives an ethical, emotional, factual education about friends, family, or life that is more important than the education he fails to receive from school. A moving example occurs in "The Girl Like a White Lily" (3: 157–181; 1974), a story about how we shape the past with our subjective memories. Nobita's father tells him and Doraemon about the time when he was a poor, hungry, exhausted boy during World War II and how he one day received chocolate and silent caring from a beautiful, lily-like girl with long black hair, white skin, and large round eyes. He's never forgotten her. Nobita takes the time machine back to that era intending to photograph the mystery girl and then present the picture to his father. Through an absurd chain of events sparked by his presence in the past, however, Nobita becomes the mystery girl. When his father faints from hunger, Nobita shaves his head in order to take his father's place in the fields. Later, when Doraemon applies too much hair-growing tonic to Nobita's hair, it grows too long. After Nobita falls into a cesspool Doraemon douses him with white deodorant powder, and he dons a girl's skirt while his own clothes dry. Although he's wearing a skirt, has long hair, white skin, and large round eyes (with his huge glasses), he looks nothing like the beautiful girl of his father's story. But he gives his father the chocolate, and Doraemon photographs him doing it. Upon returning to the present, Nobita tears up the photos because he can't bear to spoil his father's beautiful memory. The gap between reality and nostalgic vision is comical, yet poignant as well, because life in World War II Japan was so harsh that the gift of chocolate was wonderful enough to make his father transform Nobita into a beautiful girl.

One time-control goal noticeably absent from *Doraemon* is the world-saving variety common to American science fiction stories featuring time travel like Jack Williamson's *The Legion of Time* (1952), the *Terminator* movies (1984, 1991), and the *X-Men* comic books. To save the universe in a typical *X-Men* story called "To the Limits of Infinity," Gambit must "steal a shard of the [M'Kraan] crystal, send Bishop back in time, and stop Professor Xavier from being killed."[7] In comparison, Nobita's goals are refreshingly small-scale and personal. Far from saving the space-time fabric of the universe from evil (or even the planet from pollution as in *Timescape*), most often Nobita wants to do something like postpone homework, make old toys new, see the day he was born, or learn whom he'll marry. In this respect *Doraemon* also differs from Japanese "hero manga" like Tezuka Osamu's *Atom Boy*. Whereas superheroes dominate American popular comic books, in manga everyday wimps like Nobita more than hold their own against superheroes.

Fujiko also controls time in the form with which he creates *Doraemon*. Fujiko's chosen short story format that averages ten pages denies him the extreme time dilation and story decompression possible in a serialized novel. In Takehiko Inoue's popular high school basketball manga, *Slam Dunk* (1990–1996), for example, one minute lasts for 190 pages, twenty minutes for 930, and three months for 5,800. Fujiko nevertheless effectively uses several techniques to control the flow of time so as to amplify the themes and action. One of these techniques is to vary the amount of time that elapses between frames. When Nobita asks his mother to buy him the radio-controlled car he has long been asking for, and she answers yet again, "next time!," he shoots her in frame five with the Do It Now Gun (33: 122–128; 1985). In frame six she's running out of the house. In frame seven she's running back in holding a large package as though the toy magically appeared in her arms without her even leaving the house. This all speeds up the story so that it takes Nobita three frames and three seconds to get what he wants, which makes the Do It Now Gun seem all the more marvelous.

Or Fujiko slows down the pace of his stories via what Scott McCloud calls "moment to moment" transitions between panels, drawing several consecutive frames with characters in both the same position and same setting to elongate time in the scene.[8] An example appears on page 14 of "Fast-Slow Medicine" (5: 5–19; 1974), where Doraemon has accidentally taken too many Fast pills and Nobita too many Slow pills. The first six frames show Nobita in the midst of a single yawn where it's difficult to detect any movement or time passing, apart from his fragmented sentences, the different parts of which appear in separate speech balloons to simulate slow time. Fujiko also uses visual tricks to emphasize fast or slow speeds of characters within individual frames, as seen on the same page of "Fast-Slow Medicine." The eighth frame shows Nobita frozen in time and space while Doraemon's foot is about to leave the panel, the robot having just run across the panel from left to right trailing speed lines, dust clouds, and a wind sound effect.

Another aspect of form that helps Fujiko control time is his depiction of a narrative world frozen in time. Most popular Japanese manga are serialized novels with single story lines moving ever forward, and the present of our world is moving ever forward in time. But Fujiko renders the present of his manga as eternally frozen in 1970. Nobita and his friends live in the same traditional Japanese houses and play in the same vacant lot with its stack of unused sewer pipes every day for twenty-seven years. Their world foregrounds relatively few contemporary technological devices and almost no popular culture references. Only a few stories feature problems like pollution or deforestation. The "present" of his stories seems more like a nostalgic "past" outside the world of real time, and it probably felt that way from the very start of the series. There are no murders, no strange religious cults. Wounds and ethical lessons disappear by the start of the next story, and no event from an earlier story affects anything in a later one. All 824 *Doraemon* stories, apart from the occasional Christmas or summer vacation story, occur at the same time. The stories of other Japanese manga, as well as of some American newspaper comics like *Peanuts*, also take place in an unchanging time frame, but *Doraemon* is more thematically concerned with time.

Because *Doraemon* depicts the desire to control and temporarily escape time, it is not surprising that Fujiko's depiction of time manipulation is not constrained by consistent ground rules. In one story the past may not be changed; in another it may be. In one story, changing the past causes the present situation in a time-loop paradox. In another, changing the past changes the present. In one story the Time Machine moves through the fourth dimension horizontally, as through a tunnel; in another it descends, as in a well. In one story the fourth dimension is lined with soft clocks with squiggly hands; in another with soft clocks without hands; in another without any clocks. In one story adult Nobita, twenty-five years in the future, is skinny with a long pointy nose, glasses, and nerdy haircut; in another he's chunky with a short, flat nose, no glasses, and stylish haircut. Scrutiny of the stories leads to endless questions: Why don't more people from the future send back robots to urge their ancestors to improve themselves? Why doesn't Nobita return to the present at the exact moment when he left so his mother won't scold him for being late? Why don't people panic when Nobita slows time for a day?

Fujiko delights in playing with time travel conventions and paradoxes without explaining their pleasures and wonders with the rigorous logic and scientific language of American time travel fiction. Whereas in *Timescape* Benford carefully depicts how the time paradox inherent in changing the present by tampering with the past might logically be resolved, in Doraemon Fujiko blithely has Nobita spend an afternoon with his future adult self and his son, or ensure that his parents ask each other to marry, or let his dead grandmother see him as an elementary school boy before she dies. Nobita never asks, "Do the laws of space and time allow me to do this?" He just does what he wants and dream logic takes over.

Partly because *Doraemon* is not a coherent novel and the order of any of its many stories after the first could be rearranged, Fujiko is able to "forget" earlier developments that might restrict later story lines. A striking example is how in the first story Nobita learns that unless he improves himself, in addition to ruining his descendants, he will wind up marrying the sister of the neighborhood bully; however, with neither explanation nor comment, and certainly without any improvement in Nobita, by the sixth volume of stories we learn that his future wife will be his beloved Shizuchan.

Some inconsistencies may be accidents explained by Fujiko's medium: the deadline-driven, monthly short story gag manga for elementary school children. He was strenuously creating multiple manga series at the same time and probably didn't expect much rigorous questioning from his readers. Whatever the reason for the many inconsistencies, their effect is to make time feel malleable. The legions of *Doraemon* fanatics who publish their mental gymnastics rationalizing all inconsistencies may be missing the point. After all, the inconsistencies are consistent with Fujiko's and Nobita's desire to be free from constraints of time. And there is at least one overt consistency: the ethical-emotional "rules" for time control. Nobita's attempts to manipulate time lead to trouble or failure when his goals are selfish, and to success and education when they are selfless.

Why, then, are *Doraemon* and its treatment of time so popular? One reason is that Japanese children begin reading *Doraemon* just as they have been thrust from what Ian Buruma calls "the Garden of Eden-like state"[9] of timeless infancy—when they are astoundingly spoiled and allowed to do anything they want—into the incredibly difficult elementary school world of homework deadlines, elaborate and inflexible schedules, test dates, and conformity, a world in which they suddenly have so few free moments and so many school-oriented responsibilities. In the elementary school years, students have homework every day, and even during their five-week-long summer vacation they must complete various assignments called *natsuyasuminotomo* (summer vacation friend). Even though in 1992 their six-day school week became a five-day week twice a month, they still must attend school activities on the two "free" days. Recently, while I was talking with a student about her elementary school days, she said, "Childhood is no time." And this lack of free time grows even more severe as Japanese children progress through junior high school and senior high school, when they must begin attending cram schools at night and preparing for difficult, life-determining entrance examinations.

Doraemon offers a seductive fantasy of transcending the constraints of the hard time of school. Many stories concern Nobita's use of various time gadgets to make it easier to do his homework—or avoid doing it—or be on time for school or travel to a time when there was no school. The time machine is in his desk, where he is supposed to study: Nobita's place of enslavement to time is also his place of liberation from it. The soft clocks adorning the fourth dimension he travels through make the symbol of institutional hard time—the school facade clock—pliable.

However, because Nobita's use of gadgets is often subject to time limits, because he often fails to control time, and because by the end of each story Nobita has returned to the world of actual time, *Doraemon* also eases the entry of children into the world of hard time. The last frame of many stories shows Nobita hard at work at his desk; no last frame of any story shows him on the time machine.

Fujiko has said that to create successful children's manga, you "have to be at [children's] eye-level . . . with their perspective." One common ground Fujiko shares with children is his career in the deadline-driven manga world, where popular authors are worked to exhaustion by their editors. Fujiko underwent "major surgery for ulcers"[10] and had to cut back his work load in the 1990s. As Nobita has his mother and teacher pressuring him to finish his homework on time, Fujiko had his editors pressuring him to finish his stories. His manga is so popular because the strong empathy he feels for Nobita and Japanese children is so genuine. Nobita's apt full name, Nobi Nobita, is a pun meaning to relax freely or postpone, and it describes the similar desires of Fujiko and his readers.

Fujiko satirizes his career in stories about manga like "Lion Mask in Danger" (3: 5–17; 1974). Here a popular manga creator suffers from writer's block because of intense pressure from editors, so he begs Doraemon to go into the future to buy the next installments of his various manga stories. When Doraemon returns to the present carrying a bag marked "Fujiko" stuffed with manga, the manga creator is so exhausted that to meet his deadlines he asks Doraemon to copy all the future magazine stories onto blank paper. The story closes with Doraemon wearing the manga creator's beret, which is Fujiko's trademark, and wondering, "Just who is the creator of these manga?"

In any industrial country people may feel busy and uneasy about the technological future, so many of the desires in *Doraemon* are not specific only to Japan: to make unpleasant experiences end immediately and pleasant ones last longer; to have more time to complete a project; to live at a slower pace with more free time; to have something you want now; to return to the past and rectify a mistake you made or to see some interesting event you missed; to know what effect a decision will have in your future; to say something you never said to someone who died; to get one of the latest technological gadgets to (ostensibly) save you time; to have a friendly relationship with technology. Because all these desires make *Doraemon* a human and relevant manga, it is read throughout Asia and in some European countries as well as in Japan. (It will probably never be popular in the United States because Nobita is such a wimpy, whining, clumsy, sensitive protagonist.)

One reason why science fiction in general and *Doraemon* in particular are pervasive in Japanese culture is that Japan, more than any other country, is a science fiction land. It is awash in ever newer technological gadgets, from virtual chicken pets, television games, and cellular phones to money cleaners, smart toilet seats, and robot-tended convenience stores. Doraemon puts a comical and friendly face on the technological future to which the present is rushing. And because he is prone to careless mistakes and possessed of wonderful gadgets that are all too easy to misuse horribly, Doraemon is also our present. Indeed, many of his twenty-second-century tools (like the Time *Belt* and Speed *Watch*) are present-day items given a futuristic spin. Fujiko imagines but two futures: one near future twenty-five years away that is slightly more gadgetry-filled than our present; and the far future of the twenty-second century, which is a technological playground. Nobita never travels any farther into the future—Fujiko is not interested in it.

Most importantly, Doraemon embodies the imaginative use of the future to improve the present. He is in the present to help Nobita improve, though Fujiko died leaving the question of Nobita's ultimate improvement unresolved. My students often tell me the "true" conclusions to the series that have spread via word of mouth: In one, Nobita improves himself, becomes a genius inventor, grows up and invents Doraemon, and sends him back into his past. Such rumored endings, however, say more about the fans' desire for closure than about Fujiko's intentions. In any case, Nobita's temporary improvements and overall failings delight us even as they show us how to live ethically and emotionally in our present, technology and all, so our future may be a better time to live.

Notes

1. Frederik L. Schodt, quoted in *Asahi Shinbun* (Tuesday, June 3, 1997), 19.
2. Fujio F. Fujiko, *Doraemon*, Volume 1 (Tokyo: Shougakukan, 1974), 5–19. There are 45 volumes of Fujiko's *Doraemon* stories, all published by the same company between 1974 and 1996; future parenthetical references to *Doraemon* stories in the text will provide paperback volume number, pages, and publication date.
3. Frederik L. Schodt, *Dreamland Japan: Writings on Modern Manga* (Berkeley, California: Stone Bridge Press, 1996), 218.
4. Mark Schilling, "*Doraemon*: Making Dreams Come True," *Japan Quarterly*, 40:4 (1994), 409.
5. Gregory Benford, *Timescape* (1980; New York: Pocket Books, 1981), 24.
6. Benford, 24.
7. Fabian Nicieza, Salvador Larroca, and Al Milgrom, "Gambit and the Externals: To the Limits of Infinity" *X-Men Deluxe*, No. 3 (May, 1995).
8. Scott McCloud, *Understanding Comics* (Northampton, MA: Kitchen Sink Press, 1993), 70.
9. Ian Buruma, *A Japanese Mirror: Heroes and Villains of Japanese Culture* (London: Vintage, 1984), 23.
10. Both statements cited in Schodt, 220.

Part III

Time Capsules

The Curvature of Space-Time in Dante's *The Divine Comedy*

Pekka Kuusisto

In the Heaven of the Fixed Stars, Dante the pilgrim (in Canto XXVII of the *Paradiso*) turns his eyes down to the Earth and notices, drawn on the sea beyond the Pillars of Hercules at Gibraltar, the track of Ulysses's ship. The "mad track of Ulysses"[1] bends along the Earth's surface, going around a sphere with Lucifer chained at the center point. In the next canto, with Beatrice, he then ascends to the ninth and outermost sphere of the Ptolemaic universe, the Primum Mobile, where he sees "a point which radiated a light so keen that the eye on which it blazes needs must close because of its great keenness" (*Par.* 313). Recalling Aristotle's definition of the Unmoved Mover,[2] Beatrice explains how "[o]n that point the heavens and all nature are dependent" (*Par.* 315). The blinding spot of light is girded by a series of nine concentric "circle[s] of fire" (*Par.* 315), which are the angelic orders speeding around God, the center point of the Empyrean heaven.

The scene is important because Dante is here forced to seek a solution to the problems of the world's limiting boundary and the relation of the physical and metaphysical universes. From the beginning of the poem, readers have received signals on the problems of representing the transcendental in language and relating the tropes of metaphor and metamorphosis involved. Although we are advised to take the nine planetary heavens as a metaphor for the metaphysical realm beyond,[3] the poetics of ineffable metaphor is countered with Ovidian allusions—like that of Glaucus's in Canto I of *Paradiso*—which prepare for the poet's inevitable task: if the poem is to reach the Primum Mobile, how will the pilgrim be transferred beyond the boundary of the physical universe, and what lies waiting there? Underneath the theological poetics of metaphor, there runs in *The Divine Comedy* the unofficial language of metamorphosis needed to get Dante to heaven.

To support this reading, I will delineate the final articulation of the poetics of metamorphosis in service of Dante's cosmology and introduce an interpretation, dating from the 1920s, which reads Dante's Empyrean as a second hemisphere of the so-called three-dimensional spherical space, the three-sphere, double elliptical space, or simply S^3, the cosmological model of Einstein's finite but unbounded universe. While Dante could not have such conscious intentions, his cosmology is basically non-Euclidean and relativistic, and the spacetime at the other pole of Dante's cosmos, as reflected in the pilgrim's passing by the center of the Earth and in the story of Ulysses, is of relative nature.

The conceptual breakthrough involved in the pilgrim's transfer to the Empyrean became possible to articulate only when non-Euclidean geometry emerged in the nineteenth century. The first reference to Dante's Empyrean as a second hemisphere of the three-sphere is to my knowledge by Andreas Speiser in 1925,[4] and J. J. Callahan in 1976 and Mark Peterson in 1979 further substantiated the argument.[5] More recently, the Stanford mathematician Robert Osserman has repeated the argument in *Poetry of the Universe* (1995), describing the resembling of the three-sphere or hypersphere invented by Riemann to Dante's universe as "almost eerie" and leading him to speak of the "Dante-Riemann universe."[6] Still, despite its contribution to what is one of the most concrete and immediate problems of representation in the poem, the argument remains marginal within Dante scholarship.

The three-sphere was discovered by Bernhard Riemann in the nineteenth century and formulated in cosmology by Albert Einstein in his general theory of relativity. "It is still," Peterson writes, "one of the foremost cosmological models of modern astrophysics," while "Dante's account of it is unquestionably the earliest."[7] The three-sphere is a three-dimensional equivalent of two-dimensional surface of the ball. To visualize this type of curved space, Einstein asks us to imagine a point from where strings proceed to all directions, so that their free endpoints lie on a spherical surface. The amazing beauty of this model is that after a certain value, such strings start to curve until they coincide in the second counter-pole of the universe.[8] The three-sphere can be visualized as two solid balls or hemispheres that are glued along their boundary all over. These solid balls can be sliced into series of hollow two-dimensional spheres, or surfaces of ball, a configuration that the series of the planetary heavens and the hierarchies of angels in Dante's poem correspond to. The three-sphere has no boundary; therefore no point in it is outside. Crossing the boundary of one hemisphere, one always ends in the other hemisphere. In Dante, we have the center of the Earth and center of the Empyrean, or Satan and God, as the two counter-points of the three-sphere, though the latter point, of course, is valorized in symbol. Peterson also suggests the possibility of reading the speed of rotation of the heavenly spheres in Dante as a fourth, time coordinate of the continuum.[9]

Nevertheless, Dante must solve the problem of the boundary of the Ptolemaic universe within the conceptual system of Classical thought. What has not been recognized in previous studies of his three-sphere are the microcosmic elements of this tradition that may have provided him with a pre-conceptual symbolic language he needed to surpass the conceptual dogma of his day. Especially suggestive is the role of the microcosmic language in articulating certain differences between the spacetime geometry of the two counter-poles of Dante's three-sphere.

The microcosmic notion has a biological basis in agrarian cultures, where the projection of the dimensions of plants and animals and especially of human body into cosmic proportions provides eventually a picture of the universe as a living organism with the six opposite directions of the absolute "up" and "down," "right" and "left," and "front" and "behind."[10] In medieval commentaries on Aristotle's *On the Heavens*, the principle of the absolute directions was illustrated with the image of the cosmological man, the giant Atlas holding the heavens on his shoulders, his head at the Southern and his feet at the Northern pole of the universe. Thomas Aquinas, in the commentary Dante probably knew, clarifies Aristotle's thought with this image:

This will be easier to understand if we imagine a man with his head in the arctic and his feet in the antarctic poles of the heaven. His right hand will be in the west and his left in the east, provided his face is toward the upper hemisphere, i.e., the one visible to us on earth. Therefore, since the motion of the heaven is from east to west, it will follow that it is from the left to the right. On the other hand, if we place his head in the antarctic and his feet in the arctic pole, with his face as before, his right hand will be in the east and his left in the west. Then the motion would begin from the right, as it should. Thus it is clear that heaven's "up" is the pole which is hidden from us.[11]

It is one thing to postulate the absolute directions theoretically, like Aquinas following Aristotle, and another to represent this notion geometrically in poetry. Though Dante in the *Convivio* finds a premonition of the metaphysical universe, the Empyrean, already in Aristotle, no clear geometric model of it was available.[12] This problem of geometrization becomes evident in any illustration of the poem: How can the Empyrean be both the center and the circumference of the universe?

In the Primum Mobile, Dante and Beatrice approach Atlas's head. The intellectual tone of their discussions on opening the knot of the universe matches the microcosmic location of the scene. How can the physical universe be in a place, if it is the largest body that contains everything else? Why is the relation of speed of the planetary heavens inverse in relation to angelic hierarchies of the Empyrean? "[T]his heaven has no other *Where* than the divine mind," Beatrice explains in Canto XXVII, "wherein is kindled the love that revolves it, and the virtue which it rains down. Light and love enclose it in a circle, as it does the others, and this engirdment He alone who girds it understands" (*Par.* 309); it is no wonder that in the next canto Dante's "fingers are insufficient for such a knot," for "so hard has it become by not being tried" (*Par.* 317).

As Charles Singleton shows in his commentary, Dante the poet opens Beatrice's knots with one of the most original rhetorical gestures of the poem. Before Callahan and Peterson, but unaware of the connection to modern relativistic cosmology, Singleton points to the series of inversions in Dante's eight and ninth heaven, which gradually turn the physical universe inside-out into metaphysical heaven. Inversion, or chiasmus, would be the master-trope of Dante's cosmology.[13] So far physicists have been predominantly interested in the heavenly hemisphere of Dante's three-sphere, but it is also appropriate to find features of spacetime curvature at the other hemisphere. The two hemispheres are—to a degree—symmetric mirror images of each other, while Ulysses serves as a figure connecting the symmetric structure.

Rather than an intellectual tone, the tone at the mundane hemisphere relates to the lower bodily level of the cosmological man, to the functions of the endocrine rather than the mind. Whereas the spacetime curvature in the Empyrean is a marvelous phenomenon, at the center of the Earth it is uncanny, moving as we are in Atlas's intestines. Dante's Lucifer is chained at the center point of the closed ball of the Ptolemaic universe. The Earth's center in this tradition, Virgil explains in Canto XXXIV of *Inferno*, is also "the point to which all weights are drawn from every part,"[14] that is, it is the natural place of the element earth.

But what kind of a point is the center of the world? According to Aristotle, as a point it should first be a mathematical notion that in principle is indivisible, weightless, and distinguished from physical bodies.[15] However, it is also a fixed, determined point (III, 4, 311b25) with a concrete physical correlation. Since the planetary heavens by their divine nature move "always in a circle" (II, 3, 286a11), and circular motion does not have a contrary movement, for Aristotle it follows from the principle of contraries that "there must be something at rest at the centre of the revolving body" (II, 3, 286a12–13) of the heavens. The astounding deduction is that "[e]arth then has to exist; for it is earth which is at rest at the centre" (II, 3, 286a20–21). As Pierre Duhem has shown, the center point of the universe in Aristotle turns out by false conclusion of immobility of an abstract entity to be a physical object.[16]

Literalization of the center point is completed in Dante. New problems, new requirements concerning the representation of this point crop up when he shifts from philosophy to poetry. To evade these problems most easily, Dante could have transported his personage beyond the center point in a dream had this device not been used already earlier in the *Inferno*, while crossing another decisive borderline, the river Acheron. Dante therefore is obliged to make passing through the center of the world credible for his readers in a more immediate manner. His ingenious stroke was to compound the center point with the body of Lucifer, which served to justify the repression of the theoretical problems and the moral haste away from them, as voiced by Virgil (in Canto XXXIV) climbing up on Lucifer's body away "from so much evil" (*Inf.* 367). For this reason, readers never have the chance to ask the naive but inevitable questions—What does the center point look like? How big is it?—for this point is hidden, as Norman Brown's logical suggestion goes, and as Robert Durling in his studies of Dante's microcosm has supported, in Lucifer's anus.[17]

Dante's literalization of the center point involves an acute problem of geometry, not conceivable in the Euclidean terms of his tradition, that has escaped the modern commentators' attention. Moving toward the center and then turning toward the circumference of the physical universe, the pilgrim goes between the two limits of representation of the Euclidean geometry as the *Convivio* introduces them. The point and the circle are, first, principles or limits of Euclidean geometry: "as Euclid says, the point is the primary element in Geometry, and, as he also indicates, the circle is its most perfect figure, and must, therefore, be considered its end."

Therefore geometry "moves between the point and the circle as between its beginning and its end." As values of the limit, however, the point and the circle are "antithetical to the certainty characteristic of this science . . . free of any taint of error, and utterly certain," because the point "cannot be measured at all, since it cannot be divided" and the circle, because it "cannot be measured precisely, since, being curved, it cannot be perfectly squared" (II, xiii, 26–27).

The *Convivio*'s epistemology is put to its first test at the Earth's center. Anticipating Beatrice's topological knots at the rim of the universe, the tone is that of problem solving, even if Virgil eventually gives the answer in allegorical terms (*Inf.* 367, 369). Coming across the frozen lake of Cocytus at the bottom of Hell (in Canto XXXIV), Dante sees a strange edifice resembling a turning windmill (*Inf.* 361). The pilgrim realizes that it is Lucifer flapping his six huge wings, fixed tightly in the icy rocks. With Dante on his back Virgil then begins to climb down Lucifer's shaggy flanks until they are at the level of the pelvis. There Virgil turns "round his head to where his shanks had been and grappled on the hair like one who is climbing, so that I thought we were returning into Hell again" (*Inf.* 365).

What the pilgrim believes is happening here is that after his turnover, Virgil starts up and climbs back to the bottom of Hell. While Virgil hurries to continue the journey, the disoriented Dante begs Virgil to draw him "out of error" (*Inf.* 367) by explaining the confusing scene. The "error" here is interesting. As part of the pilgrim's direct discourse, the meaning of the word would express his doubt and confusion when confronting the strange spatial phenomenon.[18] More specifically, the error would be in the pilgrim's subjective illusions of his return into Hell, of Lucifer's contrary position than before, of the disappearance of the ice from Hell's bottom, and finally of the sudden change of the evening into morning in Hell.

The pilgrim is trying to orient himself according to the common sense experience of space and time on Earth's surface. But what kind of "stairs" or ladder is Lucifer providing the poets with? For the pilgrim who believes he has returned into Hell, it appears this ladder can rotate on its middle rung according to an inverted gravity. Suppose you have a ladder on the surface of the Earth that can rotate freely on its middle rung. Following our everyday sense of gravity, you can climb on such a ladder starting off from the ground up until the middle rung. If you rise higher, you are whisked upside-down with the upper half of the ladder. If you wanted to start over again, you would be whisked back one attempt after another. However, as the pilgrim now understands it, Lucifer's ladder works the other way round. It stays stable while he climbs down on it on Virgil's back, but turns downside-up once they are beyond the middle rung. The result might still be similar to the experience on the ground; this ladder might also turn over again, whisking him and Virgil back to Hell's bottom once they gather their strength for a new attempt—which is also logical given that Dante is dealing with an "edifice" resembling an infernal war machine (*Inf.* 361). The satanic geometry at Earth's core merits a closer look.

Throughout his career, from a scene in the *Vita Nuova* where "a gentle lady of quite pleasing aspect" sitting "intermediate in the direct line that proceeded from the most gentle Beatrice and ended in my eyes"[19] veils Beatrice from Dante's sight, to that geometer searching to square the circle in the end of the *Paradiso* (in Canto XXXIII), Dante displays a peculiar if medieval fascination with geometric metaphor.[20] If in the *Convivio*, geometry is given as a science "free of any taint of error, and utterly certain both in itself and its ancillary science, called Perspective" (II, xiii, 27), this area of certainty is found between two limits of uncertainty, that of the point and the circumference. The problem of squaring the circle at the other center of the universe may reference a parallel problem of perspective at the Earth's center.

Whereas the pilgrim suffers from illusions, the reality—from a modern point of view—of the scene is no less extraordinary. If Dante has not returned into Hell, but has really passed beyond the center point, we have to consider that not only the ladder, but the whole world into which it is fastened has turned downside-up. That is, the directions "down" and "up" have changed 180 degrees, which is a phenomenon of non-Euclidean geometry the commentaries of the poem do not recognize, but which Pavel Florenski pointed out in a little-known 1922 article.[21]

The image of the mirror is central to the metaphysics of light in the poem. With light pouring down from the shining point at the Empyrean's center, the pilgrim sees from the Primum Mobile (in Canto I) "[t]he Glory of the All-Mover penetrates through the universe and reglows in one part more, and in another less" (*Par. 3*), through (in Canto XXIX) "so many mirrors wherein it is reflected, remaining in itself One as before" (*Par. 333*). The brighter the light and its reflection, the closer the pilgrim is to God and truth; the darker it is, the more he is exposed to falseness and the error of signification, Lotman notes.[22] In the sequence of the poem's mirrors, Satan's mirror has gone unnoticed due to its blackness. Such is the function of this center point—to invert perspective. Anticipating the modern literary fantastic, this magic mirror serves as a gateway to another world for the one who knows the way, like Virgil, but it may have a darker side as well: when one does not know the way, like Dante, a ladder becomes a trap, that is, active manipulation of perspective with black magic.

Significantly, Dante introduces the two major images of modern literary fantastic, the Devil and subversive mirror,[23] together in a scene that puts the basic premises of his conceptual system at stake. The pilgrim's natural or commonsensical perspective is contested by Lucifer's black magic, a trap eventually avoided in Christian supernatural terms by Virgil's allegorical reading of the events. While Lucifer disorients the one who tries to pass him by on the way to salvation, eternal disorientation, my instinct says, is the cruel punishment of Lucifer himself, the one who once wanted to assume the highest position in the universe but is now the lowest of the low, reduced to a turning windmill at the center of the physical universe, where directions can be known only in relation to a transcendental principle.

How does Ulysses connect the two hemispheres of Dante's three-sphere? Ulysses says (in Canto XXVI) that he yearned to "gain experience of the world, and of human vice and worth," driving him to venture beyond the limit of the known world at Gibraltar, to transgress "where Hercules set up his markers, that men should not pass beyond," into the unknown open sea and "the world that has no people" (*Inf.* 277, 279). After five months of sailing "always gaining on the left," crossing the equator and having now the stars of "the other pole" in sight, "there appeared to us a mountain dark in the distance, and to me it seemed the highest I had ever seen" (*Inf.* 279). This must be Mount Purgatory in the southern hemisphere. Having reached the opposite side of the globe, Ulysses momentarily rejoices with his crew before "from the new land a whirlwind rose and struck the forepart of the ship . . . as pleased Another, till the sea closed over us" (*Inf.* 279, 281).

The character of Ulysses is among the poem's most discussed and debated details. While Virgil explains Ulysses's punishment among the sinners of fraud in the eight circle of the Hell by referring to the treacherous wooden horse of Troy, Ulysses's undeniable importance in the poem has divided commentators: Some emphasize the heroic element of Ulysses's quest, his desire for knowledge, while others take a moralizing stance against Ulysses for his transgression of human limits.[24]

There is a textual basis for such a controversy, for besides Virgil and Beatrice, Ulysses is the most important figure Dante meets in the other world in terms of references and allusions.[25] Based on this evidence, some critics have described him either as the pilgrim's negative double on a thematic level or as a figure of transgression in a formal level and thus as the counterpart of the poet in his work.[26] As Barolini observes, "[t]he Ulysses theme, if looked at from the angle of the poet rather than the pilgrim, forces us to challenge the theological grid with which we read the Commedia . . . whereby whatever happens in Hell is 'bad,' problematic, and whatever happens in Heaven is 'good,' problem-free."[27] The severe punishment and the obsessive revoking of Ulysses thereafter should be considered a signal of a divided authorial position: Dante the theologian serves God's plan by condemning Ulysses into deep Hell, but the more unconscious poet invests in Ulysses as a model for his own daring navigation from one center of the universe into the other. More than Ulysses's personal fate or the poet's or pilgrim's personal concerns are at stake when the pilgrim turns his eye from the world's boundary to Ulysses's track on the sea. The mad line of Ulysses's sin now becomes visible in the pilgrim's eye.

What is the modality of this curved line on the sea? Is it an ideal line of the allegory, a metaphor in the mind's eye, or a contemptuous or contemplative projection of the lifeline of the pilgrim's negative double? What undermines the allegorical reading is the position of the pilgrim's eye on the border of time and eternity. Already in Hell he has seen part of God's unfolded plan upon which no further changes are expected. Gazing down from the rim of Heaven, he now sees the surface of the Earth from an Apocalyptic point of view and sees the past track of Ulysses as a line in the eternal presence, bending from the Pillars of Hercules to the left over the equator and to the Southern Hemisphere. Allegorically, the leftward line suggests sinister movement. But he pilgrim's eye is not fascinated with the allegorical line. The theologian sentenced the Greek hero to lower Hell, but the poet wants to get his pilgrim in Heaven, if he only knew how. It is rather the literal line—the curious curve on a two-dimensional spherical surface that "Euclid the geometer" (*Inf.* 45) in the underworld shadows of Limbo (in Canto IV) cannot understand—that demands a backward glance. But there is more: There is the line seen and there is the eye that sees. So much depends on the relation between the gazing eye and curved line, the line and the stars reflecting in the eye, when the eye turns toward the Unmoved Mover. The eye reads the sea chart into Heaven, reads while the mind stares.

While the geometry of the three-sphere had to wait for the nineteenth century, an approximate two-dimensional version of it, the so-called two-sphere, was available in the surface of any ordinary sphere, particularly the spherical Earth dominant since antiquity. Leaving Circe's island in the eastern Mediterranean on the latitude of Mount Zion and curving to the opposite pole of the globe, Ulysses and his crew traverse approximately a great circle, the shortest route on a spherical surface. If the surface of the spherical Earth suggests a curved, non-Euclidean space, at least from the rational vantage point of the heaven of physics and metaphysics, the possibility decreases the nearer we are to the Earth's center, that black, irrational point that overturns the directions where Aristotle's indivisible center point breaks into infinite regression of a center point of a center point with an infinite curve of increasing weight. What we have here is a series of mimetic acts modeled on the spacetime curvature at the Earth's center. Following Lucifer's call, Ulysses navigates on a sinister surface bending around the center point. He acts out Lucifer's black magic on open seas. At the border of the physical and metaphysical world, Dante the pilgrim gets mimetically connected to Ulysses, acting out the hero's curving line in the poet's invention of the three-dimensional closed universe that follows.

In geometric terms, Dante's turnover at the center point is a change from one global orientation to another. Since it has two different orientations, Dante's cosmos would then be globally non-orientable. Noting the non-Euclidean features of Dante's center of the Earth, Florenski[28] concludes that Dante's cosmos is in terms of geometry a single elliptical space, described by Einstein (133) as a curved space where the counter-points are identical and indistinguishable from one another. A concrete model of this kind of space is the Klein bottle.[29] The non-orientable single elliptical space, Florenski argues, would account for the Moebius strip-like change of directions at the Earth's center, for here the pilgrim's path is understood as a movement on a one-sided surface that turns the perpendicular normal over.[30] This model accounts for the geometry of the center of the Earth, but not the spacetime features of the Empyrean that suggest a bipolar spherical space.

To explicate Dante's cosmology, we need not return to the dogma of absolute directions Dante circumvents, though a model that accounts for both centers of Dante's universe might be constructed in purely geometric terms. Instead, I would turn to Einstein's view of geometry "as a branch of physics" (4). Curvature of spacetime is an effect of gravitation field and an indication of presence of matter. There is a symmetry of strong force fields between the two poles of Dante's universe, the "attraction" of the element earth on one hand and "the Love which moves the sun and the other stars" (*Par.* 381) drawing the pilgrim to the Empyrean on the other (in Canto XXXIII).

Dante has become a proverbial example for modern cosmologists. Stephen Hawking evokes Dante's Hell in searching for a gate inscription of a black hole: "One could well say of the event horizon what the poet Dante said of the entrance to Hell: 'All hope abandon, ye who enter here.' Anything or anyone who falls through the event horizon will soon reach the region of infinite density and the end of time."[31] Hawking may believe that he is only recycling a dead metaphor, but here an infernal irony turns casual twists of speech into flesh. A black hole is a singularity of spacetime where laws of physics break down and from where no information, even light, can be obtained. Dante knew nothing about such laws to be broken, but he could conceive of something analogous in terms of his microcosmic body of the universe. Both scientific metaphors—the center of the Earth in Dante and the black hole of modern cosmology—collocate darkness and the breakdown of information with the infinite density of matter that causes the spacetime around it to curve. That in Dante's microcosmic language, such a point would be located in a black hole proper—so to say—matches Dante's instinct, for he wants us to shun the center point and laugh at Lucifer's upward sticking legs. This carnival laugh, largely repressed in Dante's Hell, suddenly bursts out here to help the allegorical absolute directions to be reestablished.

Let us boldly look more closely at Lucifer's black hole. Lucifer is enclosed in his middle within what Virgil calls (in Canto XXXIV) "a little sphere" (*Inf.* 369) that forms a sort of a shell around the center point and Lucifer's pelvis. What is the reason for this obscure detail? Paolo Pecoraro suggests that Dante's intuition draws with this sphere a horizon analogous to the collapse of matter in modern physics under infinite gravitation, but his idea is insufficiently developed.[32] It is within this sphere that the radical spacetime curvature takes place, between the lake Cocytus and the rock where Virgil places Dante to rest for a moment. The innermost sphere of Dante's physical universe, this little sphere separates, Pecoraro argues, an "essence-under-zero" (140) underneath the concentric sublunary spheres of earth, water, air, and fire from the ether-made superlunary spheres. It is thus heavier than earth, the heaviest of Aristotelian elements, going off the scale as it were. The element earth, we must recall, "escaped" the fallen angel in a cataclysmic horror, leaving an "empty space" (*Inf.* 369) at the Earth's center to be filled with Lucifer's middle. The little sphere, Pecoraro (139) continues, would be Lucifer's "quintessence" as an Archon of his star he once wanted to shine highest but which now has fallen to be the lowest.

Together with black holes, modern cosmology applies the metaphor of the wormhole, "a hypothetical tunnel through the fabric of spacetime" connecting two black holes or a black hole to a white hole, so that "[t]he 'other end' of a wormhole could be anywhere in space, and also anywhere in time, allowing an object that passed through the wormhole to appear instantaneously in some other part of the Universe—not just in a different place, but also in a different time."[33] Such time travel, once considered a purely mathematical construct with no physical reality, is now accepted as a true possibility.

For readers of poetry used to observing poets building the world's order with metaphorical correspondences, the metaphors of current cosmology such as black holes and wormholes do not sound unfamiliar; the language of physicists is attuned to the mythopoeic mode of poets. When Virgil carries Dante beyond the center point, he speaks of a wormhole, an "evil worm that pierces the world" (*Inf.* 367). While the reference may be to the Biblical "snake" of Eden and the apple of original sin, the strange spacetime characteristics of Dante's worm give us reason to ask: In what sense could it be analogous to the modern cosmological notion?

The analogy builds through Dante's microcosm, where Lucifer can be seen as an embedded image of Hell and "a kind of great projection of the human body,"[34] a huge torso noted by Boccaccio and explicated more fully by Durling and Martinez: "The pilgrim and Virgil begin their descent through Hell at what corresponds to the head" of the traditional Hellmouth, go then to the Limbo "associated with the traditional seat of memory, the rear ventricle of the brain," past by the sins of the gullet, as Ciacco illustrates them in Canto VI of *Inferno*, and enter the breast at the city of Dis. They then approach the Malebolge where "we find countless references to the processes and products of the human digestive system." Dante's Hell, Durling accordingly concludes, is "divided . . . at points roughly corresponding to the major divisions of the human body," so that "Flegias carries Dante across what corresponds to the division between head and breast" and "Geryon across the diaphragm." At the bottom of Hell, "Cocito, finally, corresponds to the large intestine or to the anus."[35]

As one piece of Dante's semiotic puzzle, Bruno Nardi suggested that Lucifer has the features of an inverted Atlas. Whereas Atlas is an image of cosmic harmony and order, the upside-down Lucifer with his head(s) toward the Northern celestial pole, his right to the west, and left to the east is an image of chaotic disorder.[36] To extend the analogy, according to the classical proportions, Atlas's middle, like Hell's and Lucifer's, coincides with the center of the Earth. While Atlas's body—the body of the universe—is in Dante's poem virtual, compared to the material torso of Hell and Lucifer, the three bodies are hitched to each other by their anuses. Whereas in the allegory, Lucifer's "worm" pierces the world in the Biblical sense, on the literal level, with these microcosmic figures, a digestive tract is formed that runs from the black to the white hole through the universe, from the dark wood to the Hell's "intestines" and into Lucifer's intestines, and then into Atlas's intestines and finally into his head, where the shining face of "our image" (*Par.* 379) at the Empyrean can be seen. Disturbing as this image may be for modern readers whose thoughts are alienated from the microcosmic functions of the human body, it has its own logic that allows us to understand, for instance, the contents of Dante's Hell as Atlas's excrement and Mount Purgatory as the place of purgation of humanity's sins collected in Hell's body. Throughout his journey, Dante's course goes along the spiral of this cosmic digestive tract, often at supernatural speed.

In Lucifer's body, however, this wormhole would make a fatal turn into uncontrolled time travel for wayfarers. At the bottom of Hell (in Canto XXXIV of *Inferno*), Virgil points out the punishment of the three worst sinners, Judas Iscariot, Brutus, and Cassius, whom Lucifer chews in his three mouths (*Inf.* 365). The eternal chewing is no doubt a punishment, yet for a newcomer in Hell without Virgil as his ideological guide, this act of eating follows the theme of cannibalism introduced in the story of Count Ugolino a little earlier (in Canto XXXII and XXXIII) in the Cocytus region, even if in slow motion. How did Lucifer get his meal? Minos (in Canto V of *Inferno*) threw it to him. Were the allegory to crack for a moment here, as it might at the center point, the pilgrim might see Lucifer swallowing his age-old dinner just as a possible new meal has suddenly appeared. Virgil, however, does not wait here long, but "took advantage of time and place, and when the wings were opened wide he caught hold on the shaggy flanks" (*Inf.* 365), and carries Dante to the other side of the center point.

My model for Dante's microcosmic metaphor of the center point as analogous to a black hole in modern physics is now nearly complete. In both contexts, the fall or collapse of a "star" produces a radical spacetime curvature. In Dante, the non-Euclidean change of directions is accompanied by a shift of time over twelve hours from the evening of the Northern to the morning of the Southern Hemisphere (*Inf.* 369), which constitutes time travel unless Virgil's point of reference is by poetic license on the surface of the two hemispheres. When we consider that this jump across time is followed by the two poets's climbing up of half the Earth's diameter in about twenty-four hours, a distance that would "take a train traveling at a hundred kilometers an hour four days and four nights to cover,"[37] another example of poetic license or spacetime curvature is detected.

The literalization of the world's center speeds up both the pilgrim and the poet toward the circumference, giving them experience on how to pass beyond this crucial limit. By literalizing Aristotle's Unmoved Mover into a blinding point of light, and turning the physical universe inside out, Dante the poet gains a deferral of the final confrontation of representing the transcendental in language. This confrontation may never arrive, for it is not surprising that even the poem's final flash of vision is metamorphic in essence. Gazing into Christ's anthropomorphic features, the pilgrim feels how "one sole appearance, even as I changed, was altering itself to me" (*Par.* 379). A trope not of carrying over the unmediated spirit into language, nor of language into pure spirit, but rather of speeding up the vehicles of language and thought while flying by a second critical point of the bending universe, this suddenly throws the poem's point of view back to Earth. From there the poet now contemplates the eternal wheel of the sun and stars going around the Earth in their cosmic dance, while the desire and will of the pilgrim's soul are attuned with the turning order of the angels in the Empyrean—the motion also driving the planetary heavens below.

Not only does the "wheel that is evenly moved" (*Par.* 381) transmit the harmony between the spiritual universe and the pilgrim's soul, but it relates the two systems of wheels, the metaphysical and physical universes, that move evenly with each other in opposite directions. The final image sets the two systems of spheres apart while connecting them in a closed immanent cosmology, rather than building up a further limit of categories to divide them. Time and space on one hand, and spaceless eternity on the other, undergo a chiasmic inversion with this image.

Even in an Empyrean that should be the locus of timeless eternity, Dante keeps reflecting on the passing of time, seeking to articulate its duration with an image of the Argonauts' mythic journey. The recollection of one moment in the present tense of the poet's time "makes for me greater oblivion than five and twenty centuries have wrought upon the enterprise that made Neptune wonder at the shadow of the Argo" (*Par.* 377). We have the gaze once again, this time that of the god Neptune amazed at seeing the shadow of Argo, the first ship ever built to traverse the surface of his kingdom with the Argonauts on board. Stretched across the centuries, the recollection of the Argonauts' line on Neptune's eye recalls the bending curve of the universe on the pilgrim's eye, providing a poor unit of measure for the forgetfulness that this recollection brings the poet who has returned to Earth from a visionary journey. But these images of negation, of an inability to comprehend immense measures of time, actually produce a series of presences in regard to each other. Beyond the shadow of Argo, what the eye sees is the pilgrim's line across the starry spheres—and beyond that the eternal now of poetry.

Notes

1. Dante Alighieri, *The Divine Comedy: Paradiso: Italian Text and Translation*, translated with a commentary by Charles S. Singleton, Second Printing with Corrections (Princeton: Princeton University Press, 1977), 307. All citations of *Paradiso* in the text are to this edition, parenthetically identified by the abbreviation "*Par.*" and page number.

2. Aristotle, *Metaphysics*, Book XII, Section 7, line number 1072b14 (following Becker edition), in Aristotle, *The Complete Works of Aristotle in Two Volumes: The Revised Oxford Translation*, edited by Jonathan Barnes (Princeton: Princeton University Press, 1984).

3. See Canto IV of *Paradiso* and Dante Alighieri, "Letter to Can Grande" [Epistola XIII], Section 29, in Dante Alighieri, *Literary Criticism of Dante Alighieri*, translated and edited by Robert S. Haller (Lincoln: University of Nebraska Press, 1973).

4. Andreas Speiser, *Klassische Stücke der Mathematik* (Zürich: Verlag Orell Füssli, 1925), 53–54.

5. J. J. Callahan, "The Curvature of Space in a Finite Universe," in *Scientific American* 235:2 (1976), 90–100; Mark Peterson, "Dante and the 3-sphere," in *American Journal of Physics*, 47 (1979), 1031–1035; Peterson, "Dante's Physics," in Giuseppe Di Scipio and Aldo Scaglione, editors, *The Divine Comedy and the Encyclopedia of Arts and Sciences* (Amsterdam: John Benjamins Publishing Company, 1988), 163–180.

6. Robert Osserman, *Poetry of the Universe: A Mathematical Exploration of the Cosmos* (New York: Anchor Books, 1995), 118, 90.

7. Peterson, "Dante's Physics," 171.

8. "Suppose we draw lines . . . in all directions from a point, and mark off from each of these the distance r. . . . All the free end-points of these lengths lie on a spherical surface. We can . . . measure up the area (F) of this surface. . . . If the universe is Euclidean, then $F = 4\pi r^2$; if it is spherical, then F is always less than $4\pi r^2$. With increasing values of r, F increases from zero up to a maximum value [of] . . . the 'world-radius,' but for still further

increasing values of r, the area gradually diminishes to zero. At first, the . . . lines . . . diverge farther . . . from one another, but later they approach each other, [until] they run together again at a 'counter-point' to the starting-point. . . . It is easily seen that the three-dimensional spherical space is . . . analogous to the two-dimensional spherical surface. It is finite . . . and has no bounds." Albert Einstein, *Relativity: The Special and General Theory*, translated by Robert W. Lawson (New York: Crown, 1933), 132–133. Later page references in the text are to this edition.

9. Peterson, "Dante and the 3-sphere," 1033.

10. See Giorgio Stabile, "Cosmologia e teologia nella Commedia: la caduta di Lucifero e il rovesciamento del mondo," in *Letture classensi*, 12 (1983), 139–173.

11. Thomas Aquinas, *Exposition of Aristotle's Treatise On the Heavens. Books I–III*, translated by R. F. Larcher and Pierre H. Conway, (Columbus: College of St. Mary of the Springs, 1964), Book II, Section 3, line 324.

12. Dante Alighieri, *The Banquet (Il Convivio)*, translated with introduction and notes by Christopher Ryan (Saratoga: Anma Libri, 1989), Book II, Section iii, Line 10. Later references in the text are from this edition.

13. Singleton, *The Divine Comedy: Paradiso: Commentary*, Second Printing with Corrections (Princeton: Princeton University Press, 1977), 434, 449–450.

14. Dante Alighieri, *The Divine Comedy: Inferno: Italian Text and Translation*, translated with a commentary by Charles S. Singleton, Second Printing with Corrections (Princeton: Princeton University Press, 1977), 367. All citations of *Inferno* in the text are to this edition, parenthetically identified by the abbreviation "*Inf.*" and page number.

15. Aristotle, *On the Heavens* Book III, Section 1, line number 299a28–299b11, in Barnes, editor. Later parenthetical references to Aristotle in this paragraph are from this edition.

16. Pierre Duhem, *Le Systeme du Monde: Histoire des Doctrines Cosmologiques de Platon á Copernic, Vol 1: La Cosmologie Hellânique* (Paris: A. Hermann, 1913–1959), 220.

17. According to Brown, "The persistently anal character of the Devil has not been emphasized enough. . . . Hence Dante makes the still point of the turning world, round which he passes upward to Purgatory, Satan's anus." Norman Brown, *Life Against Death: The Psychoanalytical Meaning of History*, Second Edition (Middletown: Wesleyan University Press, 1985), 207. See also Robert M. Durling, "'Io son venuto': Seneca, Plato, and the Microcosm," in Anthony L. Pellegrini, editor, *Dante Studies with the Annual Report of the Dante Society*, XCIII (Cambridge: The Dante Society of America, 1975), 95–129.

18. See Dante Alighieri, *La Divina Commedia*, commentary by Manfredi Porena (Bologna: N. Zanichelli, 1947).

19. Dante Alighieri, *Vita Nuova*, Italian text with facing English translation by Dino S. Cervigni and Edward Vasta (Notre Dame: University of Notre Dame Press, 1995), Chapter 5, lines 1–5.

20. See Thomas Hart, "Geometric Metaphor and Proportional Design in Dante's *Commedia*," in *The Divine Comedy and the Encyclopedia of Arts and Sciences*, 95–146.

21. Pavel Florenski, cited in Yuri Lotman, *Universe of the Mind: A Semiotic Theory of Culture*, translated by Ann Shukman (London: I. B. Tauris & Co. Ltd, 1990), 178–179.

22. Lotman, 179.

23. See Rosemary Jackson, *Fantasy: The Literature of Subversion* (London: Methuen, 1981), 43–44, 53–60.

24. See Theodolinda Barolini, "Dante's Ulysses: Narrative and Transgression," in Amilcare A. Iannucci, editor, *Dante: Contemporary Perspectives* (Toronto: University of Toronto Press, 1997), 113.

25. After Ulysses's own travelogue, he is twice referred to in the *Purgatorio* (Canto XIX) and *Paradiso* (Canto XXVII) and in numerous allusions through Ulyssean imagery of seafare and surrogate figures like Phaeton and Icarus. See Barolini, 115.

26. See Lotman, 183; Barolini, 117–118.

27. Barolini, 117.

28. Pavel Florenski, "Imaginäre Größen in der Geometrie," in *An der Wasserscheiden des Denkens: Ein Lesebuch*, translated by Sieglinde und Fritz Mierau (Berlin: Kontext, 1994), 133.

29. See David Gans, *An Introduction to Non-Euclidean Geometry* (San Diego: Academic Press, Inc., 1973), 201, 243.

30. "Dante . . . moving forward always in a straight line and turning over once . . . comes back to the same place in the same position as he left it in. . . . This surface then is obviously 1) a Riemannian plane since it contains enclosed straight lines, and 2) a single-sided surface since it turns over when moving along it perpendicularly. . . . Klein showed that a spherical surface is like a two-sided surface, while an elliptical surface is one-sided. Dante's space is extremely like elliptical space." Florenski, cited in Lotman, 178–179.

31. Stephen W. Hawking, *A Brief History of Time: From the Big Bang to Black Holes*, (London: Bantam Press, 1988), 89.

32. Paolo Pecoraro, *Le stelle di Dante: Saggio d'interpretazione di riferimenti astronomici e cosmografici della Divina Commedia* (Roma: Bulzoni editore, 1987), 139. Later page references in the text are to this edition.

33. John Gribbin, *Companion to the Cosmos* (Boston: Little, Brown and Company, 1996), 424.

34. Durling, "Io son venuto," 118.

35. Dante Alighieri, *The Divine Comedy of Dante Alighieri. Volume 1, Inferno*, edited and translated by Robert M. Durling, introduction and notes by Ronald L. Martinez and Durling (New York: Oxford University Press, 1996), 576, 118.

36. See Bruno Nardi, "La Caduta di Lucifero e l'Autenticità della 'Quaestio de Aqua et Terra,'" in *Lectura Dantis Romana* (Torino: Società editrice internationale, 1959), 12.

37. Vittorio Rossi, cited in Singleton, *The Divine Comedy: Inferno: Commentary*, Second Printing with Corrections (Princeton: Princeton University Press, 1977), 635.

11

Temporal Compression, Fractious History: H. G. Wells, George Orwell, and the Mutiny of "Historical Narrative"

Larry W. Caldwell

The vexed filial relationship between H. G. Wells and George Orwell is widely held to have culminated in Orwell's repudiation of his literary foster-father with *Nineteen Eighty-Four*. I have made this case myself and still believe it is largely correct: Orwell followed Wells's career carefully; read virtually everything Wells published, including his last minor collections of journalism and the seemingly senescent *Mind at the End of Its Tether* (1946); and, disillusioned, even horrified by the cumulative utopian "message" of Wells's *oeuvres*, formulated a relentless and comprehensive critique in his *dys*topian final novel. I have sought, however, to elaborate and refine this notion by focusing both on the intricacies of the Wells/Orwell nexus and on dense allusiveness and specificity of Orwell's critique. His persistent concerns are threefold: he seeks to denude the facile nature of Wells's faith in progress and hence in the inevitability of utopia; he wishes to chastise Wells for his glib embrace of catastrophic chiliasm as a means to utopian ends; and he undertakes to interrogate Wells's notions of history and time, especially insofar as these seem to entail an ineluctable recidivism.

The critical literature focuses upon the first two, inevitability and chiliasm, as have my own studies; here, however, I will shift attention to the more comprehensive category of history and time. For while Orwell condemns unequivocally the Wellsian utopia's reliance on foregone conclusions and millennial disasters, it is also true that these, as categories in their own right, merely subtend time and history. Focusing on the latter discloses the degree to which Orwell's critique, however relentless its scrutiny of Wells's historical-temporal shortcomings, *subordinates* inevitability and chiliasm, and, moving beyond the merely reactionary foreclosure of utopia which that critique seems to promise, serves to "open" utopia's discourse. This "opening"—in the postmodern sense of a rupture or hitherto unapprehended gap in a structure presumed to be contiguous and whole—corresponds to a temporal gap that *Nineteen Eighty-Four* reveals to be indispensable in utopian narrative. Thus, Orwell's text tends to subsume its own critique, perhaps even mutinously to evade its reactionary tendencies and reclaim utopia as a discursive genre.

Nineteen Eighty-Four is the last installment in a critical sequence initiated by Orwell twelve years earlier with *The Road to Wigan Pier*.[1] Despite that work's debilities—especially its puerile and indiscriminate hectoring of the literary Left— Orwell attained a number of useful insights during the extraordinary intellectual struggle that attended its composition. Preeminent among these was his recognition of a recidivist strain in utopian-socialist discourse. Suspicious of Wells's "glittering" utopias of steel, concrete, hygiene, and efficiency (202, 208), Orwell noted in these features a kind of atavism, a tendency for material progress to produce its opposite. Ameliorating the environmental conditions that have provoked human inventiveness and strength must eventuate, Orwell believed, not in Wells's garden-city of brave, hardy naturists and cosmic intellects but in a paradise of "little fat men" (210). While this represents an inexcusable gibe at Wells's physical appearance, it also posits an apparently insuperable dilemma: To remain strong and inventive, as Wells insists they will be, utopians would have to somehow preserve artificially the vicissitudes that initially led them to construct their utopia. In conditions of unprecedented indolence,

you are striving to keep yourself brave and hard. You are [thus] at the same moment furiously pressing forward and desperately holding back. It is as though a London stockbroker should go to his office in a suit of chain mail and insist on talking medieval Latin. . . . [I]n the last analysis the champion of progress is also the champion of anachronisms. (194)

This "huge contradiction" (194), as Orwell calls it, this compulsion to eliminate the past by reproducing it, mocks Wells's own mockery of eras such as the Middle Ages, revealing an immedicable fracture in temporal dialectic: contrasting an imagined future with a past that can itself only be imagined suppresses the ideological nature of such imagining and so disguises a political act as an aesthetic one. For Orwell this not only damages Socialism by enforcing a false choice between, say, the Middle Ages as an epoch of oppression, filth, and plague and the utopic future as an era of liberty, cleanliness, and health, but by urging the synthetic readmission of the Middle Ages as a period of salutary evolutionary stress, it also represents the past tendentiously, deploying it as a rhetorical expedient, a sleight-of-hand that allows Wells to both condemn and cherish history.

Throughout *The Road to Wigan Pier* this issue remains for Orwell predominantly a moral one, since to advocate conflicting claims, in politics *or* art, is at best lazy, at worst mendacious. Yet by 1941 he had begun to recognize the more distressing implications of his analysis: Contradictory representations of history, deployed as political rhetoric and embedded in quasi-aesthetic scenarios of the future, are dangerous not merely because they are dishonest—though this would persist among Orwell's concerns right through *Nineteen Eighty-Four*—but because their purveyors fail, or refuse, to account for either the contaminants they themselves inject into temporal discourse or the political consequences. In two essays published in the early 1940s, "Prophecies of Fascism" and "Wells, Hitler and the World State," Orwell elaborated his moral critique into a fully political one.[2] Wells, by imagining futures in which "barbarism" ("World State" 143) had been both superseded and preserved, had not only prevented himself from anticipating the rise of fascism, but he had made himself complicitous in its imminent victory. Arguing in the first essay that Wells as utopian prophet was inferior to Jack London because the latter had a fascist "streak" ("Prophecies" 30) himself—and so comprehended early on the latent, anachronistic savagery of ruling classes as well as revolutionaries—Orwell goes on in the second essay to demonstrate how Wells, the "champion of anachronisms" (*Road* 194), by leaving the savage past safely encysted in his imagined futures, had empowered its catastrophic reemergence. For Wells, Hitler was merely a "defective," a momentary regression,[3] but for Orwell he was anachronism triumphant, living political proof of Wells's folly with regard to the past. Far from being superseded *and* domesticated, that past had broken through Wells's glib assurances and denuded the inadequacies of his utopian schemata. What, indeed, had Wells "to set against the . . . 'defective'. . . ?" Only "the usual rigmarole," the grand rational plan for a World State and federated "world control of air power" ("World State" 140). Unlike London, Wells had no acknowledged fascist streak; he had buried it deeply and refused to acknowledge its potencies:

Hitler [according to Wells] is all the war-lords and witch-doctors in history rolled into one. Therefore [he argues], he is an absurdity, a ghost from the past, a creature doomed to disappear almost immediately. . . . The war-lords and witch-doctors *must* fail, the common-sense World-State . . . *must triumph*. . . . Hitler *cannot* be a danger. That he should finally win would be an impossible reversal of history, like a Jacobite restoration. ("World State" 143)

Yet clearly, Orwell continued, "Creatures from the Dark Ages have come marching into the present," and it would take stronger "magic" than Wells's to "lay them" ("World State" 144). Indeed, minute scrutiny of Nazi Germany disclosed it to *be* the Wellsian future:

Much of what Wells has imagined and worked for is physically there. . . . The order, the planning, the State encouragement of science, the steel, the concrete, the aeroplanes, are all there, but all in the service of ideas appropriate to the Stone Age. ("World State" 143)

   Understandably, this rhetorical collapsing of Wells into Hitler seemed, even to Orwell, a "kind of parricide" against his literary foster-father ("World State" 143). Wells himself, stung to outrage by this and subsequent provocations, roared at Orwell in a letter, "you shit."[4] Yet by 1946, the year of Wells's death, Orwell had already outlined what would become his final provocation. *Nineteen Eighty-Four* had been conceived, and many of its key concepts laid out, during the period of the two authors' wariest, most perturbed encounters—for example, the dinner debate depicted by both Bernard Crick and Norman and Jeanne Mackenzie—during which Wells read aloud from "Wells, Hitler and the World State" and bulldogged Orwell point for point. Their reconciliation that same evening, effected by mutual friends, appears to have been largely superficial, with Inez Holden reporting that the two men had managed to agree on one item only: Wells was preoccupied with *what* the future would look like; Orwell with *how* it could be achieved.[5]

Readers of *Nineteen Eighty-Four* will perhaps recognize the mutation of this what/how dichotomy into the how/why dichotomy articulated by Winston Smith in his diary. Winston, falsely confident that he understands the *how* by understanding merely the manner in which Oceanian society operates but not *how it arose*, suppresses this crucial latter sense, displacing the historical investigations, through which he had originally intended to "blow the Party to atoms,"[6] with a premature quest to penetrate the *why*: why should the Party, with its vast resources, elect hierarchy, universal surveillance, brutality, and material squalor? Winston is unaware that this deflection is the critical moment in O'Brien's strategy to entrap him utterly; or that by leapfrogging the *how* he violates a logical sequence which Orwell has laid out along an essentially temporal axis. The what/how dichotomy of Orwell's debate with Wells is here revealed as incomplete, the proper structure of utopian discourse being WHAT, then HOW, then WHY, with HOW as the crucial mediator. This is, clearly enough, Orwell's fundamental rationalism at work, and in itself subject to critique; what must be emphasized is that without a thorough apprehension of the Wells-Orwell nexus, the tragic error of Winston's deflection from the past, from history, from the issue of *how* Oceanian society arose or was *caused to come into being*, is occluded. Further, by configuring logic as a problem of time, Orwell also signals his intention to treat time as a problem of logic.

Orwell is not, of course, expressing in this matter an interest in theoretical physics, for unlike Wells he appears to have been as bored by such things as he claims to have been by academic philosophy; and in his own cognitive operations he betrays a distinctly Newtonian, mechanical orientation.[7] His concern with time is a concern with proper analytical procedure—logic—and with history—construed as a developmental-causal sequence laid out along the line of the classic episteme past-present-future. By compelling utopian discourse into a particular developmental form—what/how/why—and then laying this form alongside the causal sequence past/present/future, Orwell problematizes utopian causation, confronting us, and Wells, with a sort of cognitive estrangement from both syllogism and dialectic, that is, from tripartite logico-historical structures of prediction.

How, not *what* or *why*, is the crucial question both Wells and Winston ignore. How can utopia be brought into being over time? If the causative sequence entails, as Orwell believed it did in Wells's case, a sleight-of-hand regarding the past, an expedient deployment of history as a pseudo-aesthetic but actually political construct, then utopia would be contaminated beyond repair; and this is precisely what happened in Oceania. The encysted medieval primitive whom Wells both repudiates and cherishes is the manifest causal agency in bringing this *dys*topia into being over time. This becomes obvious when Winston encounters O'Brien as inquisitor, complete with torture chamber and Ptolemaic cosmos; but it is emblematized earlier through Winston's musings on the nature of the Party's official history. Out of a "children's history textbook" (49) borrowed from neighbors Winston copies a long passage for his diary. In the pre-Party era, it reads, London was "dark, dirty [and] miserable" (49); the impoverished multitudes went bootless; the children labored twelve hours a day, were "flogged . . . with whips if they worked too slowly" (49) and were "fed . . . on nothing but stale breadcrusts and water" (49). The capitalist masters, by contrast, lived in "great big beautiful houses" with "as many as thirty servants" (49) and had the power to starve or throw into prison anyone they wished. Their "chief," the passage continues,

> "was called the king, and—" But [Winston] knew the rest of the catalogue. There would be mention of the bishops in their lawn sleeves, the judges in their ermine robes, the pillory, the stocks, the treadmill, the cat-o'-nine-tails, the Lord Mayor's Banquet, and the practice of kissing the Pope's toe. There was also something called the *jus primae noctis*, which would probably not be mentioned in a textbook for children. It was the law by which every capitalist had the right to sleep with any woman working in one of his factories. (50)

Among the extraordinary features of this passage is its deliberate compression of two (or more) historical eras into one. Even the most vulgar Marxists distinguish feudalism from capitalism as indispensable *but sequential* eras in the logic of historical dialectic, so we are not simply dealing here with Orwell's caricature of Marxist reasoning.[8] Rather, this outrageous compaction, which consigns the entire narrative of pre-Party history to the Middle Ages, satirizes Wellsian history as Orwell knew it, not only in Wells's best-selling *Outline* (1920) but also in publications contemporaneous with the composition of *Nineteen Eighty-Four*: *Guide to the New World* (1941), *'42 to '44* (1944), and *Crux Ansata* (1944). In *Outline*, with the same magisterial disdain glimpsed in the child's history of the Party, Wells dismisses the whole of European history, from the crowning of Charlemagne to the "catastrophe of 1914," as medieval, as little more than an attempt, generation after generation, to perpetuate the Holy Roman Empire. Napoleon, whom Orwell held to be Wells's chief villain in *The Outline of History*, is indeed depicted as a principal character in the process, a ghost of a ghost, a Holy Roman revenant.[9]

The types that emerge as quintessential representatives of the so-called "period" 800–1914, however, are the Catholic priest—any Catholic priest—and Gilles de Rais, the fifteenth-century serial child-murderer.[10] These figures recur throughout Wells's critical journalism in the 1940s as anachronisms, anomalies, obstacles on the way to the order of the enlightened World State. Yet for Wells they are also necessary antecedents to that order inasmuch as they reflect, in primitive and destructive form, the discipline and ruthless energy which the utopian elite will require. Thus, once again, the champion of progress is the champion of anachronisms, embedding in his projected future a medieval man whose *how*, whose explicit process of transformation from mass-murdering repressed pervert to utopian *Übermensch*, cannot be adumbrated. In Orwell's Oceania, the Party manifests the same antecedents, and in the closed loop of Ingsoc, Party members perpetuate these antecedents in saecula saeculorum. Embedding the Middle Ages in the future has caused to come into being over time—only the Middle Ages.

The Party's slogan, "Who controls the past controls the future; who controls the present controls the past" (*Nineteen Eighty-Four* 25), is disclosed in this context as one of the most opulent logico-temporal sites in the novel. Rhetorically it is a truncated syllogism, the unspoken conclusion to which must be, "Who controls the present controls the future"; but since the past has been embedded in the future and the present is identical to the past (that is, the Party claims to have superseded the Middle Ages, but only by instituting the Middle Ages), the syllogism is really a tautology: "Who controls the present controls the present." Consequently, the developmental sequence *what-how-why* and the temporal-causal sequence *past-present-future* collapse into single terms, and *Nineteen Eighty-Four* administers to Wells a cathartic dose of what Orwell might have called plain realism. "What is the use," Orwell demanded to know in "Wells, Hitler and the World State," of advocating globally federated air power and a World State? "The whole question is how we are to get [them]"—especially in the face of Wells's own failure to grasp the consequences of medievalizing vast stretches of history and projecting its villains onto the future as heroes ("World State" 140). Winston's tormentor, O'Brien, is an agent of a *de facto* World State whose federated air power routinely bombs its own citizens; he is also a disciplined, ascetic, ruthless, deranged medieval cleric who professes to believe that the sun goes round the Earth and the order he depicts as constituted within a species of eternity—the persistent present—is a repudiation of the Middle Ages that spawned him (*Nineteen Eighty-Four* 176). *How*, then, has Oceania been caused to come into being over time? "Ask H. G. Wells," is Orwell's reply.

Of course, those who know the full extent of Wells's work—in fifty years he published over 100 books—or the range and complexity of that work—science textbooks, popular history and economics, realistic fiction, science fiction, topical journalism, and utopias—may observe that Orwell's representation is not especially representative. John Huntington explicitly asserted in his volume on Wells and "the logic of fantasy" that characterizations of Wells as a proto-fascist—one obvious entailment of Orwell's critique—simply do not pass muster.[11] And one need not read much of Wells's wartime journalism to realize that he did not merely despise and dismiss Hitler, as Orwell maintained. He was a fervent, even jingoistic anti-Nazi who considered Hitler a criminal lunatic and legitimate candidate for extermination. Orwell's Wells, then, viewed from a broader perspective, looks suspiciously like a straw man who, already widely repudiated by Orwell's generation and especially by senior Modernists, had become a familiar polemical target for quasi-reactionary aesthetes (as in Virginia Woolf's "Mr. Bennett and Mrs. Brown"). It was thus easy for Orwell to configure Wells as a glib, shallow utopianist with ideas that were increasingly inadequate, even sinister, as the wary peace of the 1930s yielded to total war. Yet, though several of Orwell's essays and *Nineteen Eighty-Four* are deeply critical of *certain aspects* of Wells's notions of time and causation, Orwell actually knew the full story, as it were, and elsewhere—

in his review of Wells's final book *Mind at the End of Its Tether*, for example—acknowledged "a kind of grandeur" in Wells's treatments of evolutionary and cosmic time.[12] Orwell implies on several occasions that he had read virtually all of Wells's works, so he must have been far more aware than anyone might infer from his critical analysis that Wells's recurrent figure of the evolved savage—the animal beneath the frock coat—always appears as both a promise and threat, from *The Island of Dr. Moreau* through *Mr. Blettsworthy on Rampole Island* to *Secret Places of the Heart* and *The Croquet Player*—to say nothing of several wartime essays in the very collection Orwell responded to in "Wells, Hitler and the World State." Wells's representations of time and causation are more sophisticated than Orwell wishes to grant in his critical analysis, and nowhere does Wells say, as Orwell claims, that "utopia is just around the corner." At his most optimistic, as Warren Wagar and other scholars note, Wells says that utopia *may* be just around the corner *if* man can assimilate and transmute the energy of his beast-nature to evolve beyond it.

Yet even with Orwell's evidentiary debilities acknowledged, his critique remains powerful and meritorious, not merely a component of his presumed "reactionary" repudiation of utopia.[13] For the totalizing closure ascribed to *Nineteen Eighty-Four*—O'Brien's success in lifting Winston "clean out of the stream of history" (169) and dropping him into the static, permanent medieval present—is subverted in turn by the extraordinary narrative device of the novel's "Appendix: The Principles of Newspeak." Much discussion has centered on this remarkable authorial impertinence, from Crick's observation that when the novel concludes, "He loved Big Brother. The End," it is "not 'THE END'" at all, to my own essay on the utility of such anti-closure for "reclaim[ing] utopia for productive doubt."[14] The present consensus on the "Appendix" is that its ambiguous temporal locutions, its complex verb tenses and nonreferential adverbs, as well as its narrator's striking tone of confidence, serve to discompose the relentless dystopian certitude of the "novel proper." Not only is it impossible to determine where or when in the novel's chronology the "Appendix" fits, or who its narrator may be in relation to the "main" narrator, but it is impossible to determine how it came to be written and appended—that is, how it was caused to come into being over time. Its narrator's temporal and ideological orientations are those of an intellectual, in full possession of what we would call liberty, and with abundant records of the past, including the pre-Oceanian past, at his disposal, looking back over time to the era of the Party as something that has failed and passed away.

If this is so, what has happened to the Party to make it fail, and what empowered the distinctly *eu*topian moment—the yet more distant future beyond 1984, perhaps even beyond 2050—where the "Appendix" appears to be located? Once more: how has this moment been caused to come into being by the cumulative effect of preceding moments? On this matter, Orwell is as silent as Wells; and while I have long believed that Orwell was perfectly conscious of his own design in the novel at every point, so that this suppression of the *how* is a parodic reflection of Wells's logico-temporal debilities, it is conceivable that Orwell's text has simply mutinied, refusing to bear the particular ideological freight Orwell has assigned to it. In such a reading, the "Appendix" would be a species of preciousness, a bit of narrative detritus too clever to leave out but rhetorically too expository to work in. To read it as a moment in a *eu*topic future that cannot have come into being by any agency in the novel proper would be a splendid irony, a practical joke on Orwell merited by his tendentious reading of Wells.

But whether "intentional" or "mutinous," the "Appendix" exists across a structural, temporal-historical, and causal gap that should, by Orwell's own criteria, be filled with a narrative of *how*: "A brotherhood of enlightened libertarians rose up and destroyed the Party, instituting a reign of true equality and justice." The absence of this narrative highlights the frequent tendency of Wellsian utopias, and utopias in general, to operate as closed narrative structures assembled around a *what*, a finished or "given" form like ideology that forecloses all other possibilities. In this respect, Orwell's real accomplishment in *Nineteen Eighty-Four* is to rupture that form, to apprehend, as postmodernists say, the "opening" which deauthorizes its oppressive program and frees us to both consider other forms and construct detailed, practical narrations of *how*. Perhaps even, eventually, of *why*.

Notes

1. George Orwell, *The Road to Wigan Pier* (1937; New York: Harcourt, 1958). Page references in the text are to this edition.

2. George Orwell, "Prophecies of Fascism," *Tribune* (12 July 1940); and Orwell, "Wells, Hitler and the World State," *Horizon* (August 1941); reprinted in Ian Angus and Sonia Orwell, editors, *The Collected Essays, Journalism and Letters of George Orwell*, Volume 2 (New York: Harcourt, 1968), 30–33 and 139–145. Later references in the text are to these editions.

3. H. G. Wells, *Guide to the New World* (London: Victor Gollancz, 1941), 31.

4. Cited by Orwell in his "War-Time Diary" entry for March 27, 1942; *Collected Essays, Journalism and Letters*, volume 2, 415. The editor of Wells's complete correspondence, however, has found no other record of such a letter; see David C. Smith, *The Correspondence of H. G. Wells*, 4 volumes (London: Pickering and Chatto, 1998), volume 4, 326n.

5. See Bernard Crick, *George Orwell: A Life* (Harmondsworth: Penguin, 1980), 429–430, and Norman Mackenzie and Jeanne Mackenzie, *H. G. Wells* (New York: Simon and Schuster, 1973), 430–431.

6. George Orwell, *Nineteen Eighty-Four: Text, Sources, Criticism*, Second Edition, Irving Howe, editor (New York: Harcourt, 1982), 53. Later page references in the text are to this edition. Novel first published in 1949.

7. Letter to Richard Rees, March 3, 1949; *Collected Essays. Journalism and Letters*, volume 4, 478.

8. See Raymond Williams, *George Orwell* (New York: Columbia University Press, 1971), 60–61, and especially Alex Zwerdling, *Orwell and the Left* (New Haven: Yale University Press, 1974), 13–14, and John Rodden, *The Politics of Literary Reputation: The Making and Claiming of "St. George" Orwell* (New York: Oxford University Press, 1989), 171–211.

9. H. G. Wells, *The Outline of History*, Third Edition (New York: Macmillan, 1921), 903–904.

10. H. G. Wells, *Crux Ansata* (New York: Agora Publishing, 1944), 41 ff. and 113 ff.

11. John Huntington, *The Logic of Fantasy: H. G. Wells and Science Fiction* (New York: Columbia University Press, 1982), 119. See also W. Warren Wagar, *H. G. Wells and the World State* (New Haven: Yale University Press, 1961), 211–226.

12. George Orwell, "Are We Really Done For?" Review of *Mind at the End of Its Tether* by H. G. Wells, *Manchester Evening News*, 8 November 1945, 2.

13. See Rodden, 322–374.

14. Bernard Crick, "Reading *Nineteen Eighty-Four* as Satire," in Robert Mulvihill, editor, *Reflections on America, 1984: An Orwell Symposium* (Athens: University of Georgia Press), 42–43; Larry W. Caldwell, "Wells, Orwell, and Atwood: (EPI)Logic and Eu/Utopia," *Extrapolation*, 33, No. 4 (Winter, 1992), 333–345.

12

Play It Again, Sam: Ken Grimwood's *Replay* and Time Travel as Reincarnation

Andrew Gordon

> "O, call back yesterday, bid time return."
> —William Shakespeare, *Richard the Second*, III, ii, 69

There is a story about a tenor who was performing in an opera at La Scala in Milan. He came to the close of a famous aria, and the audience began shouting vociferously, "Encore, encore!" So he sang it again. At the end, there was a repeated cry from the audience, "Encore, encore!" So he sang it a third time. Once again, the demand was loudly repeated: "Encore!" At this point, the tenor paused and addressed the crowd: "I am very flattered by your requests, but my voice may give out, so tell me, please, how often do you want me to sing this aria?" And a voice from the balcony cried out, "Until you get it right!"

I concern myself here with time-travel stories that seem to illustrate the repetition compulsion—the mechanical need to repeat human experience unreflectively and endlessly—or else the desire to repeat the past out of the need to correct mistakes, gain greater self-knowledge, and work through trauma. I am thinking of a variant on the time travel story in which protagonists return to their bodies in the past but retain present consciousness, with the chance to relive their lives. This is not physical time travel so much as consciousness transfer. Such stories express a common wish: "If only I were eighteen again, and knew then what I know now. . . ." These could be termed narratives of time travel as reincarnation.

Every waking moment, we make choices, and the sum of these choices constitutes a life. We metaphorize life as a journey and tend to spatialize time.[1] Way leads on to way, irreversibly. Robert Frost speaks of two roads that diverged in a wood and Jorge Luis Borges of the garden of the forking paths. A lot of life consists of making mistakes, so at times we all want to return to a crossroads to do it right or at least to do it differently.

In the unconscious, there is no such thing as temporal sequence. In our dreams, we can twist time into any shape to fulfill our desires: the dead walk again, old lovers return to us. We also do this consciously as well, as we mull over memories and revise the narratives of our lives. And we often repeat the past in present actions, either unconsciously repeating mistakes or consciously trying to correct them. Much of life consists of such repetition. Stories of time travel as reincarnation enact the universal human desire for a second chance or, rather, for endless chances, since it seems unfair that we only get one brief life. When he turned seventy, a friend of mine compared life to a pinball game, saying,"Since I've reached so high a score, you'd think I deserve a replay."

The popularity of time travel narratives in recent years is part of the wave of nostalgia suggesting a growing dissatisfaction with a present that is sensed as dehumanized, diseased, out of control, and perhaps doomed. Somewhere along the line, the unspoken feeling goes, something went drastically wrong, in both contemporary American history and individual lives. If we could only return to the appropriate crossroads in the past and correct things, we could mend history and return to a revised, glorious present, the timeline we truly deserve. During the Reagan era, that crucial time to which we should return became identified with the relative innocence of the Eisenhower or Kennedy eras, roughly 1955–1962, in the halcyon years after the Korean War but before the murder of Kennedy and the military buildup in Vietnam.[2] George Lucas's *American Graffiti* (1973) began the wave of nostalgia films; it was the first to return to the prelapsarian time of 1962.

The proliferation of such narratives also reflects new, more accepting popular attitudes about time travel, or rather, "time shifting," and a flattening of our perspective of time. The media critic Tom Shales noted that one of the most popular films of the 1980s was a time travel story: "*Back to the Future*, a phrase that almost sums the Eighties up, and that's partly because the movie made time travel a joke, a gag, a hoot. We are not amazed at the thought of time travel because we do it every day." Shales called the 1980s "The Re Decade," a decade of replays, reruns, and recycling of popular culture, epitomized by videorecorders. "Television is our national time machine."[3] The technology of the 1980s reinforced the postmodern, collapsed sense of time and history, so that the decades since World War II seem to coexist, especially while switching channels on late-night TV. The computer revolution of the 1990s only deepened this collapse of temporal sequence; the Web is a vast storehouse of endlessly recycled and scrambled images from decades of popular culture.

Time travel as reincarnation occurs in both recent fantasy and sf literature and film. In works toward the fantasy end of the spectrum, the time travel can be passed off as a possible hallucination caused by a near-death experience, as in the film *Peggy Sue Got Married* (1986), or can be left unexplained, as in the film *Groundhog Day* (1993). The heroine and hero in these films get the chance to return to their pasts while retaining present knowledge and thus to change their lives. In science fiction, the consciousness transfer is rationalized through mechanical means, as in the tv series *Quantum Leap*: scientist Sam Beckett is stuck in a time travel experiment gone awry. He temporarily displaces the consciousness of people from the past, usually strangers, but sometimes famous people, friends, family, or, on one occasion, his younger self. Sam acts as a guardian angel to prevent tragedies. The mystical element in the series is that Sam is uncertain who is guiding his leaps; it may be some higher power. In another sf work, the reincarnation is explained as the intervention of an extraterrestrial, "Tralfamadorian" perception of time or else as the wanderings of an unsound mind: Either explanation fits Kurt Vonnegut, Jr.'s seminal novel *Slaughterhouse-Five* (1969), in which hero Billy Pilgrim has come unstuck in time, replaying at random his past, present, or future, although without the power to alter any of it. Finally, time travel as reincarnation can be justified as the effect of a space warp or cosmic disaster, as in "Time Squared," an episode of *Star Trek: The Next Generation* and many sf stories. Characters caught in a time loop operate like clockwork mechanisms, endlessly repeating the same sequence until one of them recognizes the eerie sense of *déjà vu* and tries to escape the pattern. According to Mark Rose, "the paradox at the heart of the time loop is that both free will and determinism are asserted simultaneously."[4]

Stories of time travel as reincarnation almost always have a utopian dimension. The implicit hope is that, through repetition, the heroine or hero or the world will finally reach a state of moral perfection or perfect enlightenment. In actuality, in such stories, things usually get a lot worse before they improve, and sometimes they stay the same.

Here I will focus on two Reagan-era stories of time travel as reincarnation, both released in 1986—the film *Peggy Sue Got Married* and Ken Grimwood's sf novel *Replay*—and on the later film *Groundhog Day*. In *Peggy Sue*, things essentially remain the same, but in both *Replay* and *Groundhog*, they get much worse before they get better. All three stories have a moral dimension, for the heroine and the heroes are improved by the experience of reincarnation, especially in *Groundhog*, a narrative like Charles Dickens's *A Christmas Carol* about the moral transformation of a misanthrope into a philanthropist.

Peggy Sue is the simplest of the three works. The film was compared to *Back to the Future*, which preceded it by a year.[5] Both juxtapose two periods of postwar American history in a small town setting: *Back to the Future* compares 1985 with 1955, *Peggy Sue* compares 1985 with 1960, and both contrast the innocence and promise of the past with the disillusionment of the present. Even the title of the movie evokes Buddy Holly and the 1950s. *Peggy Sue* is a funny and frequently poignant film that views the past through rose-colored lenses.

The premise is simple: In 1985, Peggy Sue, a forty-two-year-old woman, attends her twenty-fifth high school reunion. The event is awash in nostalgia; Peggy Sue wears a dress from 1960 and is reunited with her classmates. She had been the most popular girl in high school, a majorette and Prom Queen. But her life has not turned out as she had hoped.

Peggy Sue grows increasingly nervous when her estranged husband Charlie shows up. She and Charlie married right out of high school and never left town. She tells a friend, "We just got married too young and started blaming each other for all the things we missed." Charlie never became the professional singer he wanted to be, he started running around, and the two are about to divorce. Peggy says, "I've got two great kids, my own business. Still, if I knew then what I know now, I'd do a lot of things differently." When Peggy Sue is crowned Queen of the reunion, she collapses onstage.

When she wakes up, she is seventeen again, back in high school in 1960, her senior year, and given her second chance. But Peggy Sue is, as she says, "a walking anachronism," a middle-aged woman impersonating a teenager, thrust back into a more naive era with foreknowledge of what is going to happen to all the people around her. She is pulled by strong, conflicting emotions: happiness at being reunited in her childhood home with her parents and her little sister, horror that her grandparents will soon die, and love and anger toward Charlie, whom she sees simultaneously as the charming, hopeful teenager and the unhappy, middle-aged husband who will cheat on her.

Peggy Sue finds herself with the luxury of deciding between three very different men: Richard Norvick, the high school brain who will become a famous inventor, the only one in town to whom she can entrust her secret; Michael Fitzsimmons, a beatnik loner on whom she had a crush; and Charlie. All three propose marriage. But Richard, who will be the most successful of the three, does not interest her except as a friend; besides, she met Richard's pregnant wife at the high-school reunion. Michael is a brooding, romantic poet, and they have a thrilling one-night stand under the stars. But all he offers her is a *menage-a-trois* on a chicken farm out west. She is glad she had one perfect night with Michael, but she tells him they are "light years apart." Once again, she is left with Charlie, but she decides not to marry anyone, because she sees her early marriage (Charlie got her pregnant on her eighteenth birthday) as the big mistake of her life.

On her eighteenth birthday, she instead flees Charlie and leaves town for a final visit with her beloved grandparents, to whom she confesses her time traveling and yearning to go home because she misses her children. Grandpa claims that his lodge was founded by a time traveler and that they can send her home. The old men perform a batty ceremony, the lights go out, and Peggy Sue disappears. But she has only been captured by the persistent Charlie. When Charlie proposes, she says, "You betrayed me. You were never there for the children. . . . I may be crazy but I'm not crazy enough to marry you twice!" Then he offers her as an engagement present a silver locket, the locket she always wore with pictures of her children. So they make love, just as before.

She awakens in a hospital bed in 1985. Charlie has kept a vigil by her bedside, says he has left his girlfriend, and asks for another chance. Peggy Sue's time traveling is explained as a near-death experience, a dream in which she replayed her life, which does not explain the book at her bedside by Michael Fitzsimmons, dedicated "To Peggy Sue and a starry night."

She is reunited at the end with Charlie and her daughter. It was a foregone conclusion that she could do nothing else than marry Charlie again; for all his flaws, the marriage produced two children whom she loves and who would not exist if she had chosen differently. So nothing really changes, and the elaborate reincarnation fantasy seems to suggest that we should accept life as it is, rather than yearning futilely for something different. At one point, she asks her grandfather, "If you could do it over again, what would you do differently?" But grandpa, a truly happy man, says only, "I'd have taken better care of my teeth."

Replay is the most complex work of the three I am discussing. Since it is a science fiction novel rather than a Hollywood film, the author is free to work many variations on the theme of time travel as reincarnation and speculate at length on the human experience of time. Central to *Replay* is the Hindu notion of karma, of being reincarnated as punishment or reward, repeating the cycles of life until one attains complete enlightenment. The hero, Jeff Winston, thinks of "Wheels, mandalas: symbols of eternal cycles, of illusory change that merely led back to where the change had begun and would begin again."[6] A passage from the *Bhagavad Gita* is repeated twice: "'You and I, Arujna, have lived many lives. I remember them all. You do not remember'" (110, 238).

Like Peggy Sue, Jeff is thrust back twenty-five years so that he is eighteen again; Peggy Sue goes from 1985 to 1960 and Jeff from 1988 to 1963. Peggy Sue has a heart attack and a near-death experience; Jeff has a heart attack and dies. Both are middle-aged and miserable, but Jeff is worse off than Peggy Sue: childless, stuck in an unhappy marriage and a dead-end job.

The view of the 1980s is far more jaundiced in this novel: "The future: hideous plagues . . . city streets haunted by null-eyed punks in leather and chains and spiked hair, death-beams in orbit around the polluted, choking earth" (15). And his first time around, the 1980s were a decade of personal defeat for Jeff: "The eighties: a decade of loss, of broken hopes, of death" (90). He contrasts the 1980s with the innocence of the prelapsarian era of 1963: "Girls—women—her age in the eighties didn't look like this . . . weren't this young, this innocent; hadn't been since the days of Janis Joplin, and certainly weren't in the aftermath of Madonna" (20).

Jeff finds himself back in college his freshman year, with his whole adult life to live over. As in *Peggy Sue*, it is a move that attempts to reverse the flow of time: from middle age to youth, from disappointment to hope, from experience to innocence. But as Jeff replays his life, he finds that his advance information is a mixed blessing. He attempts to prevent the original sin that began postmodern American history: the assassination of John F. Kennedy. Jeff arranges for Lee Harvey Oswald to be arrested, but instead another assassin kills Kennedy and is, in turn, killed by Jack Ruby. So apparently he cannot improve history. His knowledge also isolates him from the people around him, who are no longer his contemporaries. He becomes a multimillionaire by betting on sports events and investing in stocks, but Linda, his wife in his previous life, spurns him. His women are a bimbo mistress and then his wife, a coldhearted heiress.

His only compensation is his beloved daughter, the first child he has ever had. But when he reaches age forty-three, he dies as before, and so loses everything he had gained, including his daughter, who has ceased to exist except in the timeline Jeff had created.

In his second replay he goes for love instead of money, marries his college sweetheart, and lives a comfortable middle-class life. He decides never again to have children, but he adopts some. However, it all comes to nothing again when he dies on schedule, at age forty-three. He seems doomed to lose everyone he loves, over and over again: "[T]hey were all dead all of them dead except for him and he couldn't die no matter how many times he died. He was the wheel; he was the cycle" (94).

In the third replay, he feels nothing matters and lives only for sex and drugs. Finally, repelled by the depressed hedonist he has become, he retreats for years as a hermit farmer. What brings him out of his shell is the discovery in 1974 of a science fiction film that employs the talents of George Lucas and Steven Spielberg. This film is an anomaly: it never existed in any of his previous timelines. He tracks down the writer-producer, Pamela Phillips, and she proves to be another replayer.

Jeff and Pamela fall in love and try to stay together for their remaining replays, although circumstances sometimes prevent that, as when Pamela returns age fourteen, a prisoner in her parents' home and in high school, or later, when she returns already married and pregnant with her second child. Together, they try to understand their fate but never succeed. They search for other replayers, but find only one: an insane serial killer confined to a mental institution. Their replays become progressively shorter. Trying to find scientists to explain their condition, they reveal themselves to the world media but become prisoners of the CIA, who put their information to terrible uses, so that soon they are in a destabilized world they no longer recognize. "In making themselves known to the world and in dealing with the government in exchange for the paltry information they had received, they had sown the seeds of a vicious whirlwind" (202). Pamela becomes so angry that for years she won't speak to Jeff.

Eventually, time runs out as their replays grow ever briefer. "For all that they'd struggled, all they'd once achieved, the end result was null. . . . They had squandered far too much of the priceless time that had been granted them . . . when they themselves, their love for each other, had been all the answer either of them should have ever needed" (232).

The cycles speed up until they are dying over and over, faster and faster. Finally, it ends and they are thankful to discover miraculously that they are still alive, but now living in the uncharted present, not in the past. "The unfathomable cycle in which he and Pamela had been caught had proved to be a form of confinement, not release" (247).

Like King Midas or Swift's immortal Strulbruggs, Jeff and Pamela have been given a gift that proves to be a curse rather than a blessing. They are isolated and lonely people sharing an unhappy fate, with only each other to confide in. "Even the happiness they had managed to find together had been frustratingly brief . . . transient moments of love and contentment like vanishing specks of foam in a sea of lonely, needless separation" (232). To be forced to return over and over again to the past, to live one's life only to die repeatedly and lose everything, is a trap and a punishment. "Many lives. . . . Many pains," a lover tells Jeff.

The replayers also know too much. As a character says in Ursula K. Le Guin's

The Left Hand of Darkness, "The unknown . . . the unforetold, the unproven, that is what life is based on. Ignorance is the ground of thought."[7] They learn and grow from their experiences, but they are grateful at the end to be freed into the unknown present. One cannot transcend the limitations and inevitable losses of the human condition, suggests *Replay*, and to attempt to do so is self-defeating.

In the last work I will discuss, *Groundhog Day*, reincarnation also proves to be a curse until the hero takes control and uses the replays to change himself for the better. *Groundhog Day* is a moral fable like *A Christmas Carol*, a comedy about a misanthrope who is forced to relive his life until he learns to love humanity. Like the unfortunate tenor, Phil must repeat it again and again until he gets it right. Interestingly, Bill Murray, who plays the unlikable Phil in *Groundhog Day*, played a similar role in a filmed update of Dickens's tale, *Scrooged* (1988).

The protagonist, Phil, is a weatherman at a Pittsburgh TV station who hates his job, hates people, and hates himself. For the fourth consecutive year, he is sent to cover the Groundhog Day celebration in Punxsutawney, Pennsylvania. The little rodent emerges from hiding and, according to legend, if it sees its shadow and retreats, there will be six more weeks of winter. Like the loner Scrooge, who hates Christmas, Phil is supremely bored with the festivities and with the "hicks" of Punxsutawney. He responds to everything with cynicism and sarcasm. The only new element in the day is his new producer, Rita, a cheery optimist and people lover who is the complete opposite of Phil, and he enjoys goading her.

After they tape the ceremony in a public park, they head back to Pittsburgh, only to be forced to return to Punxsutawney by a blizzard whose path weatherman Phil incorrectly predicted.

When he wakes the next morning, it is not February 3, but February 2, Groundhog Day, all over again. Inexplicably, as if by divine punishment, Phil must relive the day, and, he discovers, not once but again and again. He finds himself trapped in a boring small town he hates, forced to replay seemingly infinite variations on Groundhog Day. Phil is linked with the groundhog, who is also named Phil: a loner who lives in a hole, is scared of his own shadow, and retreats for another round of winter.

Phil rapidly grows tired of facing the same boring small talk and the same aggressive insurance salesman, whom he finally slugs. It's *déjà vu* again and again. He tells Rita he is reliving the same day and she sends him to a doctor, who refers him to a psychiatrist who is no help.

He gets drunk. He asks his drinking buddies, Punxsutawney working men, "What if you were stuck in one place and every day was exactly the same and nothing you did mattered?" One says, "That about sums it up for me."

Realizing there are no consequences, he decides to become an outlaw. First he takes a car for a joyride, is chased by the police and arrested. He pigs out at the diner before a disgusted Rita while telling her that "I don't worry about anything anymore. . . . I don't even have to floss." He seduces a pretty but dumb local woman, robs an armored bank truck, and attends a movie dressed as Clint Eastwood in a Sergio Leone western.

All this is too easy. He starts to become interested in Rita and decides to gain her love, a much harder task because she detests him. Day by day he learns all her likes and dislikes, even memorizes French poetry to impress her, until finally he gets her back to his room one night. But Phil ruins a perfect day by forcing the issue, so that Rita believes the whole day has been a setup, which it has.

Phil tries again and again with Rita, but each time he fails and she slaps his face. He grows increasingly depressed and makes a dire weather forecast in his daily Groundhog Day speech for the TV camera: "It's gonna be cold, it's gonna be grey, and it's gonna last the rest of your life." Like Jeff in *Replay*, not even death will free him from the cycles: He attempts various forms of spectacular suicide, but he always returns the next morning.

Finally, he decides to try a new tactic with Rita: honesty. He tells her, "I'm a god. . . . I am an immortal." He wants her to believe him and proves it by introducing her to all the people in the diner and telling intimate details about each one, by predicting what will happen in the next ten seconds, and by telling her everything he knows about her. They spend the day together, waiting to see what happens at the end of the day. Rita grows fond of him. He says, "The worst part is that tomorrow you will have forgotten all about this and treat me like a jerk again."

But she says, "I don't know, Phil. Maybe it's not a curse. Depends on how you look at it."

As she sleeps, he declares his love for her. For the rest of his replays, he tries to become worthy of her by attempting to fulfill her description of her ideal man: "Humble, intelligent, supportive, funny, romantic, and courageous. . . . Kind, sensitive, gentle. He likes animals, children. . . . He plays an instrument. And he loves his mother." Phil uses his days to systematically transform himself into this man: He becomes a philanthropist and repeatedly tries to save an old homeless man from death. He rescues a child who falls from a tree, a man who chokes in a restaurant, and two little old ladies whose car breaks down. He learns to sculpt ice and to play the piano. His speeches at the Groundhog Day celebration become heartfelt and moving.

In the climax, which takes place at a party in the hotel, Phil has become the most popular man in town and has won Rita's love. They spend the night together, and the next day is not February 2 but February 3. The cycle is broken. Outside, the ground is covered with a beautiful blanket of freshly fallen snow from the blizzard. Phil declares to Rita, "It's beautiful! Let's live here."

Like George Bailey in Frank Capra's film *It's a Wonderful Life* (1946), Phil learns to love a small town that once seemed like a trap, to love his fellow man, and to enjoy the small, everyday, repeated pleasures of life.

The protagonists of narratives of time travel as reincarnation are at first unhappy people, unable to enjoy life, to love or to be loved, and so time seems to mock them. What precipitated Peggy Sue's collapse and retreat to the past was a cake with twenty-five candles representing the inexorable passage of the years. In a repeated motif in *Replay*, Jeff over and over faces the "glowing red numerals on the digital clock atop his bookshelf: 1:06 PM, OCT 18 88" (3). This is the last thing he sees as he dies and dies again, the limit point of his life. In a sequence in *Groundhog*, the depressed and angry Phil repeatedly smashes a clock radio as it wakes him at 6 AM, over and over, to the same day. Time, represented by the candles or the clock, becomes the enemy of these heroes. In attempting to escape time by repeating the past, Peggy Sue, Jeff, Pamela, and Phil ironically become hyperconscious of the passage of time, become even more prisoners of the clock. Whether you stare at the clock or smash it, you are equally time-obsessed.

What time-travel narratives of reincarnation such as *Peggy Sue*, *Replay*, and *Groundhog Day* all suggest is nothing more complicated than that what we need is not more life but the ability to enjoy whatever brief life we are granted, to live in the present, to savor the moment, to love life, and to be able to love others. Not repeating the past but seizing the day is their message. In the words of the *Rubaiyat*:

> Come, fill the Cup, and in the fire of Spring
> The Winter Garment of Repentance fling:
> The Bird of Time has but a little way
> To fly—and Lo! the Bird is on the Wing.[8]

Notes

1. Mark Rose, *Alien Encounters: Anatomy of Science Fiction* (Cambridge, MA: Harvard University Press, 1981), 100.

2. Fredric Jameson, "Postmodernism, or the Cultural Logic of Late Capitalism," *New Left Review*, 146 (July/August 1984), 67.

3. Tom Shales, "The Re Decade," *Esquire* (March 1986), 67, 68.

4. Rose, 109.

5. Roger Ebert, *Roger Ebert's Movie Home Companion* (Kansas City: Andrews and McMeel, 1988), 478.

6. Ken Grimwood, *Replay* (New York: Arbor House, 1986), 92. Later page references in the text are to this edition.

7. Ursula K. Le Guin, *The Left Hand of Darkness* (New York: Ace Books, 1969), 72.

8. Omar Khayyam, *The Rubaiyat of Omar Khayyam*, translated by Edward FitzGerald (Garden City, NY: Doubleday, 1952), 44. Translation originally published in 1859.

13

Time Travel at the Crossroads: The Search for New Paradigms in Science and Science Fiction

Bradford Lyau

While time travel stories in science fiction are common, such stories that also qualify as hard science fiction are rare. Since many scientists believe time travel is impossible, stories must stress the plausibility of an untried concept or unexplored theoretical direction to be regarded as rigorously scientific. For that reason such works help readers focus on problems of scientific inquiry and the nature of historical scientific paradigms.

These time travel stories constitute a longstanding, if intermittent, tradition in science fiction. Writers have used time travel to drive their plots, but few discuss in terms of existing scientific theory and methods, sometimes even presenting it in a whimsical manner. Often these stories come from scientifically trained writers infusing their stories with ideas based on recent research to serve as plausible foundations for the possibility of some form of time travel. Three examples are John Taine's *The Time Stream* (1946), with perhaps the earliest mention of Minkowski in American science fiction; Robert A. Heinlein's *Time for the Stars* (1956), a juvenile novel that describes Einstein's Theory of Relativity; and Gregory Benford's *Timescape* (1981), with its detailed use of tachyons and a realistic portrayal of scientists at work.

Another outstanding example is Stephen Baxter's *The Time Ships*.[1] Published on the one-hundredth anniversary of the first appearance of H. G. Wells's paradigmatic *The Time Machine*, it is both a literary tribute to Wells and an up-to-date example of how contemporary science can be used to explain still unproven concepts such as time travel. Further, due to the pervasive importance of the concept of time in science, the novel examines the problem of the limits of knowledge in science.

This last point is important due to the appearance in the 1990s of the controversial best-seller, John Horgan's *The End of Science: Facing the Limits of Knowledge in the Twilight of the Scientific Age*.[2] This work is derived from interviews with the leading thinkers in various scientific fields and reveals their opinions on the future of science. Horgan obtained both affirmative and negative responses as to whether science has finally reached its limits, and therefore its end. Horgan eventually concluded that science ("true, pure, empirical science") has indeed run its course (266). Though Horgan's book may reflect a certain perception of the uncertainty of science, religion, and culture in this "postmodern" era, it does not really deal with the nature of science's historical development nor its method of adapting to challenges.

Horgan is familiar with scientists and their work as a senior writer for *Scientific American*. However, once a college English major, he employs a text of literary criticism, Harold Bloom's *The Anxiety of Influence* (1973), as a framework for his analysis of the perception that scientific progress is ending.[3]

According to Bloom, Shakespeare and writers of the English Renaissance represent the peak of English literature and they "are not matched by their Enlightened descendants, and the whole tradition of the post-Enlightenment, which is Romanticism, shows a further decline in its Modernist and post-Modernist heirs" (10). Writers following this literary high point experience what Bloom terms "an anxiety of influence," and this anxiety

comes out of a complex act of strong misreading, a creative interpretation that I call "poetic misprision." What writers may experience as anxiety . . . are the *consequences* of poetic misprision, rather than the *cause* of it. . . . Without Keats' misreading of Shakespeare, Milton, and Wordsworth, we could not have Keats' odes and sonnets and his two *Hyperions*. (xxiii, author's italics)

Today's writers are invariably consumed by the past, whether they realize it or not. As Bloom observes, "The dead may or may not ever return, but their voice comes alive" (xxiv).

Horgan applies this method of analysis to the ideas of some modern scientists. Building upon Bloom's description of "strong poets" who admit to the perfection of their predecessors and strive to transcend them by "various subterfuges, including a subtle misreading of their predecessors' works," he transfers this mode of analysis to what he terms "strong scientists:" those who "are seeking to misread the great modern paradigms of science" (7).

This he considers the only option for those scientists, for he concludes—after interviewing leading scientific figures—that science has reached the limit of its capabilities to further understand the true nature of reality. All that remains is "to pursue science in a speculative, post-empirical mode,"which Horgan labels "ironic science." Also influenced by Northrop Frye's *Anatomy of Criticism*, Horgan uses this term to reveal today's theories as having multiple meanings, none of them definitive (7). Horgan does not refer to all scientists, just those who attempt to transcend the ideas of the giants whose paradigms remain the basis for today's science, like Einstein and the founders of quantum mechanics. For Horgan, the most common approach of this group consists of revealing the shortcomings of present-day scientific knowledge as well as all remaining unanswered questions (3).

If studying the philosophical problems of the limits of knowledge in science were identical to analyzing the problems facing literary critics as seen by Bloom, then Horgan has produced a definitive text for popular consumption that will become a standard starting point for those interested in understanding how science is working today. But he has not. A historical study of both the changing philosophical bases of science and the process of these changes must be taken into account.

The epistemological problems Horgan deals with have existed (at least in what is recognized as the "Western Tradition") since the days of Plato and Aristotle. Charles Coulston Gillispie provides a rigorous historical analysis of this in *The Edge of Objectivity: An Essay in the History of Scientific Ideas*. He details the ongoing tension between the Platonic and Aristotelian modes of knowledge and how these two systems of epistemology (Platonic mathematics and Aristotelian physics) were combined in the work of Galileo, thus launching the era of classical physics. It is with Newton that the two traditions reach their full synthesis by making his natural philosophy a general approach to the new science. One of Newton's major achievements is his axioms of absolute space and absolute time.[4]

Einstein's theories of relativity made the Platonic tradition ascendant all over again. Space and time are no longer absolute, now being dependent on the observing researcher. More than the relativity of space, it was the relativity of time that shocked the scientific establishment. As Gillispie relates,

And thus classical physics ended as it begun in Galileo's law of falling bodies—with a redefinition of the physical property of time. Time seems the intimate aspect of the continuum, and the consequence was to move science one step further into the impersonal generality of things. There is no privilege left in quality in Galileo's physics . . . and now no privileged frame of reference or geometry left by Einstein.[5]

The resulting era of quantum mechanics served to further push people not only from absoluteness to relativity, from certainty to uncertainty, from exactness to probability, but also from realism to idealism. As Nick Herbert puts it in *Quantum Reality: Beyond the New Physics*,

Most physicists use quantum theory as a mere recipe for calculating results and don't trouble themselves about "reality."

However, it is hard to believe that this theory could be so successful without corresponding in some way to the way things really are.[6]

This leads to many interpretations, some quite provocative, regarding what the world is really like. Herbert identifies no less than eight major schools in quantum mechanics to which scientists subscribe to explain what goes on behind the mathematical equations. Still, no matter which interpretation scientists select, they will agree with all others on the measured results that quantum mechanics has successfully predicted for decades.

As noted, the historical process of these series of changes must also be taken into account, especially in response to Horgan's application of Bloom's method of literary criticism to contemporary science. His usage is incorrect if a person wishes to truly understand the way in which science adjusts from one philosophical paradigm or worldview to another when the results of observation either conflict with the present way of looking at things or present a seemingly impenetrable obstacle to understanding.

This issue of how scientists relate to the accomplishments of the past is dealt with more properly by historians of science such as Herbert Butterfield, Thomas Kuhn, and I. Bernard Cohen. In philosophical as well as historical terms, they discuss how science has traversed a sometimes tumultuous path in trying to attain a more accurate description of, and hopefully an understanding of, how the universe works. Studying the succession of paradigm shifts reveals not an anxiety of equaling or transcending the masters through post-empirical speculations, but rather a succession of challenges to certain or all (if the experiment is ambitious and comprehensive enough) aspects of a prevailing method of describing the world based on new empirical findings. No matter how wild and diversified the speculations may be, they all derive from the quantitative, corroborative results of a community of researchers.

Horgan is correct that today's sciences face many daunting challenges and that some speculations seem more like pure fantasy than scientific probabilities. However, he is incorrect when discussing the history of scientific research. Though accurately noting how differing speculations and interpretations have divided the scientific community, he fails to emphasize that first, it has always been that way (after all, Leibniz argued with Newton, Einstein with Bohr), and second, there is little, if any, disagreement on the actual results of the experiments themselves. The interpretations are just ways of trying to find the proper explanation of what a scientist's findings mean. They present possible new avenues of testing, not indications of final limits.[7]

The Time Ships is a most relevant book to the topic of limits of knowledge in scientific endeavors, providing an interesting counterpoint to Horgan's view of science; for throughout the novel the theme of scientific knowledge, its advancements, and its open-endedness pervades. As protagonists go on a wondrous journey of exploration, the novel introduces scientific theories that further explain the universe while also expanding the scope—and knowledge—of human endeavor.

The novel follows the further adventures of the Time Traveller as he moves backward and forward in time, explores alternate histories of Earth, and discovers new ideas of science that developed after his era of the 1890s. He first stops in the year 657,208, where he encounters a world of Morlocks who are a peaceful race in this version of the future. He befriends a Morlock, Nebogipfel, who will be his companion for the rest of the novel. They briefly return to the 1890s, meeting the Time Traveller before the time machine is built, then travel to the 1930s to find England and Germany involved in a decades-long war, with both sides employing time travel as a result of the Time Traveller's experiments.

Next, 50 million years in the past, they encounter an English colony established as a prehistoric base to guard against the Germans, but the Germans destroy most of the camp with an atomic bomb. The English who survive start to rebuild with the aid of the scientific and technical knowledge that Nebogipfel imparts. After witnessing the incredible progress made by their colonists' descendants, they again return to the 1890s to discover this time that humanity has departed the Earth, leaving humanity's machines—which continued developing on their own—in control.

These immortal machines, devoted to the pursuit of ultimate truth, travel back to the beginning of time with the two time travelers accompanying them to achieve their goal. They witness the beginning of the universe, tour a newly constructed universe, and finally grasp the ultimate purpose of the universe. Having accomplished this, the Time Traveller returns to his original 1890s, discovering that the universe exists on even a larger scale than previously imagined. Finally, the Time Traveller arrives back at the year 802,701 of Wells's novel, finds his lost love Weena, and looks forward to a happy life by her side.

In this novel the Time Traveller's machine is powered by a metal called Plattnerite. Those familiar with Wells's stories will recognize the reference to "The Plattner Story," wherein a teacher is thrown into the fourth dimension by an explosion caused by a chemistry experiment. He emerges in a strange, decaying world dominated by a pale green sun. While exploring this world, he is accompanied by eerie floating heads that he soon refers to as the Watchers. By mere chance he duplicates his accident and is propelled back to his own world, finding on his return that the sides of his body have been reversed.[8] Obviously this story can be viewed as a brief reprise of *The Time Machine.* For Baxter, however, it provides another source of literary inspiration, as he incorporates into his novel both the greenish color of the sun, to describe the Plattnerite that powers his time machine, and the Watchers, who accompany the Time Traveller and Nebogipfel through their temporal journeys.

From the beginning of the novel the theme of understanding the nature of the universe through the analysis and expansion of scientific knowledge is apparent. On the first page of the "Prologue" the Time Traveller reports that he is waiting for a journal with an article on Michelson and Morley's experiments on light. As this study would become important for Einstein and the resulting scientific revolution of the early twentieth century, the novel's reference might warn readers that the Time Traveller will soon encounter some revolutions of his own. This is also the first mention of an actual scientific theory. As the novel progresses, Baxter introduces other theories from physics and cosmology as possible guides in better understanding the universe.

Also at the novel's beginning the Time Traveller associates the constant speed of light described by Michelson and Morley with the constant behavior of the Plattnerite that he developed to power his time machine (50–51). Thus Baxter updates the time machine's abilities by combining Wells's explanation with the results of actual research completed during the latter's era. This sets the stage for Baxter's subsequent use of theoretical speculations as vehicles through which the Time Traveller expands his awareness of scientific knowledge and how it affects the universe.

When the Time Traveller reaches the world of 657,208 and meets Nebogipfel for the first time, he also gets his first exposure to future scientific theory. Here the Morlocks have constructed a Dyson sphere around the sun in which to live and have basically abandoned the Earth. The Morlocks are dedicated to the acquisition of knowledge by means of scientific inquiry. This comprises the first actual statement of this goal, serving as a crucial moment in the story as this goal becomes the novel's central theme.

When the Time Traveller asks what would happen if the Morlocks succeeded in understanding all that there is to know about the universe, Nebogipfel replies that it would be impossible, bringing up the work of mathematician Kurt Goedel. Citing his Incompleteness Theorem (that any complex mathematical axiom must bring up questions that the axiom cannot answer), Nebogipfel explains,

"Godel showed that our quest, to acquire knowledge and understanding, *can never be completed.*"
I understood. "He has given you an infinite purpose. The Morlocks were like a world of patient Monks . . . working tirelessly to comprehend the workings of our great universe." (95, author's italics)

This introduction of Goedel's ideas comprises the novel's first step in defining scientific knowledge as open-ended and not confined by any inherent limits. Coupling the Incompleteness Theorem with the goal of pursuing knowledge will be the thematic backdrop for the remainder of the novel.

This becomes clear when the two travel back to meet the Time Traveller before his time machine is built. This episode, along with the new future of the Morlocks, makes the Time Traveller think about the possible existence of a multiplicity of histories. When he asks Nebogipfel about the existence of these alternate histories when they encounter the English-German war, the latter introduces the concept of quantum mechanics. The use of probability as a central notion and Heisenberg's Uncertainty Principle is explained. When the Time Traveller asks how this is relevant to the multiple histories he is experiencing, Nebogipfel brings up an alternative explanation of quantum mechanics developed by Hugh Everett while still a graduate student in physics at Princeton in 1957, the Many Worlds Interpretation of quantum mechanics (198–201).

Because of the probability factor in observing the atomic world, multiple possibilities always emerge with each action or experiment. This particular interpretation claims that, if several alternatives are possible from a single action, then *all* of them will occur. New universes will be created every time, all identical except for the consequences of that single action. So when the Time Traveller started journeying through time, new universes emerged from each action, and this will continue as long as he travels.

To reinforce the basic theme introduced earlier, Baxter arranges for the two of them to meet the Kurt Goedel of this history, who fled Germany to work for the English time travel project inspired by the Time Traveller's efforts. For Goedel, the purpose of time travel is to search for the truth, not for political or military advantage. Like the real Goedel, this fictional Goedel is a mathematician, but he ironically dreams of discovering an ideal "World where all Meaning is resolved" (230) even though his real-world counterpart has demonstrated the ultimate futility of this goal.

It is out of this ingenious contrast between the Goedel of our history and the Goedel constructed by the Time Traveller's journeys that Baxter presciently constructs a rebuttal to Horgan a year before the latter's book was published. On one hand, the Incompleteness Theorem demonstrates that comprehensive, definitive knowledge is impossible, which might appear to sanction Horgan's vision of future scientists endlessly engaged in fruitless and inconclusive "ironic science." Yet the Incompleteness Theorem still allows for *ever-continuing improvements* in the state of human knowledge, so that science can continue to progress by eliminating flawed theories and making new discoveries, even if a "World where all Meaning is resolved" remains impossible. By presenting time travel as a means of generating new universes—guaranteeing the inexhaustibility of knowledge—and by imaginatively envisioning a multiplicity of future worlds where humans and machines perpetually strive to gain more and more knowledge, Baxter puts colorful and persuasive flesh on an otherwise skeletal argument against the postmodern skepticism of Horgan.

The Time Ships thus stands as a testament to scientific optimism and the endless pursuit of knowledge, refuting any notion of limits to scientific endeavor. Every time Baxter applies a twentieth-century theory to the novel, he demonstrates that the theory serves as not only an explanation of what has been observed, but also a starting point for further exploration. The theories of relativity and quantum mechanics may have presented a severe challenge to humanity's attempt to understand nature, and the epistemological limits imposed by modern science may have forced scientists to philosophize and speculate more daringly on what the hard data of their experiments really mean. Still, the hard data they continue to compile make these speculations the starting points for further study, not limits to human knowledge. Baxter's novel, like other science fiction novels, ultimately endorses both rigorous fact-finding and creative speculation as necessary means for people to make breakthroughs in understanding the world around them, and the history of science also shows this to be true. Despite Horgan's claims, then, the future of science remains an open book.

Notes

1. Stephen Baxter, *The Time Ships* (New York: Harper, 1995). Later page references in the text are to this edition.

2. John Horgan, *The End of Science: Facing the Limits of Knowledge in the Twilight of the Scientific Age* (Reading, MA: Helix Books, 1996). Later page references in the text are to this edition.

3. Harold Bloom, *The Anxiety of Influence*, Second Edition (New York: Oxford

University Press, 1997); first edition published in 1973. Later page references in the text are to this edition.

4. Charles Coulston Gillispie, *The Edge of Objectivity: An Essay in the History of Scientific Ideas* (1960; Princeton: Princeton University Press, 1973), especially 16–19 and 141–50.

5. Gillispie, 158–159.

6. Nick Herbert, *Quantum Reality: Beyond the New Physics* (New York: Anchor Books, 1985), 196. See also 15–29.

7. See Herbert Butterfield, *The Origins of Modern Science, 1300–1800* (London: G. Bell and Sons, 1949); I. Bernard Cohen, *Revolution in Science* (Cambridge, MA: Belknap Press, 1985); Thomas S. Kuhn, *The Structure of Scientific Revolutions* (Chicago: University of Chicago Press, 1962); Gillispie; and Herbert.

8. H. G. Wells, "The Plattner Story," in Wells, *The Complete Short Stories of H. G. Wells* (London: Ernest Benn, 1927), 325–345.

14

Tall, Dark, and a Long Time Dead: Epistemology, Time Travel, and the Bodice-Ripper

Erica Obey

"A text cannot belong to no genre," Jacques Derrida claims: "there is no genreless text; there is always a genre and genres, yet such participation never amounts to belonging."[1] Paradoxically, if there is one sort of literature to which this claim would not seem to apply, it would be the work that is conventionally termed "genre fiction." Indeed, genre fiction is, in its way, *plus royaliste que le roi*, or, at least, more canonical than the canon, adhering to a set of rules and prescriptions more precise than those of Boileau. It is a paradox that gives new meaning to the tautology (or is it an oxymoron?) inherent in the category of "popular culture."

Yet, genre fiction does change. One such obvious change, as of late, is the combination of science fiction and romance writing, two genres whose traditionally antithetical nature can be best seen in their gender associations. Romance writing always has been, and still is, a genre written by women, for women.[2] Twenty-five years ago, a similar claim might have been advanced for men and science fiction, despite the fact that the most obvious precursor of science fiction, *Frankenstein*, was not only written by a woman, but is concerned primarily with a search for a mate. This clear-cut split in the demographics of science fiction began to change in the 1970s, with the upsurge in popularity of fantasy, which was lumped together with science fiction under the new rubric of "speculative fiction." Still, most would be hesitant to identify as science fiction such passages as "I will find you . . . I promise. If I must endure two hundred years of purgatory, two hundred years without you—then that is my punishment, which I have earned for my crimes. . . . [But] when I shall stand before God, I shall have one thing to say, to weigh against the rest . . . Lord, ye gave me a rare woman and God! I loved her well,"[3] before the heroine leaps into the cleft rock in the druid circle to escape the approaching English soldiers and bear the hero's baby in the twentieth century.

The passage in question comes from Diana Gabaldon's *Dragonfly in Amber*, the second in what is perhaps the most successful of an odd hybrid in romance publishing: the time travel romance. The time travel romance is actually one of a series of genres that make up a subgenre of romance writing commonly termed "Alternative Reality" romance. According to Kristin Ramsdell in *Romance Fiction: A Guide to the Genre*: "One of the newest—or at least most recently recognized—of the romance subgenres, Alternative Reality, is . . . actually . . . not a true subgenre at all, but, rather a collection of separate mini-subgenres linked by the common thread of fantasy or 'unreality.' "[4] The subgenre of alternative reality is subdivided, at least according to Ramsdell, into fantasy, futuristic, paranormal, and time travel romance.

Ramsdell sees the immediate precursors of the subgenre as rising from the more "female" science fiction and fantasy that began to emerge between 1968 and 1978, in particular the work of Anne MacCaffrey. Perhaps the earliest true alternative reality romance was June Lund Shiplett's *Journey to Yesterday* (1979). The genre continued to grow as such prominent romance writers as Jayne Ann Krentz (*Sweet Starfire*, 1986, and *Crystal Flame*, 1986), Jude Devereaux (*A Knight in Shining Armor*, 1989), and Johanna Lindsey (*Warrior's Woman*, 1984) experimented with the genre. In 1991, Gabaldon's series began with *Outlander*, anticipating the subgenre's official recognition in 1992, when the Romance Writers of America added a Futuristic/Fantasy/Paranormal category to its annual Rita and Golden Hearts awards.[5]

Gabaldon's work, the flagship of the genre, is a seemingly interminable saga in which—over the course of some 4,500 pages, the majority of them involving lusty sexual encounters—Claire Randall, a nurse from 1941 who matures to a doctor in 1968 by the second book, is mysteriously transported back in time to Jacobean Scotland, where she falls in love with Jamie Fraser, a Scots loyalists, and ineffectually attempts to prevent Bonnie Prince Charlie from launching the rebellion that will result in the bloody massacre of Culloden. It takes her 1,800 pages to fail in that task, but Jamie also fails in his intention to die at Culloden, opening up a whole new set of adventures on the American frontier.

Perhaps an immediate reaction is to claim that these novels are not science fiction, even though Gabaldon is herself a trained scientist, with a master's degree in marine biology and a Ph.D. in ecology. She is also a self-professed science fiction fan, though it may be indicative of her peculiarly genre-bridging perspective that she claims to have watched *Doctor Who* primarily because it gave her "just enough time to do her nails."[6] Her lack of interest in scientific specifics is far from atypical of the genre. One tip sheet I examined, for example, specified that "The methods of time travel are unimportant and should not be emphasized." Yet, couched however it might be in thoroughly awful prose, Gabaldon's work, and the entire subgenre of alternative reality romance, does pursue, consciously or unconsciously, the project described by Derrida—a project not dissimilar to the avowedly literary intentions of the precursor of both science fiction and romance writing, the Gothic novel. As Horace Walpole explains in the preface to the second edition of *The Castle of Otranto*, his project was "to blend the two kinds of romance, the ancient and the modern. In the former all was imagination and improbability: in the latter, nature is always intended to be . . . copied with success."[7] Even as it invents itself as a genre, thus, the Gothic follows Derrida's formulation by showing itself resistant to generic classification. However, Michael Gamer has shown that, no matter what the Gothic novel's intentions or formal proclivities for the "laws" of genre, Gothic writers "were forced to realize the innate differences between legal category and literary genre and to see that the power of the former could displace the play of the latter." Following the lead of Frederic Jameson, Gamer argues that literary genre is primarily an act of social participation, "where various parties combine to determine textual meaning and where all must agree on the nature of a text's participation before any act of belonging, however temporary, can occur."[8] For feminist critics, however, the Gothic novel represents a much more important act of participation, that of earning one's own living by the pen, a practicality that is echoed by Gabaldon in her discussion of her own work:

> I had come to the conclusion—based on experience—that the only real way of learning to write a novel was probably to write a novel. . . . So . . . what kind of novel should this be? Well, I read everything, and lots of it, but perhaps more mysteries than anything else. Fine, I thought, I'd write a mystery. But then I began to think. Mysteries have plots. I wasn't sure I knew how to do plots. Perhaps I should try something easier for my practice book, then write a mystery when I felt ready for a real book. (*Companion* xx)

While a great deal of this disclaimer speaks of a savvy, self-conscious authorial modesty, the association of the female writer with cheerful, bourgeois economic practicality has long been recognized. Indeed, economics and its twin brother, politics, have long been used to distinguish between the "male" and "female" Gothic novels. Maggie Kilgour's summary of the difference between the two is succinct and representative. The male Gothic, as represented customarily by the work of Matthew Lewis or Walpole, traces a teleological development to detachment, centering a conflict with precursors. Since this moving toward individuality makes society impossible, the "male" Gothic is "revolutionary" in intent and meaning. In contrast, the "female" Gothic is circular in structure, depending on repetition, continuity, and identification with precursors, making its political stance essentially bourgeois. As Kilgour neatly sums up *The Mysteries of Udolpho*, "After 700 pages of suspicion and suspense, Emily turns out to be exactly who she thought she was at the beginning."[9]

It is perhaps a further truism, perpetrated by every male waiting in a movie line, that women's stories are more concerned about "relationships" and "feelings," while men's are more concerned about "action" and "plot." It would be difficult, especially with Gabaldon's own 1,000 pages of authorial self-justification mostly revolving around the coy claim, "I am a storyteller," to argue for a serious postmodern intent to challenge genre, beneath 4,500 pages of sex in the haylofts of the Scottish highlands. However, Gabaldon does manage to out-Walpole Walpole in her *oeuvre*, creating a fiction that blends two genres; and, in doing so, does manage to call into the question some of the commonly assumed boundaries between "women's fiction" and "men's fiction." In particular, her works plays out an interesting tension between "personal," "psychological," or "interior" writing, and "social," "historical," or "exterior" writing.

The tension of the "female" Gothic novel, as critics from Claire Kahane to Ellen Moers have pointed out, depends on primal women's fears, usually those of sex, motherhood, and birth.[10] Gabaldon's work, too, revolves around issues of motherhood, birth, and sex. However, although the broad conventions of the story do focus on "conventional, conservative" valuations of true love, heterosexual sex, and parent-child loyalty, there is a sadistic subtext to Gabaldon's treatment of these issues that is radical to the point of abusiveness.

Perhaps the most disturbing gesture in Gabaldon's work is the replacement of the time-traveling heroine's husband, Frank, with his eighteenth-century *döppelganger*, Captain Randall, the villain of the piece, who is, not incidentally, associated with repression, in terms of both male control of property and English control of Scotland. Presumably this transformation of an innocuous history professor—who, offstage between *Outlander* and *Dragonfly in Amber*, foots the bill for Claire to go medical school, raises Jamie's daughter as his own, and then obligingly dies—into a bisexual sadist is designed to obviate any guilt Claire (and the reader) might feel about abandoning her husband for the lusty Scotsman, Jamie. However, the fact that Jamie allows himself to be raped by Captain Randall in order to save Claire, at the point that can perhaps too aptly be described as the climax of *Outlander*, seems to raise to an abusive level Gabaldon's determination that her heroine never be a victim. (Claire is never raped during the course of the entire narrative.) Further, *Outlander* ends with a bizarre and distasteful ritual, in which Claire reenacts the rape scene with Jamie, taking the role of the rapist, in order to allow him to, as it were, "work through the memories." While the feminist can applaud Gabaldon's desire not to present her heroine as victimized, such posturings seem like nothing but gratuitous exhibitionism or repressed rage.

The novel presents a similar anxiety about parenting and precursors. While the conventional time travel romance, in Gabaldon's own discussion, is concerned primarily with the intellectual paradoxes of time travel,[11] Gabaldon's theory of time travel is highly personal. According to her theory, which is accompanied by what can only be hoped to be tongue-in-cheek Mendelian diagrams, the ability to time travel is an inherited genetic characteristic, not requiring any arcana such as blood sacrifice.[12] As a result, the characters' main concern about the consequences of time travel (when they exhibit any concern at all) is to keep their descendants alive in the future. (Claire's one consistent gesture of loyalty to her husband is keeping alive his evil, bisexual predecessor, at least long enough to father a son, so his line will continue.)

Indeed, Gabaldon's original title for her novel had been *Cross Stitch* (the title the novel is sold under in England), a title that reinforces the cozy nature of Gabaldon's two rules of time travel:

1. A time-traveler has free choice and individual power of action; however, he or she has *no more* power of action than is allowed by the traveler's personal circumstances.
2. Most notable historical events (those affecting large numbers of people and thus likely to be recorded) are the result of the *collective* actions of many people. (*Companion* 335)

The net result of these rules is that, even when Claire is attempting to prevent the disastrous battle at Culloden, it is not out of any sense of historical tragedy, but instead out of a desire to save the man she loves. In this aspect, Gabaldon's fiction falls squarely in the domain of romance writing, particularly of the historical "bodice-ripping" ilk, which has long been accused of setting aside conventional historical practice in favor of unabashedly personal narrative, usually with historical characters such as Napoleon making cameo appearances to adjust the heroine's dress. The subjective nature of this vision is highlighted, excruciatingly, in Gabaldon's work, with a shift from third person narration in the present to first person narration in the past. However, it is impossible to categorize Claire's experiences as purely subjective, because the very fact of time travel endows her with "objectivity," not only by making her a representative of twentieth-century "enlightenment," but also by providing her with the knowledge of how the other characters' stories will end. Such a belief in objectivity about history, however, is also called into question, for Claire's much abused husband is, in fact, a professor of history. Indeed, perhaps the only way to explain, if not justify or understand, the unfair venom the author seems to feel for him is as a displacement of her rage against "objective," male history.

Interestingly, though, such a concern with attacking objectivity and empiricism is conventionally seen as more closely related to the "revolutionary," male Gothic novel, which, in Ian Watt's view, "was a rebellion against a mechanistic or atomistic past—a desire to regain an organic medieval model in which individuals were bound by a symbolic system of analogies and correspondences to their families, societies, and the world around them" (Kilgour 11). One does not have to go as far as modern thinkers such as Kristeva and Cixous to see the time travel romance, despite its iron thews and lockjawed dialogue, as taking up this same epistemological project, in which empiricism is replaced with an epistemology based on analogy, in this case between contemporary humans and their historical counterparts.

Further, the revolutionary nature of this epistemology is reinforced by the stories' being set during the Scottish nationalist uprisings and the American revolution.[13] It may come as no surprise that Gabaldon denies any conscious project in her choice of eighteenth-century Scotland as setting, claiming nothing more than Doctor Who's young Scots companion, Jamie MacCrimmon, as her inspiration. However, she does offer a sort of *summa* of her theory of history at the end of *Dragonfly in Amber*—perhaps the only real evidence that there is in fact a clear epistemological project underlying her work. In this scene, Claire, returned to 1968, delivers the not terribly earth-shattering revelation that Bonnie Prince Charlie was a "fool and a drunkard and a weak, silly man" to a Jacobean scholar. Unlike the other 4,500 pages of her prose, the passage bears extensive citation:

"I suppose you must feel some bitterness against the historians," Roger ventured. "All the writers who got it wrong—made him out to be a hero. . . ."

"Not the historians. No, not them. Their greatest crime is that they presume to know what happened, how things come about, when they have only what the past chose to leave behind. . . . No, the fault lies with the artists. . . . The writers, the singers, the tellers of tales. It's them [sic] that take the past and re-create it to their liking. Them that could take a fool and give you back a hero, take a sot and make him a king."

"Are they all liars, then?" Roger asked. Claire shrugged. . . .

"Liars?" she asked, "or sorcerers?"

"And are they wrong to do it, then?" Roger asked. . . .

"You still don't understand, do you? . . . You don't *know* why. . . . You don't know, and I don't know, and we never *will* know. Can't you see? You don't know, because you can't say what the end is—there isn't any end. You can't say, 'This particular event' was 'destined' to happen, and therefore all these other things happened. What Charles did to the people of Scotland—was that the 'thing' that had to happen? Or was it 'meant' to happen as it did, and Charles's real purpose was to be what he is now—a figurehead, an icon?" (*Amber* 907–908)

According to this passage, history acquires its significance when it is transmuted to representation, rather than representation being used to understand the "reality" of history, as in "objective" historical practice. This understanding renders unimportant the most common criticism of women's writing: that the "female" Gothic minimizes the "external" historical, philosophical, or occult concerns of the "male" Gothic, by moving them to the arena of the psychological—or, more broadly speaking, that the female novel recasts quest romance in essentially domestic terms. It is this aspect of the female Gothic novel that has become the most identifiable aspect of the contemporary romance novel, from *Jane Eyre* and *Rebecca* to the trappings of Victoria Holt, and it is the romance novel's transference of male quest romance to a domestic situation, placing the woman's desire and resourcefulness completely in the service of not a Grail, or even the saving of a homeland, but love and marriage with the hero, that has opened the romance novel to its current vilification, particularly among feminist critics.

It is also this view that is most easily subverted by the trappings of time travel. It is, after all, Claire Randall, the time traveler, who is possessed of the outcome of the quest. In fact, because they are historically fixed, she knows the outcome of each character's own quest, the time and nature of their death. Indeed, it is with this foreknowledge that Claire curses the villain of the piece. Finally, in what is perhaps the *piece de resistance* of time travel problematization, Claire Randall is a married woman, sexually experienced, while, on their wedding night, the sword-wielding Jamie Fraser blushingly confesses himself to be a virgin.

Jamie, of course, follows his instinct as a farmer, and is soon up to speed, yielding what is perhaps the commonest attribute of the bodice-ripper: robust, rampant, continual sex—in the hayloft, the marital bed, or the Scottish glens near Inverness. Yet although at least 30 percent of its pages are devoted to escapades whose only variety seems to be in the positioning, or perhaps because of that very fact, there is a distinct lack of sexual tension in the saga. Gabaldon herself remarks on this peculiar lack on energy, claiming:

romance novels are courtship stories. They deal with the forming of a bond between a couple, and once that bond is formed, by marriage and sexual congress (in that order, we hope)—well, the story's over. That was never what I had in mind.

I didn't want to tell the story of what makes two people come together, although that's a theme of great power and universality. I wanted to find out what it takes for two people to *stay* together for fifty years— or more. I wanted to tell not the story of a courtship, but the story of a marriage. (*Companion* xxxviii)

Sadly, however well-meant her intentions, the book itself sounds very much like a mother spending 4,500 pages in order to describe to her daughter what sex was like with her dad.

The issue has been discussed more formally in the Freudian tradition, which claims that signification derives its energy from lack, whether that lack is the mother's love, as Freud asserts while introducing the Oedipus complex in *The Interpretation of Dreams*, or the lack of a phallus in Lacan's and Kristeva's formulations. What is consistent in these interpretations is both the sexual, and largely female, nature of what is missing, as well as the fact it is missing. In quest romance, in particular, attainability not only destroys the lady's ability to motivate action, but also destroys her signifying function. Without the lady as a signifier, quest romance would degenerate into the realist novel—precisely the sort of literature Walpole is attempting to graft back onto the "ancient" form of romance.

Yet attainability is the solution that not only Gabaldon but the romance genre in general has turned to, and in turning to, has destabilized the entire symbolic underpinnings of the genre. Only in Christian romances, and the most conservative lines of category romances, which routinely and awfully describe themselves as "sweet," do the authors, in the memorable words of Violet Winspear, "prefer to draw a veil over the lovemaking."[14] Endlessly, repetitively, from Judith Krantz to Catherine Coulter, thews throb and manhoods stiffen, seemingly oblivious to the fact that their very existence has dealt a fatal blow to the genre that has created them. Sexually unattainable, the hero of a romance is endowed with vast significative energy—regardless of our feelings about *what* and *how* he signifies. Made attainable by the twin pressures of feminism and charting the sexual realities of the 1990s, the hero of a romance novel loses his status as Other, and with it, his symbolic function in the text.

Time travel romance, thus, seems to be one of many attempts, ranging from improbable obstacles to crime and intrigue to loss of memory, to restore the hero of a romance novel to the status of Other and, in doing so, to restore his symbolic energy. The anxiety underlying these attempts is evident from a quick scan of publisher's guidelines: Dorchester Books invites not only time travel romance, but also paranormal romance and angel romance; Avon Books, as well as the redoubtable Harlequin has purchased a murder mystery house. It is too early to determine whether these attempts will succeed, but Kilgour's claim about the Gothic novel would appear to offer a poor prognosis: "The Gothic thus originates in a sense of historical difference and the desire to transcend it, which lays in recovering a lost past. What it increasingly demonstrates is the disappearance of historical difference. . . . The potential solution reproduces the problem" (30).

Of course it would be easy to claim that romance always has had a dearth of significance and that what appears to be the death of romance writing may in fact be euthanasia. However, although the genre may die, or, as is more likely, reinvent itself, what is perhaps most interesting about the current situation is the opportunity it offers to consider its implications for postmodernist thinking. The separation of signification from any fixed truth value is a *sine qua non* of postmodernist thinking. Time travel romances such as Gabaldon's, inadvertently or not, go a step further, offering a conscious interpretive project within a sharply destabilized symbolic structure. If the postmodernist novel sees a series of signifiers endlessly playing each other out into the *mise en abime*, Gabaldon's novel seems to create an interesting variation in which a signifier has no real meaning, except to generate an endless series of interpretations, each of which creates a new reality as a signification is inferred.

Indeed, there was a certain postmodern simplicity to the original Harlequin Romance plot (girl meets older, mysterious man; complications ensure; older man confesses love; girl weds man) that reminds one of nothing so much as Paul Auster's mysteries featuring characters named simply Blue, White, and Black. The contexts of Harlequin Romances may shift, but the signifiers always play out the logic of the romance. Moreover, the very interchangeability of these signifiers, their lack of psychological individuation, closely relates them to Peter Brooks's melodramatic signifiers.[15] Indeed, the very prolixity of Gabaldon's narrative seems to hint at a desperate attempt to make use of Brooks's notion that narrative is itself a form of signification. Her modest claim that she knows nothing about plot is well borne out by her work. For, despite the endless succession of episodes, her narrative remains oddly static: a sword fight; a robbery; meeting Prince Charlie; sex; more swordfights, more robberies, a misstep with a wine importer; Jamie's capture by the English; more sex; and then more sex. Moreover, the plot simply sprawls from book to book, the ending of each volume seemingly determined by page count, rather than by any organic coherence.

Such a looseness of structure—going far beyond the nineteenth century "loose, baggy monsters" or even the ongoing narratives of Arthurian romance, where variety is ensured since the characters change—is reflected also in another oddity of recent publishing, the serial novels, such as Stephen King's *The Green Mile* series. It is a phenomenon that started in the science fiction/fantasy camp, but has swiftly moved over to the realm of romance with Jackie Collins's *L.A. Connections* series. While I would be the first to reiterate that it is dangerous to discuss epistemological projects in conjunction with the publishing industry, it is at least instructive to remember Todorov's claim that modern psychology makes unnecessary the fantastic story, which shares the Gothic and Gabaldonian epistemological project of subverting Enlightenment thinking by introducing hesitation in its reader, since it is no longer necessary to displace difficult issues to an irreal, or purely symbolic plane. Might not our current concern with open-ended plotting reflect an attempt to recapture such interpretive hesitation in a genre whose purpose is to conceal nothing, but instead, presents its heroes, as being "raked from nape to buttocks, [spurred] to rear and scream in his turn" (*Amber* 437)?

Notes

1. Jacques Derrida, "The Law of Genre," *Glyph*, 7 (1980), 212.

2. So much so, that, in a weird reversal of Marian Evans recreating herself as George Eliot, male authors are forced to hide behind female pseudonyms, most famously that of Beatrice Small.

3. Diana Gabaldon, *Dragonfly in Amber* (New York: Delacorte, 1992), 888. Later page references in the text are to this edition.

4. Kristin Ramsdell, *Romance Fiction: A Guide to the Genre* (Englewood, CO: Libraries Unlimited, Inc., 1999), 211.

5. Ramsdell, 215.

6. Diana Gabaldon, *The Outlandish Companion* (New York: Delacorte, 1999), xx. Later page references in the text are to this edition.

7. Horace Walpole, *The Castle of Otranto* (1761; New York: Oxford University Press, 1985), 7. The methodology that he outlines for combining the two is to "allow the possibility of the facts, and all the actors comport themselves as persons would do in their situation," which, although it refers to outsized helmets crushing heirs and ghosts instead of fourth dimension travel, is perhaps the most succinct summary of speculative fiction technique on record.

8. Michael Gamer, "Genres for the Prosecution: Pornography and the Gothic," *PMLA*, 114, No. 5 (October, 1999), 1052, 1043.

9. Maggie Kilgour, *The Rise of the Gothic* (New York: Routledge, 1995), 128. Later page references in the text are to this edition.

10. See, for a representative selection, Ellen Moers's *Literary Women*, Claire Kahane's "The Gothic Mirror" in *The (M)other Tongue*, Barbara Johnson's "My Monster/My Self" in *Diacritics* 12:2, and Mary Poovey's "My Hideous Progeny: Mary Shelley and the Feminization of Romanticism" in *PMLA*, 95.

11. Gabaldon refers specifically to Robert Heinlein's "By His Bootstraps" and David Gerrold's *The Man Who Folded Himself* in *Companion*, 335.

12. Such as that, for instance, practiced by Geillis Duncan, a time-traveling witch in Gabaldon's work who, in an unparalleled example of man-hating, lures her husband to a stone circle to murder him in order to facilitate her own time travel.

13. It is also interesting, but beyond the scope of this article, to consider the current relationship between Scottish nationalism and American reactionary politics, especially in the deep South.

14. Violet Winspear, cited in Kathryn Falk, *How to Write a Romance Novel and Get It Published* (New York: Crown Publishers, Inc., 1983), 22.

15. See Peter Brooks, *The Melodramatic Imagination: Balzac, Henry James, Melodrama, and the Mode of Excess* (New Haven: Yale University Press, 1976).

A Bibliography of Works Related to Time and Time Travel

Inasmuch as a comprehensive bibliography of works related to time and time travel would demand years of obsessive research and occupy a volume in itself, our goals in compiling this bibliography were necessarily more modest. In three sections devoted to novels and short stories (along with a few poems and plays), films and television programs, and nonfiction and critical studies, we selectively include works that in our view are most familiar, most representative of larger categories of texts, and most interesting and significant to our contributors. A useful resource for further research is the extensive bibliography in the Second Edition of Paul J. Nahin's *Time Machines: Time Travel in Physics, Metaphysics, and Science Fiction*, cited below.

I. Novels and Short Stories

Abbott, E. A. [as by A Square] *Flatland: A Romance of Many Dimensions*. London: Seeley, 1884.

Aksyonov, Vassily. *The Island of Crimea*. 1981. Translated from the Russian by Michael Henry Hein. London: Abacus, 1986.

Aldiss, Brian W. *An Age*. 1967. London: Sphere, 1969. Published in America as *Cryptozoic*.

———. "Ahead." In Aldiss, *Who Can Replace a Man?* 1965. New York: Signet Books, 1967, 63–75. Story first published as "The Failed Men" in 1957.

———. *Frankenstein Unbound*. London: Cape, 1973.

———. "Man in His Time." 1966. In Aldiss and Harry Harrison, editors, *Nebula Award Stories Number Two*. 1967. New York: Pocket Books, 1968, 203–229.

———. "The Night That All Time Broke Out." In Harlan Ellison, editor, *Dangerous Visions #1*. 1967. New York: Berkley Books, 1968, 207–219.

———. "The Ultimate Millennia: Visiting Amoeba." In Aldiss, *Galaxies Like Grains of Sand*. New York: New American Library, 1960, 116–144.

Amis, Kingsley. *The Alteration*. 1976. London: Penguin, 1988.

Amis, Martin. *Time's Arrow*. London: Penguin, 1992.

Anderson, Poul. *The Corridors of Time*. 1965. New York: Berkley Books, 1978.

———. *The Guardians of Time*. New York: Ballantine Books, 1960.

———. *The Shield of Time*. New York: Tor Books, 1990.

———. *Tau Zero*. Garden City, NY: Doubleday & Co., 1970.

———. *There Will Be Time*. Garden City, NY: Doubleday & Co., 1972.

Anstey, F. *Tourmalin's Time Cheques*. New York: D. Appleton, 1891.

Asimov, Isaac. "The Dead Past." In Asimov, *Earth Is Room Enough*. 1957. New York: Fawcett Crest Books, 1970, 7–54. Story first published in 1956.

———. *The End of Eternity*. 1955. New York: Lancer, 1963.

———. "The Ugly Little Boy." In Asimov, *Nine Tomorrows*. 1959. New York: Fawcett Crest Books, 1969, 184–224. Story first published in 1958.

Ballard, J. G. "The Garden of Time." In Ballard, *Chronopolis*. 1971. New York: Berkley Books, 1972, 241–250. Story first published in 1962.

———. "The Index." In Ballard, *War Fever*. London: Collins, 1990, 171–176.

———. "Mr F. Is Mr F." In Ballard, *The Disaster Area*. 1967. London: Panther, 1969, 103–121.

Banks, Iain M. *Use of Weapons*. London: Orbit, 1990.

Barnes, John. *The Timeline Wars*. New York: Science Fiction Book Club, 1997. Omnibus of *Patton's Spaceship*, *Washington's Dirigible*, and *Caesar's Bicycle*, all first published in 1997.

Barrie, J. M. *Peter Pan and Wendy*. 1921. New York: Charles Scribner's Sons, 1925.

Bates, Harry. "Alas, All Thinking." In Robert Silverberg and Martin H. Greenberg, editors, *Great Tales of Science Fiction*. 1983. New York: Galahad Books, 1994, 182–209. Story first published in 1935.

Baxter, Stephen. *The Time Ships*. New York: Harper, 1995.

Bayley, J. Barrington. *Collision with Chronos*. London: Allison and Busby, 1977.

Bear, Greg. "Judgment Engine." In Gregory Benford, editor, *Far Futures*. New York: Tor Books, 1995, 23–55.

Bellamy, Edward. *Looking Backward, 2000–1887*. 1888. Boston: Houghton Mifflin, 1988.

Benford, Gregory. "Of Space-Time and the River." In Benford, *In Alien Flesh* (New York: Tor Books, 1986), 196–227. Story originally published in 1985.

———. *Timescape*. New York: Pocket Books, 1981.

Bester, Alfred. "The Men Who Murdered Mohammed." In Robert Silverberg and Martin H. Greenberg, editors, *Great Tales of Science Fiction*. 1983. New York: Galahad Books, 1994, 371–381. Story first published in 1958.

———. "Of Time and Third Avenue." In Damon Knight, editor, *A Century of Science Fiction*. 1962. New York: Dell Books, 1963, 59–67. Story first published in 1951.

Bishop, Michael. *No Enemy but Time*. 1982. New York: Book of the Month Club, 1990.

Blake, William. "The Mental Traveller." In Geoffrey Keynes, editor, *Blake: Complete Writings*. London: Oxford University Press, 1969, 424–427.

Blaylock, James P. *Lord Kelvin's Machine*. New York: Berkley, 1992.

Blish, James. "Beep." In Blish, *Galactic Cluster*. 1954. London: Faber and Faber, 1960, 103–143.

———. "Common Time." In Blish, *Galactic Cluster*. 1954. London: Faber and Faber, 1960, 9–31.

———. *Jack of Eagles*. 1952. New York: Avon, 1958.

Bloch, Robert. "A Toy for Juliette." In Harlan Ellison, editor, *Dangerous Visions #1*. 1967. New York: Berkley Books, 1969, 167–174.

Borges, Jorge Luis. "The Garden of Forked Paths." Translated by Donald A. Yates. In Borges, *Labyrinths: Selected Stories and Other Writings*. 1962. New York: New Directions, 1964, 19–29.

Boulle, Pierre. "Time Out of Mind." In Boulle, *Time Out of Mind*. Translated by Xan

Fielding and Elisabeth Abbott. 1966. New York: Signet Books, 1969, 7–35. Story first published in 1957.

Bradbury, Ray. "The Fox and the Forest." In Bradbury, *The Illustrated Man*. 1951. New York: Bantam Books, 1952, 114–127. Story first published in 1950.

———. "Frost and Fire." In Bradbury, *R Is for Rocket*. 1962. New York: Bantam Books, 1965, 124–163. Story first published in 1946.

———. "A Sound of Thunder." In Bradbury, *The Golden Apples of the Sun*. 1953. New York: Bantam Books, 1954, 88–99. Story first published in 1952.

Brennert, Alan. "Her Pilgrim Soul." In Brennert, *Her Pilgrim Soul*. New York: Tor Books, 1990, 194–244.

———. *Time and Chance*. New York: Tor Books, 1990.

———. "Voices in the Earth." In Brennert, *Her Pilgrim Soul*. New York: Tor Books, 1990, 161–193. Story first published in 1987.

Brin, David. "The River of Time." In Brin, *The River of Time*. 1986. New York: Bantam Books, 1987, 282–295. Story first published in 1981.

Brown, Fredric. "The End." In Brown, *The Best Short Stories of Fredric Brown*. London: New English Library, 1982, 447.

Brunner, John. *The 100th Millennium*. New York: Ace, 1959. Revised as *Catch a Falling Star* in 1968.

Burdekin, Katharine. *The Burning Ring*. New York: W. Morrow, 1929.

Burgess, Anthony. *1985*. Boston: Little, Brown, 1978.

Butler, Octavia E. *Kindred*. 1979. Boston: Beacon Press, 1988.

Buzzati, Dino. "The Time Machine." In David G. Hartwell, editor, *The Science Fiction Century*. New York: Tor Books, 1997, 261–264.

Campbell, John W., Jr. "Night." In Campbell, *Who Goes There?* Chicago: Shasta Publishing Co., 1948, 206–230. Story first published in 1935.

———. "Twilight." In Robert Silverberg, editor, *The Science Fiction Hall of Fame, Volume I*. 1970. New York: Avon Books, 1971, 40–61. Story first published in 1934.

Card, Orson Scott. *Pastwatch: The Redemption of Christopher Columbus*. New York: Tor Books, 1996.

Carroll, Lewis. *Alice through the Looking Glass*. In Martin Gardner, editor, *The Annotated Alice*. London: Anthony Blond, 1960, 167–345. Novel first published in 1872.

———. *Sylvie and Bruno*. In Carroll, *The Complete Illustrated Works of Lewis Carroll*. London: Chancellor Press, 1987, 235–433. First published in 1889.

———. *Sylvie and Bruno Concluded*. In Carroll, Lewis. *The Complete Illustrated Works of Lewis Carroll*. London: Chancellor Press, 1987, 435–641. First published in 1893.

Clarke, Arthur C. "All the Time in the World." In Clarke, *The Other Side of the Sky*. 1958. New York: Signet Books, 1959, 97–108. Story first published in 1952.

———. *Childhood's End*. New York: Ballantine, 1953.

———. "Time's Arrow." In Clarke, *Reach for Tomorrow*. New York: Ballantine Books, 1956, 112–127. Story first published in 1952.

———. "Transcience." In Clarke, *The Nine Billion Names of God*. New York: Harcourt Brace Jovanovich, 1967, 264–270. Story first published in 1949.

———. *2001: A Space Odyssey*. New York: Signet, 1968.

Clarke, Arthur C., and Stephen Baxter. *The Light of Other Days*. New York: Tor Books, 2000.

Compton, D. G. *Chronocules*. New York: Ace Books, 1970.

Cook, William Wallace. *A Round Trip to the Year 2000*. 1903. Westport, CT: Hyperion Press, 1974.

Cooper, Edmund. *Deadly Image*. New York: Ballantine, 1958.

Cummings, Ray. *The Shadow Girl*. New York: Ace, 1962.

Dalos, György. *1985: A Historical Report (Hongkong 2036)*. 1982. Translated by Stuart Hood and Estella Schmid. New York: Pantheon Books, 1983.

Dante Alighieri. *The Divine Comedy: Inferno: Italian Text and Translation*. Translated by Charles S. Singleton. Princeton: Princeton University Press, 1975–1977.

———. *The Divine Comedy: Purgatorio: Italian Text and Translation*. Translated by Charles S. Singleton. Princeton: Princeton University Press, 1975–1977.

———. *The Divine Comedy: Paradiso: Italian Text and Translation*. Translated by Charles S. Singleton. Princeton: Princeton University Press, 1975–1977.

de Camp, L. Sprague. "A Gun for Dinosaur." *Galaxy*, 11 (March, 1956), 6–35.

———. "The Isolinguals." In Damon Knight, editor, *First Flight*. 1963. New York: Lancer Books, 1966, 9–26. Story first published in 1937.

———. *Lest Darkness Fall*. 1941. New York: Pyramid Books, 1963.

del Rey, Lester. ". . . And It Comes Out Here." *Galaxy*, 2 (February, 1951), 62–74.

Deveraux, Jude. *A Knight in Shining Armor*. New York: Pocket Books, 1989.

Dick, Philip K. *Counter-Clock World*. 1967. London: Sphere, 1968.

———. "Jon's World." In August Derleth, editor, *Time to Come*. New York: Pyramid Books, 1969, 111–144.

———. "A Little Something for Us Tempunauts." In Edward L. Ferman and Barry N. Malzberg, editors, *Final Stage: The Ultimate Science Fiction Anthology*. 1974. New York: Penguin Books, 1975, 259–282.

———. *The Man in the High Castle*. 1962. Toronto: Popular Library, 1964.

———. *Now Wait for Last Year*. Garden City, NY: Doubleday & Co., 1966.

———. *Ubik*. 1969. New York: Dell, 1970.

Dickens, Charles. *A Christmas Carol*. In Dickens, *Works of Charles Dickens*. New York: Avenel Books, 1978, 469–494. Novel first published in 1843.

Dickson, Gordon R. *Time Storm*. New York: Bantam Books, 1977.

Dvorkian, David. *Timetrap*. New York: Pocket Books, 1988.

Eddison, E. R. *The Worm Ouroboros: A Romance*. London: J. Cape, 1922.

Egan, Greg. *Permutation City*. New York: Harper Prism Books, 1994.

Eklund, Gordon. *Serving in Time*. Don Mills, Ontario: Laser Books, 1975.

Ellison, Harlan. "Jeffty Is Five." In Ellison, *Shatterday*. 1980. New York: Berkley Books, 1982, 4–24. Story first published in 1977.

———. "One Life, Furnished in Early Poverty." In Ellison, *Approaching Oblivion: Road Signs on the Treadmill toward Tomorrow: Eleven Uncollected Stories*. New York: Walker, 1974, 157–177.

———. "Paladin of the Lost Hour." In Ellison, *Angry Candy*. Boston: Houghton Mifflin, 1988, 3–25. Story first published in 1985.

———. "Soldier." In Ellison, *From the Land of Fear*. New York: Belmont Books, 1967, 114–135. Story first published in 1957.

Farmer, Philip Jose. "Sail On! Sail On!" In Damon Knight, editor, *A Century of Science Fiction*. 1962. New York: Dell Books, 1963, 68–77. Story first published in 1952.

Finch, Sheila. *Infinity's Web*. New York: Bantam Books, 1985.

Finney, Jack. *Time and Again*. New York: Simon & Schuster, 1970.

FitzGerald, Edward. *The Rubaiyat of Omar Khayyam*. In A. J. Arberry, editor, *The Rubaiyat of Omar Khayyam and Other Persian Poems: An Anthology of Verse Translations*. London: Dent, 1976, 3–32.

Fitzgerald, F. Scott. "The Curious Case of Benjamin Button." In Fitzgerald, *The Bodley*

Head Scott Fitzgerald, Volume 3. London: Bodley Head, 1960, 299–327.

Friedell, Egon. *The Return of the Time Machine.* 1946. Translated by Eddy C. Bertin. New York: DAW Books, 1972.

Friesner, Esther M. *Yesterday We Saw Mermaids.* 1992. New York: Tor Books, 1993.

Fujiko, Fujio F. *Doraemon.* 45 volumes. Tokyo: Shougakukan, 1974–1996.

Gabaldon, Diana. *Dragonfly in Amber.* New York: Delacorte, 1992.

———. *Drums of Autumn.* New York: Delacorte, 1997.

———. *The Fiery Cross.* New York: Delacorte, 2001.

———. *Outlander.* New York: Delacorte, 1991.

———. *Voyager.* New York: Delacorte, 1994.

Geoffroy, Louis. *Napoléon apocryphe, 1812–1832: Histoire de la conquête du monde et de la monarchie universelle.* 1836. Paris: Tallandier, 1983.

Gerrold, David. *The Man Who Folded Himself.* New York: Random House, 1973.

Gibson, William. "The Gernsback Continuum." In Gibson, *Burning Chrome.* 1986. New York: Ace Books, 1987, 23–35. Story first published in 1981.

Gibson, William, and Bruce Sterling. *The Difference Engine.* 1991. New York: Bantam, 1992.

Gordon, Rex. *First through Time.* New York: Ace Books, 1962.

Grimwood, Ken. *Replay.* New York: Arbor House, 1986.

Guttin, Jacques. *Épigone, histoire du siècle future.* Paris: Pierre Lamy, 1659.

Haldeman, Joe. *The Forever War.* New York: St. Martin's Press, 1975.

———. *The Hemingway Hoax.* New York: Morrow, 1990.

Hamilton, Edmund. "The Man Who Evolved." In Isaac Asimov, editor, *Before the Golden Age: A Science Fiction Anthology of the 1930s.* Garden City, NY: Doubleday & Co., 1974, 23–38. Story first published in 1931.

Heinlein, Robert A. " 'All You Zombies—.' " In Robert P. Mills, editor, *The Worlds of Science Fiction.* 1963. New York: Paperback Library, 1965, 103–114. Story first published in 1959.

———. "By His Bootstraps." In Heinlein, *The Menace from Earth.* 1959. New York: Signet Books, 1962, 39–88. Story first published in 1941.

———. *The Door into Summer.* Garden City, NY: Doubleday & Co., 1957.

———. "Elsewhen." In Heinlein, *Assignment in Eternity.* New York: Signet Books, 1953, 68–95. Story first published in 1941.

———. *The Number of the Beast.* New York: Fawcett Columbine, 1980.

———. *Time Enough for Love.* 1973. New York: Berkley Books, 1974.

———. *Time for the Stars.* 1956. New York: Ace Books, 1969.

Herbert, Frank. *Dune.* 1965. New York: Ace Books, 1990.

Hodgson, William Hope. *The House on the Borderland.* 1908. Westport, CT: Hyperion Press, 1976.

———. *The Night Land: A Love Tale.* London: E. Nash, 1912.

Hogan, James P. *Thrice upon a Time.* New York: Del Rey/Ballantine Books, 1980.

Hoyle, Fred. *October the First Is Too Late.* Greenwich, CT: Fawcett Crest, 1966.

Jakes, John. *Black in Time.* New York: Paperback Library, 1970.

Jeter, K. W. *Morlock Night.* New York: DAW Books, 1979.

Jeury, Michel. *Chronolysis.* Translated by Maxim Jakubowski. New York: Macmillan, 1980.

Kinsella, W. P. *The Iowa Baseball Confederacy.* Boston: Houghton Mifflin, 1986.

———. *Shoeless Joe.* Boston: Houghton Mifflin, 1982.

Kornbluth, C. M. "The Little Black Bag." In Silverberg, editor, *The Science Fiction Hall of Fame, Volume I.* 1970. New York: Avon Books, 1971, 410–439. Story first published in 1950.

———. "Time Bum." In Kornbluth, *A Mile Beyond the Moon*. 1958. New York: MacFadden, 1966, 73–80.

Krentz, Jayne Ann. *Crystal Flame*. Thorndike, ME: Thorndike Press, 1996.

———. *Sweet Starfire*. New York: Warner Books, 1986.

Kress, Nancy. "The Price of Oranges." In Robin Scott Wilson, editor, *Paragons: Twelve Master Science Fiction Writers Ply Their Craft*. New York: St. Martin's Press, 1996, 4–28. Story first published in 1989.

Kuttner, Henry, and C. L. Moore. [as Lewis Padgett] "Mimsy Were the Borogoves." In Robert Silverberg, editor, *The Science Fiction Hall of Fame, Volume I*. 1970. New York: Avon Books, 1971, 226–260. Story first published in 1943.

Kuttner, Henry, and C. L. Moore. [as Lawrence O'Donnell] "Vintage Season." In Ben Bova, editor, *The Science Fiction Hall of Fame, Volume IIA*. 1973. New York: Avon Books, 1974, 257–301. Story first published in 1946.

Lafferty, R. A. "The Six Fingers of Time." In Lafferty, *Nine Hundred Grandmothers*. New York: Ace Books, 1970, 43–73. Story first published in 1960.

———. "Thus We Frustrate Charlemagne." In Lafferty, *Nine Hundred Grandmothers*. New York: Ace Books, 1970, 171–184. Story first published in 1969.

Laumer, Keith. *Dinosaur Beach*. New York: DAW Books, Inc., 1971.

———. *The Great Time Machine Hoax*. New York: Simon and Schuster, 1964.

Le Guin, Ursula K. *The Left Hand of Darkness*. New York: Ace Books, 1969.

Leiber, Fritz. *The Big Time*. New York: Ace Books, 1961. First published in magazine form in 1958.

———. "Time Fighter." In Leiber, *A Pail of Air*. 1957. New York: Ballantine, 1964, 66–71. Story first published in 1957.

Leinster, Murray. "Dear Charles." In Leinster, *Twists in Time*. New York: Avon, 1960, 28–44. Story first published in 1953.

———. "Sidewise in Time." In Isaac Asimov, editor, *Before the Golden Age*. Garden City, NY: Doubleday & Co., 1974, 496–539. Story first published in 1934.

Lem, Stanislaw. *Return from the Stars*. 1961. Translated by Barbara Marszal and Frank Simpson. New York: Avon, 1982.

L'Engle, Madeleine. *A Wrinkle in Time*. New York: Farrar, 1962.

Lewis, Jack. "Who's Cribbing?" In Isaac Asimov, Martin Greenberg, and Joseph Olander, editors, *Isaac Asimov's Science Fiction Treasury*. New York: Bonanza Books, 1980, 460–466. Story first published in 1952.

Lindsey, Johanna. *Warrior's Woman*. New York: Avon Books, 1990.

Loudon, Jane. *The Mummy! A Tale of the Twenty-Second Century*. 3 volumes. London: Henry Colburn, 1827.

Lovecraft, H. P. "The Shadow Out of Time." In Lovecraft, *The Best of H. P. Lovecraft*. New York: Del Rey/Ballantine, 1982, 325–375.

MacDonald, John D. *The Girl, the Gold Watch, and the Everything*. New York: Fawcett Books, 1962.

Maine, Charles Eric. *The Isotope Man*. Philadelphia: J. B. Lippincott Co., 1957.

Manning, Laurence. "The Man Who Awoke." In Isaac Asimov, editor, *Before the Golden Age*. Garden City, NY: Doubleday & Co., 1974, 317–344. Story first published in 1933.

McKenna, Richard. "The Secret Place." In Brian W. Aldiss and Harry Harrison, editors, *Nebula Award Stories Number Two*. 1967. New York: Pocket Books, 1968, 1–15. Story first published in 1966.

Miller, P. Schuyler. "As Never Was." In Robert Silverberg and Martin H. Greenberg, editors, *Great Tales of Science Fiction*. 1983. New York: Galahad Books, 1994, 227–238. Story first published in 1943.

Miller, Walter M., Jr. *A Canticle for Leibowitz*. 1959. New York: Bantam Books, 1961.

Mitchell, Edward Page. "The Clock That Went Backward." In Mitchell, *The Crystal Man*. Garden City, NY: Doubleday & Co., 1973, 71–86. Story first published in 1881.

Moorcock, Michael. *An Alien Heat*. New York: Harper & Row, 1972. Dancers at the End of Time #1.

———. *Behold the Man*. New York: Avon Books, 1968. Based on the novella of the same name published in 1966.

———. *The End of All Songs*. New York: Harper & Row, 1976. Dancers at the End of Time #3.

———. *The Hollow Lands*. New York: Harper & Row, 1974. Dancers at the End of Time #2.

———. *The Time Dweller*. 1969. New York: Berkley Medallion, 1971.

Moore, Ward. *Bring the Jubilee*. New York: Farrar, Straus, & Young, 1953.

Morris, William. *News from Nowhere; or an Epoch of Rest, Being Some Chapters from a Utopian Romance*. Boston: Roberts, 1890.

Murphy, Pat. *The Falling Woman*. New York: Tor Books, 1986.

Nelson, Ray. "Time Travel for Pedestrians." In Harlan Ellison, editor, *Again, Dangerous Visions I*. 1972. New York: Signet Books, 1973, 163–185.

Niven, Larry. "The Return of William Proxmire." In Niven, *N-Space*. New York: Tor Books, 1990, 399–406.

———. *A World Out of Time*. New York: Holt, Rinehart & Winston, 1976.

Noguez, Dominique. *Les trois Rimbaud*. Paris: Minuit, 1986.

Norton, Andre. *The Time Traders*. Cleveland: World Publishing Company, 1958.

Nourse, Alan E. "Tiger by the Tail." In Isaac Asimov and Groff Conklin, editors, *Fifty Short Science Fiction Tales*. New York: Collier Books, 1963, 185–191. Story first published in 1951.

Nowlan, Philip Francis. *Armageddon 2419 A.D.* 1928. New York: Ace Books, 1962.

O'Brien, Fitz-James. "What Was It?" In Damon Knight, editor, *A Century of Science Fiction*. 1962. New York: Dell Books, 1963, 195–208. Story first published in 1859.

O'Brien, Flann. *The Third Policeman*. London: MacGibbon & Kee, 1967.

Orwell, George. *Nineteen Eighty-Four: Text, Sources, Criticism*. Second Edition, edited by Irving Howe. New York: Harcourt, 1982. Novel first published in 1949.

Ouspensky, P. D. *The Strange Life of Ivan Osokin*. London: Faber and Faber, 1948.

Pal, George, and Joe Morhaim. *Time Machine II*. New York: Dell Books, 1981.

Piercy, Marge. *Woman on the Edge of Time*. New York: Alfred A. Knopf, 1976.

Poe, Edgar Allan. "Mellonta Tauta." In Poe, *The Complete Tales and Poems of Edgar Allan Poe*. New York: Barnes & Noble Books, 1992, 683–694. Story first published in 1849.

Pohl, Frederik. *The Age of the Pussyfoot*. 1969. New York: Ballantine, 1982.

———. "The Day of the Boomer Dukes." In Pohl, *Tomorrow Times Seven*. 1956. New York: Ballantine, 1959, 55–73. Story first published in 1956.

Pratchett, Terry. *Johnny and the Bomb*. London: Doubleday & Co., 1996.

Priest, Christopher. *Indoctrinaire*. Richmond Hill, Ontario: Pocket Books, 1971.

Priestley, J. B. *Time and the Conways: A Play in Three Acts*. London, W. Heinemann, Ltd., 1937.

Renouvier, Charles. *Uchronie (L'utopie dans l'histoire), esquisse historique apocryphe du développement de la civilisation européenne, tel qu'il n'a pas été, tel qu'il aurait pu être*. 1876. Paris: Fayard, 1988.

Reynolds, Mack. "Compounded Interest." In Judith Merril, editor, *SF: The Best of the Best.* New York: Dell Books, 1967, 199–212. Story first published in 1956.

Roberts, Keith. *Pavane.* 1968. London: Panther, 1970.

Ross, Malcolm. *The Man Who Lived Backward.* New York: Farrar, Straus and Company, 1950.

Rucker, Rudy. "Message Found in a Copy of *Flatland*." In David G. Hartwell and Kathryn Cramer, editors, *The Ascent of Wonder: The Evolution of Hard SF.* New York: Tor Books, 1994. Story first published in 1983.

Russ, Joanna. *The Female Man.* New York: Bantam Books, 1975.

Schachner, Nat. "Past, Present, and Future." In Isaac Asimov, editor, *Before the Golden Age.* Garden City, NY: Doubleday & Co., 1974, 843–877. Story first published in 1937.

Shaw, Bob. "Light of Other Days." In Brian W. Aldiss and Harry Harrison, editors, *Nebula Award Stories Number Two.* 1967. New York: Pocket Books, 1968, 17–25. Story first published in 1966.

Shaw, George Bernard. *Back to Methuselah.* 1921. Revised Edition with Postscript. London: Oxford University Press, 1947.

Sheckley, Robert. *Immortality, Inc.* New York: Bantam Books, 1959. Published in shorter form in 1958.

Sheffield, Charles. "At the Eschaton." In Gregory Benford, editor, *Far Futures.* New York: Tor Books, 1995, 280–348.

Shelley, Mary. *The Last Man.* London: H. Colburn, 1826.

———. "The Mortal Immortal." In Shelley, *The Mortal Immortal: The Complete Supernatural Short Fiction.* San Francisco: Tachyon Publications, 1996, 1–11. Story first published in 1834.

Sherred, T. L. "E for Effort." In Ben Bova, editor, *The Science Fiction Hall of Fame Volume IIB.* 1973. New York: Avon Books, 1974, 380–432. Story first published in 1947.

Shiplett, June Lund. *Journey to Yesterday.* New York: Signet Books, 1979.

Silverberg, Robert. "Absolutely Inflexible." In Silverberg, *Needle in a Timestack.* New York: Ballantine Books, 1966, 94–108.

———. *Hawksbill Station.* 1968. New York: Warner Books, 1986. Based on a story published in 1967.

———. *The Time Hoppers.* Garden City, NY: Doubleday & Co., 1967.

———. *Up the Line.* New York: Ballantine Books, 1969.

Simak, Clifford D. *Highway of Eternity.* 1986. New York: Ballantine, 1988.

———. *Mastodonia.* New York: Del Rey/Ballantine Books, 1978.

———. *Our Children's Children.* 1974. New York: Berkley Books, 1975.

———. *Time and Again.* New York: Ace Books, 1951.

Simmons, Dan. *The Fall of Hyperion.* Garden City, NY: Doubleday & Co., 1990.

———. *Hyperion.* 1989. New York: Bantam Books, 1990.

Singer, Isaac Bashevis. "Jachid and Jechida." In Jack Dann, editor, *Wandering Stars: An Anthology of Jewish Fantasy and Science Fiction.* New York: Harper & Row, 1974, 202–209.

Stableford, Brian. *The Walking Shadow.* 1979. New York: Carroll & Graf, Inc., 1989.

Stapledon, Olaf. *Star Maker.* 1937. London: Penguin, 1988.

———. *Last and First Men.* 1930. In Stapledon, *Last and First Men and Star Maker.* New York: Dover, 1968, 3–246.

Sturgeon, Theodore. "Microcosmic God." In Robert Silverberg, editor, *The Science Fiction Hall of Fame, Volume I.* 1970. New York: Avon Books, 1971, 115–144. Story first published in 1941.

Taine, John. *The Time Stream*. 1946. New York: Dover Publications, 1971. Novel first published in magazine form in 1931 and 1932.

Tenn, William. "Brooklyn Project." In Groff Conklin, editor, *17 X Infinity*. 1963. New York: Dell Books, 1969, 263–272. Story first published in 1948.

Tucker, Wilson. *The Lincoln Hunters*. 1958. New York: Ace Books, 1968.

———. "The Tourist Trade." In Robert A. Heinlein, editor, *Tomorrow, the Stars*. 1952. New York: Berkley Books, 1967, 53–63. Story first published in 1950.

———. *The Year of the Quiet Sun*. New York: Ace Books, 1970.

Turtledove, Harry. *Departures*. New York: Ballantine Books, 1993.

———. *The Guns of the South: A Novel of the Civil War*. New York: Ballantine Books, 1992.

———. *A World of Difference*. New York: Ballantine Books, 1990.

———. *Worldwar: In the Balance*. New York: Ballantine Books, 1994.

———. *Worldwar: Striking the Balance*. New York: Ballantine Books, 1996.

———. *Worldwar: Tilting the Balance*. New York: Ballantine Books, 1995.

———. *Worldwar: Upsetting the Balance*. New York: Ballantine Books, 1996.

Twain, Mark. *A Connecticut Yankee in King Arthur's Court*. 1889. New York: Signet Books, 1963.

———. "From the *London Times* of 1904." In H. Bruce Franklin, editor, *Future Perfect: American Science Fiction of the Nineteenth Century*. New York: Oxford University Press, 1966, 382–392.

van Vogt, A. E. *Children of Tomorrow*. New York: Ace Books, 1970.

Varley, John. "Air Raid." In Varley, *The Persistence of Vision*. New York: Dell Books, 1978, 43–58. Story first published in 1977.

Verne, Jules. *Paris in the Twentieth Century*. Translated by Richard Howard. New York: Random House, 1996.

———. "In the Twenty-Ninth Century: The Day of an American Journalist in 2889." Translated by I. O. Evans. In Verne, *Yesterday and Tomorrow*. New York: Ace Books, 1965. Story first published in 1910.

Vidal, Gore. *Live from Golgotha*. New York: Random House, 1992.

———. *The Smithsonian Institution*. New York: Random House, 1998.

Vonnegut, Kurt, Jr. *Galapagos*. New York: Delacorte Press, 1985.

———. *The Sirens of Titan*. New York: Dell Books, 1959.

———. *Slaughterhouse-Five*. New York: Dell Publishing Co., Inc., 1969.

Watson, Ian. "The Very Slow Time Machine." In Watson, *The Very Slow Time Machine*. New York: Ace Books, 1979, 1–30. Story first published in 1978.

Wells, H. G. *The Definitive "Time Machine": A Critical Edition of H. G. Wells's Scientific Romance*. Introduction and notes by Harry M. Geduld. Bloomington and Indianapolis: Indiana University Press, 1987.

———. "The New Accelerator." In Wells, *The Complete Short Stories of H. G. Wells*. London: Ernest Benn, 1927, 927–942. Story first published in 1901.

———. "The Plattner Story." In Wells, *The Complete Short Stories of H. G. Wells*. London: Ernest Benn, 1927, 325–345. Story first published in 1897.

———. *The Time Machine: An Invention*. A Critical Text of the 1895 London First Edition, with an Introduction and Appendices, edited by Leon Stover. Jefferson, NC: McFarland, 1996.

———. *When the Sleeper Wakes*. New York: Harper & Row, Publishers, 1899.

White, T. H. *The Once and Future King*. London: Collins, 1958.

Williamson, Jack. *The Legion of Time*. 1952. New York: Pyramid Books, 1967. First published in magazine form in 1938.

Willis, Connie. "Fire Watch." In David G. Hartwell, editor, *The Science Fiction Century*. New York: Tor Books, 1997, 435–461.

———. *Lincoln's Dreams*. New York: Bantam, 1987.

Wollheim, Donald A. [as David Grinnell] *Edge of Time*. New York: Ace, 1958.

Woolf, Virginia. *Orlando*. New York: Harcourt Brace, 1928.

Wyndham, John. "Opposite Number." In Wyndham, *The Seeds of Time*. London: Michael Joseph, 1956, 140–161.

Zelazny, Roger. "Divine Madness." In Zelazny, *The Doors of His Face, The Lamps of His Mouth, and Other Stories*. Garden City, NY: Doubleday & Co., 1971, 198–205.

———. *Lord of Light*. 1967. New York: Avon, 1969.

II. Films and Television Programs

"All Good Things . . ." *Star Trek: The Next Generation*. Syndicated, week of May 23, 1994.

"All Our Yesterdays." *Star Trek*. New York: NBC-TV, March 14, 1969.

"The Alternative Factor." *Star Trek*. New York: NBC-TV, March 30, 1967.

The Amazing Mr. Blunden. Hemdale/Hemisphere, 1972.

Apex. Green Communications/Republic Pictures, 1994.

Army of Darkness. Western Renaissance Pictures, 1993.

"Assignment: Earth." *Star Trek*. New York: NBC-TV, March 29, 1968.

The Atomic Man. Merton Park Productions, 1956.

"Babylon Squared." *Babylon 5*. Syndicated, August 10, 1994.

Back to the Future. Amblin' Entertainment, 1985.

Back to the Future II. Amblin' Entertainment, 1989.

Back to the Future III. Amblin' Entertainment, 1990.

"The Bard." *The Twilight Zone*. New York: CBS-TV, May 23, 1963.

Beastmaster II: Through the Portal of Time. Films 21/Republic, 1991.

"Behold, Eck!" *The Outer Limits*. New York: ABC-TV, October 3, 1964.

Berkeley Square. Twentieth-Century Fox, 1933.

Beyond the Time Barrier. Robert Clarke Productions, 1960.

Biggles: Adventures in Time. Compact Yellowbill/Tambarle Productions, 1985.

Bill and Ted's Excellent Adventure. Orion Pictures, 1989.

"Blink of an Eye." *Star Trek: Voyager*. New York: UPN-TV, January 19, 2000.

Brazil. Embassy International Pictures/Universal Pictures, 1985.

Brigadoon. Metro-Goldwyn-Mayer, 1954.

"Camera Obscura." *Night Gallery*. New York: NBC-TV, December 8, 1971.

"Captain's Holiday." *Star Trek: The Next Generation*. Syndicated, week of April 2, 1990.

Catweazle. Television series, 1970–1971.

"Cause and Effect." *Star Trek: The Next Generation*. Syndicated, week of March 23, 1992.

"Children of Time." *Star Trek: Deep Space Nine*. Syndicated, May 3, 1995.

"The City on the Edge of Forever." *Star Trek*. New York: NBC-TV, April 6, 1967.

A Connecticut Yankee. Twentieth-Century Fox, 1931.

A Connecticut Yankee in King Arthur's Court. Paramount, 1949.

"Controlled Experiment." *The Outer Limits*. New York: ABC-TV, January 13, 1964.

"The Convict's Piano." *Twilight Zone*. New York: CBS-TV, December 11, 1986.

"The Counter-Clock Incident." *Star Trek* [animated]. New York: NBC-TV, October 12, 1974.

"Crossover." *Star Trek: Deep Space Nine.* Syndicated, May 14, 1994.

Cyborg 2087. Feature Films Corporation, 1966.

Daleks—Invasion Earth 2150 A.D. Amicus/Continental, 1965.

"The Dead Past." *Out of the Unknown.* London: BBC-TV, October 23, 1965.

"The Deconstruction of Falling Stars." *Babylon 5.* Syndicated, October 27, 1997.

Dimension 5. United Pictures/Harold Goldman Associates, 1966.

Dr. Who. Television series, 1963–1989.

Dr. Who and the Daleks. Amicus/Continental, 1965.

"Don't Open till Doomsday." *The Outer Limits.* New York: ABC-TV, January 20, 1964.

Early Edition. Television series, 1996–2000.

"The Emperor's New Cloak." *Star Trek: Deep Space Nine.* Syndicated, February 2, 1999.

"Encounter at Farpoint." *Star Trek: The Next Generation.* Syndicated, week of September 28, 1987.

The End of the World. Irwin Yablans Company/Charles Band, 1977.

"Endgame." *Star Trek: Voyager.* New York: UPN-TV, May 23, 2001.

Erasmus Microman. Television series, 1988–1989.

Escape from the Planet of the Apes. Twentieth-Century Fox, 1971.

"Execution." *The Twilight Zone.* New York: CBS-TV, April 1, 1960.

"Extra Innings." *Twilight Zone.* Syndicated, 1988.

The Fantastic Journey. Television series, 1977.

Field of Dreams. Gordon Company, 1989.

The Final Countdown. Bryna Company, 1980.

"Flashback." *Star Trek: Voyager.* New York: UPN-TV, September 11, 1996.

Flight of the Navigator. Walt Disney, 1986.

"The Forms of Things Unknown." *The Outer Limits.* New York: ABC-TV, May 4, 1964.

"The Fox and the Forest." *Out of the Unknown.* London: BBC-TV, November 22, 1965.

Freejack. Morgan Creek Productions, 1992.

Frequency. New Line Cinema, 2000.

"Future Imperfect." *Star Trek: The Next Generation.* Syndicated, week of November 12, 1990.

"Future's End." Two-part episode, *Star Trek: Voyager.* New York: UPN-TV, November 6 and November 13, 1996.

The Girl from Tomorrow. Television series, 1991–1993.

"The Girl I Married." *Twilight Zone.* New York: CBS-TV, July 17, 1987.

Goodnight Sweetheart. Television series, 1993–1996.

Groundhog Day. Columbia Pictures, 1993.

"The Guests." *The Outer Limits.* New York: ABC-TV, March 23, 1964.

"Her Pilgrim Soul." *Twilight Zone.* New York: CBS-TV, December 13, 1985.

A Hitch in Time. Eyeline/Children's Film Foundation, 1978.

Hu-Man. Romantique Films/Yves Pauthe/M. F. Mascaro Productions, 1975.

"A Hundred Yards over the Rim." *The Twilight Zone.* New York: CBS-TV, April 7, 1961.

I Killed Einstein, Gentlemen. Czechoslovensky Films, 1970.

"Immortality, Inc." *Out of the Unknown.* London: BBC-TV, January 7, 1969.

"The Incredible World of Horace Ford." *The Twilight Zone.* New York: CBS-TV, April 18, 1963.

Into the Labyrinth. Television series, 1981–1982.

It's About Time. Television series. New York: CBS-TV, 1966–1967.

Jamie. Television series, 1971.

Je T'Aime, Je T'Aime. Parc Film/Fox Europa, 1967.

La Jetée. Argos Films, 1963.
Journey to the Beginning of Time. Studio Gottwaldow, 1955.
Journey to the Center of Time. Borealis/Dorad, 1967.
"The Junction." *Twilight Zone.* New York: CBS-TV, February 21, 1987.
Just Imagine. Twentieth-Century Fox, 1930.
Kappatoo. Television series, 1990–1992.
"A Kind of Stop Watch." *The Twilight Zone.* New York: CBS-TV, October 18, 1963.
"The Little Black Bag." *Night Gallery.* New York: NBC-TV, December 23, 1970.
"Little Boy Lost." *Twilight Zone.* New York: CBS-TV, October 18, 1985.
"Little Green Men." *Star Trek: Deep Space Nine.* Syndicated, November 4, 1995.
"A Little Piece and Quiet." *Twilight Zone.* New York: CBS-TV, September 27, 1985.
"Living Witness." *Star Trek: Voyager.* New York: UPN-TV, April 29, 1998.
"Lone Survivor." *Night Gallery.* New York: NBC-TV, January 13, 1971.
"The Long Morrow." *The Twilight Zone.* New York: CBS-TV, January 10, 1964.
Lost in Space. Irwin Allen Productions/New Line Cinema/Prelude Pictures, 1998.
The Man from the First Century. Czechoslovensky Films, 1961.
"The Man Who Was Never Born." *The Outer Limits.* New York: ABC-TV, October 28, 1963.
The Man with Nine Lives. Columbia, 1940.
"A Matter of Minutes." *Twilight Zone.* New York: CBS-TV, January 24, 1986.
"A Matter of Time." *Star Trek: The Next Generation.* Syndicated, week of November 18, 1991.
"Meridian." *Star Trek: Deep Space Nine.* Syndicated, November 14, 1994.
Millennium. First Millennium Partnership/Gladden Entertainment, 1989.
"Mirror, Mirror." *Star Trek.* New York: NBC-TV, October 6, 1967.
"A Most Unusual Camera." *The Twilight Zone.* New York: CBS-TV, December 16, 1960.
My Science Project. Touchstone Films, 1985.
The Navigator: A Medieval Odyssey. Aerna Films/John Maynard Productions, 1988.
"No Time Like the Past." *The Twilight Zone.* New York: CBS-TV, March 7, 1963.
"Non Sequitor." *Star Trek: Voyager.* New York: UPN-TV, September 25, 1995.
"Of Late I Think of Cliffordville." *The Twilight Zone.* New York: CBS-TV, April 11, 1963.
"The Once and Future King." *Twilight Zone.* New York: CBS-TV, September 27, 1986.
"Once Upon a Time." *The Twilight Zone.* New York: CBS-TV, December 15, 1961.
"One Life, Furnished in Early Poverty." *Twilight Zone.* New York: CBS-TV, December 8, 1985.
"One Small Step." *Star Trek: Voyager.* New York: UPN-TV, November 17, 1999.
Otherworld. Television series, 1985.
"The Painted Mirror." *Night Gallery.* New York: NBC-TV, December 15, 1971.
"Paladin of the Lost Hour." *Twilight Zone.* New York: CBS-TV, November 8, 1985.
"Parallels." *Star Trek: The Next Generation.* Syndicated, week of November 29, 1993.
"Past Tense." Two-part episode, *Star Trek: Deep Space Nine.* Syndicated, December 31, 1994 and January 7, 1995.
Paul's Awakening. Sigla Emme, 1985.
Peggy Sue Got Married. Tristar Pictures/Zoetrope Studios, 1986.
The Philadelphia Experiment. New World Pictures/Cinema Group Venture/New Pictures Group, 1984.
The Philadelphia Experiment II. Trimark Pictures, 1993.
Planet of the Apes. Twentieth-Century Fox, 1968.
Planet of the Apes. Twentieth-Century Fox/Zanuck Company, 2001.

"Playing God." *Star Trek: Deep Space Nine.* Syndicated, February 26, 1994.

"The Premonition." *The Outer Limits.* New York: ABC-TV, January 9, 1965.

"Profile in Silver." *Twilight Zone.* New York: CBS-TV, March 7, 1986.

"Q Who." *Star Trek: The Next Generation.* Syndicated, week of May 8, 1989.

Quantum Leap. Television series, 1989–1994.

"Quarantine." *Twilight Zone.* New York: CBS-TV, February 7, 1986.

Quest for Love. Peter Rogers Productions, 1971.

"Relativity." *Star Trek: Voyager.* New York: UPN-TV, May 12, 1999.

"Relics." *Star Trek: The Next Generation.* Syndicated, week of October 12, 1992.

"Remember Me." *Star Trek: The Next Generation.* Syndicated, week of October 22, 1990.

"Resurrection." *Star Trek: Deep Space Nine.* Syndicated, November 17, 1997.

"The Rip Van Winkle Caper." *The Twilight Zone.* New York: CBS-TV, April 21, 1961.

Sapphire and Steel. Television series, 1979–1982.

"Shattered." *Star Trek: Voyager.* New York: UPN-TV, January 17, 2001.

"Shattered Mirror." *Star Trek: Deep Space Nine.* Syndicated, April 20, 1996.

"The Sixth Finger." *The Outer Limits.* New York: ABC-TV, October 14, 1963.

Slaughterhouse-Five. Universal/Vanadas Productions, 1972.

Sleeper. Jack Rollins and Charles Joffe Productions, 1973.

Sliders. Television series, 1995–2000.

"Soldier." *The Outer Limits.* New York: ABC-TV, September 19, 1964.

Somewhere in Time. Rastar Pictures/Universal, 1980.

"Spectre of the Gun." *Star Trek.* New York: NBC-TV, October 25, 1968.

"Spur of the Moment." *The Twilight Zone.* New York: CBS-TV, February 21, 1964.

Star Trek: First Contact. Paramount, 1996.

Star Trek: Generations. Paramount, 1994.

Star Trek: The Motion Picture. Paramount, 1979.

Star Trek IV: The Voyage Home. Paramount, 1988.

"Static." *The Twilight Zone.* New York: CBS-TV, March 10, 1961.

"Tapestry." *Star Trek: The Next Generation.* Syndicated, week of February 15, 1993.

"Tell David . . ." *Night Gallery.* New York: NBC-TV, December 29, 1971.

The Terminator. Cinema 84/Pacific Western Productions, 1984.

Terminator 2: Judgment Day. Carolco Pictures/Lightstorm Entertainment/Pacific Western Productions, 1991.

Terror from the Year 5,000. American International, 1958.

"Things Past." *Star Trek: Deep Space Nine.* Syndicated, November 18, 1996.

"Through the Looking Glass." *Star Trek: Deep Space Nine.* Syndicated, April 15, 1995.

Time after Time. Warner Brothers/Orion, 1979.

"Time and Again." *Star Trek: Voyager.* New York: UPN-TV, January 30, 1995.

The Time Bandits. Handmade Films, 1981.

Time Express. Television series. London: BBC-TV, 1979.

Time Flies. Gainborough, 1944.

The Time Guardian. 1987. Chateau/FGH/International Film Management, 1987.

Time Is the Enemy. Television series. 1958.

The Time Machine. Galaxy Films/MGM, 1960.

The Time Machine. Television movie. Sunn Classic Pictures, 1978.

The Time Machine. DreamWorks/Warner Brothers, 2002.

Time Riders. Television series, 1991.

Time Slip. Toei, 1981.

"Time Squared." *Star Trek: The Next Generation.* Syndicated, week of April 3, 1989.

"Time Trap." *Star Trek* [animated]. New York: NBC-TV, November 24, 1973.
The Time Travellers. Dobil/American International, 1964.
Time Trax. Television series, 1994–1995.
The Time Tunnel. Television series. New York: ABC-TV, 1966–1967.
Timecop. Universal Pictures, 1994.
"Timeless." *Star Trek: Voyager*. New York: UPN-TV, November 18, 1998.
Timerider: The Adventures of Lyle Swann. Zoomo Productions/Jensen-Farley Pictures, 1983.
"Time's Arrow." Two-part episode, *Star Trek: The Next Generation*. Syndicated, weeks of June 15, and September 21, 1992.
"Time's Orphan." *Star Trek: Deep Space Nine*. Syndicated, May 16, 1998.
"Timescape." *Star Trek: The Next Generation*. Syndicated, week of June 14, 1993.
Timeslip. Television series, 1970–1971.
Timestalkers. Television movie. Fries Entertainment, 1987.
"Tomorrow Is Yesterday." *Star Trek*. New York: NBC-TV, January 26, 1967.
Trancers. Lexyn Productions, 1984.
A Traveller in Time. Television series, 1978.
"Trials and Tribble-ations." *Star Trek: Deep Space Nine*. Syndicated, November 2, 1996.
"The Trouble with Temptation." *The Twilight Zone*. New York: CBS-TV, December 9, 1960.
12 Monkeys. Universal Pictures, 1995.
12:01. Television movie. Chanticleer Films/New Line Cinema, 1993.
"20/20 Vision." *Twilight Zone*. Syndicated, 1988.
The Twilight Zone—The Movie. Warner Brothers, 1983.
The Twilight Zone: Rod Serling's Lost Classics. Television movie. O'Hara-Horowitz Productions, 1994.
2001: A Space Odyssey. Metro-Goldwyn-Mayer, 1968.
The Two Worlds of Jennie Logan. Television movie. Fries Productions, 1978.
Unidentified Flying Oddball. Walt Disney, 1979.
"Visionary." *Star Trek: Deep Space Nine*. Syndicated, February 25, 1995.
"The Visitor." *Star Trek: Deep Space Nine*. Syndicated, October 7, 1995.
"Voices in the Earth." *Twilight Zone*. New York: CBS-TV, July 10, 1987.
Voyagers. Television series, 1982–1983.
"Walking Distance." *The Twilight Zone*. New York: CBS-TV, October 30, 1959.
"The Wall." *Twilight Zone*. Syndicated, 1988.
"War without End." Two-part episode, *Babylon 5*. Syndicated, May 13 and May 20, 1996.
"We'll Always Have Paris." *Star Trek: The Next Generation*. Syndicated, week of May 2, 1988.
"Where No One Has Gone Before." *Star Trek: The Next Generation*. Syndicated, week of October 26, 1987.
The Windows of Time. Studio 4/Mafilm, 1968.
"Wink of an Eye." *Star Trek*. New York: NBC-TV, November 29, 1968.
"Wolf 359." *The Outer Limits*. New York: ABC-TV, November 7, 1964.
World without End. Allied Artists, 1956.
"Year of Hell." Two-part episode, *Star Trek: Voyager*. New York: UPN-TV, November 5 and November 12, 1997.
"Yesterday's *Enterprise*." *Star Trek: The Next Generation*. Syndicated, week of February 19, 1990.
"Yesteryear." *Star Trek* [animated]. New York: NBC-TV, September 15, 1973.
Zardoz. Twentieth-Century Fox, 1973.

III. Nonfiction and Literary Criticism

Alkon, Paul K. *Origins of Futuristic Fiction*. Athens: University of Georgia Press, 1987.

Asimov, Isaac. "Time Travel." In Asimov, *Gold: The Final Science Fiction Collection*. 1995. New York: HarperPrism, 1996, 301–306.

St. Augustine. *Confessions*. Edited by R. S. Pine-Coffin. Harmondsworth: Penguin, 1977.

Bainbridge, William Sims. *Dimensions of Science Fiction*. Cambridge, MA: Harvard University Press, 1986.

Baxter, Stephen. "Further Visions: Sequels to *The Time Machine*." *Foundation: The Review of Science Fiction*, No. 65 (Autumn, 1995), 41–50.

———. "The Technology of Omniscience: Past Viewers in Science Fiction." *Foundation: The International Review of Science Fiction*, No. 80 (Autumn, 2000), 97–107.

Benford, Gregory. *Deep Time: How Humanity Communicates across Millennia*. New York: Avon Books, 1999.

———. "Time and *Timescape*." *Science-Fiction Studies*, 14 (July, 1993), 184–190.

Bontly, Susan W., and Carol J. Sheridan. *Enchanted Journeys beyond the Imagination: An Annotated Bibliography of Futuristic, Supernatural, and Time Travel Romances*. Tijeras, NM: Blue Diamond Publications, 1996.

Brier, Bob. *Precognition and the Philosophy of Science: An Essay on Backward Causation*. New York: Humanities Press, 1974.

Cahn, Steven M. *Fate, Logic, and Time*. New Haven: Yale University Press, 1974.

Capra, Fritjof. *The Tao of Physics: An Exploration of the Parallels between Modern Physics and Eastern Mysticism*. Boston: New Science Library, 1975.

Clarke, Arthur C. "About Time." In Clarke, *Profiles of the Future: An Inquiry into the Limits of the Possible*. 1962. New York: Warner Books, 1984, 144–165.

Clarke, I. F. *Tale of the Future, from the Beginning to the Present Day: An Annotated Bibliography of Those Satires, Ideal States, Imaginary Wars and Invasions, Coming Catastrophes and End-of-the-World Stories, Political Warnings and Forecasts, Interplanetary Voyages and Scientific Romances—All Located in an Imaginary Future Period—That Have Been Published in the United Kingdom between 1644 and 1976*. Third Edition. London: Library Associates, 1978.

Cleugh, Mary Frances. *Time and Its Importance in Modern Thought*. London: Methuen, 1937.

Clevenger, Lisa, Jeanne Macho, and Shannon MaCravy. *The Alternate Reality Romance Guide*. Tijeras, NM: Blue Diamond Publications, n.d.

Clute, John. "Alternate Worlds." In Clute, *SF: The Illustrated Encyclopedia*. London: Dorling Kindersley, 1995, 62–63.

———. "Time in Faerie." In Clute and John Grant, editors, *The Encyclopedia of Fantasy*. New York: St. Martin's Press, 1997, 948.

———. "Time Travel." In Clute, *SF: The Illustrated Encyclopedia*. London: Dorling Kindersley, 1995, 60–61.

———. "Timeslips." In Clute and Grant, editors, *The Encyclopedia of Fantasy*. New York: St. Martin's Press, 1997, 948–949.

Cohen, Jack, and Ian Stewart. *The Collapse of Chaos*. London: Penguin, 1994.

Coveney, Peter and Roger Highfield. *The Arrow of Time*. London: Flamingo, 1991.

Davies, Paul. *About Time: Einstein's Unfinished Revolution*. New York: Simon & Schuster, 1995.

———. *God and the New Physics*. New York: Simon & Schuster, 1983.

de Camp, L. Sprague. "Language for Time-Travelers." *Astounding Science Fiction*, 21 (July,

1938), 63–72.

Douglas, Alfred. *Extra-Sensory Powers: A Century of Psychical Research.* Woodstock, NY: Overlook, 1977.

Dunne, J. W. *An Experiment with Time.* London: A. & C. Black Ltd., 1927.

Earman, John. *Bangs, Crunches, Whimpers, and Shrieks: Singularities and Acausalities in Relativistic Spacetime.* New York: Oxford University Press, 1995.

Edwards, Malcolm J., and Brian Stableford. "Time Travel." In John Clute and Peter Nicholls, editors, *The Encyclopedia of Science Fiction.* New York: St. Martin's Press, 1993, 1227–1229.

Einstein, Albert. "Autobiographical Notes." Translated by Paul Arthur Schlipp. In Schlipp, editor, *Albert Einstein: Philosopher-Scientist.* 1949. New York: Tudor Publishing Company, 1951, 1–95.

Foote, Bud. *The Connecticut Yankee in the Twentieth Century: Travel to the Past in Science Fiction.* Westport, CT: Greenwood Press, 1991.

Fraser, J. T. *Time: The Familiar Stranger.* Redmond, Washington: Tempus Books, 1987.

Fredericks, Casey. *The Future of Eternity: Mythologies of Science Fiction and Fantasy.* Bloomington: Indiana University Press, 1982.

Gabaldon, Diana. *The Outlandish Companion.* New York: Delacorte, 1999.

Galbreath, Robert. "Ambiguous Apocalypse: Transcendental Versions of the End." In Eric S. Rabkin, Martin H. Greenberg, and Joseph D. Olander, editors, *The End of the World.* Carbondale: Southern Illinois University Press, 1983, 53–72, notes 176–80.

Gale, Richard, editor, *The Philosophy of Time: A Collection of Essays.* Atlantic Highlands, NJ: Humanities Press, 1968.

Gardner, Martin. *Time Travel and Other Mathematical Bewilderments.* New York: W. H. Freeman, 1988.

Gernsback, Hugo. "The Mystery of Time." *Amazing Stories,* 2 (September, 1927), 525.

Gillespie, Bruce R. "Contradictions." *SF Commentary,* 4 (1969), 76–78.

Gordon, Andrew. "*Back to the Future*: Oedipus as Time Traveller." *Science-Fiction Studies,* 14 (November, 1987), 372–385.

Goswami, Amit and Maggie. *The Cosmic Dancers: Exploring the Physics of Science Fiction.* New York: Harper & Row, 1983.

Gott, J. Richard, III. *Time Travel in Einstein's Universe: The Physical Possibilities of Travel through Time.* Boston: Houghton Mifflin, 2001.

Gribbin, John. *In Search of Schrodinger's Cat.* London: Black Swan, 1991.

———. *Timewarps.* New York: Delacorte Press, 1979.

Griffin, Brian, and David Wingrove. *Apertures: A Study of the Writings of Brian W. Aldiss.* Westport, CT: Greenwood Press, 1984.

Hawking, Stephen W. *A Brief History of Time: From the Big Bang to Black Holes.* London: Bantam Press, 1988.

Heffern, Richard. *Time Travel: Myth or Reality?* New York: Pyramid Books, 1977.

Herbert, Nick. *Quantum Reality: Beyond the New Physics.* New York: Anchor Books, 1985.

Hollinger, Veronica. "Deconstructing the Time Machine." *Science-Fiction Studies,* 14 (July, 1987), 201–221.

Huet, Marie-Heléne. "Anticipating the Past: The Time Riddle in Science Fiction." In George Slusser, Colin Greenland, and Eric S. Rabkin, editors, *Storm Warnings: Science Fiction Confronts the Future.* Carbondale: Southern Illinois University Press, 1987, 34–42.

Hunt, Robert. "Visionary States and the Search for Transcendence in Science Fiction." In George Slusser, George R. Guffey, and Mark Rose, editors, *Bridges to Science Fiction.* Carbondale: Southern Illinois University Press, 1980, 64–77.

Jaques, Elliott. *The Form of Time*. New York: Crane Russak, 1982.

Ketterer, David. *Imprisoned in a Tesseract: The Life and Work of James Blish*. Kent, OH: Kent State University Press, 1987.

Lambourne, Robert, Michael Shallis, and Michael Shortland. *Close Encounters? Science and Science Fiction*. Bristol, England: Adam Hilger, 1990.

Leiby, David A. "The Tooth That Gnaws: Reflections on Time Travel." In George Slusser and Eric S. Rabkin, editors, *Intersections: Fantasy and Science Fiction*. Carbondale: Southern Illinois University Press, 1987, 107–118.

Lem, Stanislaw. "The Time-Travel Story and Related Matters of Science-Fiction Structuring." Translated by Thomas H. Hoisington and Darko Suvin. *Science-Fiction Studies*, 1 (1974), 143–154.

Lightman, Alan P. *Time Travel and Papa Joe's Pipe*. New York: Scribner's, 1984.

Macvey, John W. *Time Travel*. Chelsea, MI: Scarborough House, 1990.

Moore, Patrick. *Science and Fiction*. 1957. n.p.: Norwood Editions, 1976.

Moyle, David. "Beyond the Black Hole: The Emergence of Science Fiction Themes in the Recent Work of Martin Amis." *Extrapolation*, 36 (Winter, 1995), 305–315.

———. Letter. *Extrapolation*, 37 (Fall, 1996), 273.

Nahin, Paul J. *Time Machines: Time Travel in Physics, Metaphysics, and Science Fiction*. Second Edition. New York: American Institute of Physics, 1999.

———. *Time Travel*. Cincinnati: Writer's Digest Books, 1997.

Nicholls, Peter. *The Science in Science Fiction*. New York: Alfred A. Knopf, 1983.

Niven, Larry. "The Theory and Practice of Time Travel." In Niven, *All the Myriad Ways*. New York: Ballantine, 1971, 110–123.

Parrinder, Patrick. *Shadows of the Future: H. G. Wells, Science Fiction, and Prophecy*. Syracuse: Syracuse University Press, 1995.

Paul, Terri. "The Worm Ouroboros: Time Travel, Imagination, and Entropy." *Extrapolation*, 24 (Fall, 1983), 272–279.

Plato. *The Statesman*. Edited and translated by J. B. Skemp. New Haven: Yale University Press, 1952.

Rucker, Rudy. *The Fourth Dimension: A Guided Tour of the Higher Universes*. Boston: Houghton Mifflin Company, 1984.

Russell, W. M. S. "Time in Folklore and Science Fiction." *Foundation: The Review of Science Fiction*, No. 43 (Summer, 1988), 5–24.

Sachs, Robert Green. *The Physics of Time Reversal*. Chicago: University of Chicago Press, 1987.

Saint-Gelais, Richard. *L'empire du pseudo: Modernités de la science-fiction*. Québec: Nota Bene, 1999.

Shales, Tom. "The Re Decade," *Esquire* (March, 1986), 67–72.

Slusser, George E. "Storm Warnings and Dead Zones: Imagination and the Future." In Slusser, Colin Greenland, and Eric S. Rabkin, editors, *Storm Warnings*. Carbondale: Southern Illinois University Press, 1987, 3–20.

Slusser, George, and Danièle Chatelain. "Spacetime Geometries: Time Travel and the Modern Geometrical Narrative." *Science-Fiction Studies*, 22 (July, 1995), 151–186.

Slusser, George, Patrick Parrinder, and Danièle Chatelain, editors. *The Perennial Time Machine*. Athens: University of Georgia Press, 2001.

Stableford, Brian M. "Immortality." In John Clute and Peter Nicholls, editors, *The Encyclopedia of Science Fiction*. New York: St. Martin's Press, 1993, 615–617.

———. "Time Travel." In David Wingrove, editor, *The Science Fiction Source Book*. New York: Van Nostrand, 1984, 31–33.

Talbot, Michael. *Beyond the Quantum: God, Reality, Consciousness in the New Scientific Revolution*. New York: Macmillan, 1986.

————. *Mysticism and the New Physics*. New York: Bantam, 1981.

Thorne, Kip. *Black Holes and Time Warps*. New York: W. W. Norton, 1994.

Turner, George. "Paradigm and Pattern: Form and Meaning in *The Dispossessed*." *SF Commentary*, 41/42:4 (February, 1975), 65–74.

Wachhorst, Wyn. "Time-Travel Romance on Film: Archetypes and Structures." *Extrapolation*, 25 (Winter, 1984), 340–359.

Waldrop, M. Mitchell. *Complexity*. Penguin: London, 1994.

Westfahl, Gary. "Partial Derivatives: Popular Misinterpretations of H. G. Wells's *The Time Machine*." In Westfahl, *Science Fiction, Children's Literature, and Popular Culture*. Westport, CT: Greenwood Press, 2000, 129–141.

————. "Pastwonder: The Redemption of Orson Scott Card." *Interzone*, No. 144 (June, 1999), 50–52.

Westphal, Jonathan and Levenson, Carl. *Time*. Indianapolis: Hackett Publishing Company, 1993.

Whitrow, G. J. *Time in History*. Oxford: Oxford University Press, 1989.

Wilcox, Clyde. "Social Science in Space and Time." In Gary Westfahl, editor, *Space and Beyond: The Frontier Theme in Science Fiction*. Westport, CT: Greenwood Press, 2000, 143–150.

Wolf, Fred Alan. *Star Wave: Mind, Consciousness, and Quantum Physics*. New York: Collier Books, 1984.

Zelazny, Roger. "Some Science Fiction Parameters: A Biased View." *Galaxy*, 36 (July, 1975), 6–11.

Zukav, Gary. *The Dancing Wu Li Masters: An Overview of the New Physics*. New York: Bantam Books, 1979.

Index

About the Contributors

LARRY W. CALDWELL is a professor of English at the University of Evansville, where he teaches an advanced writing class that incorporates utopian texts.

ANDREW GORDON is Associate Professor of English at the University of Florida and Director of the Institute for the Psychological Study of the Arts. His essays have appeared in *Science Fiction Studies*, *Extrapolation*, *Journal of the Fantastic in the Arts*, and various anthologies.

KIRK HAMPTON is the author of *The Moonhare*, a "Wakean science fantasy," as well as the forthcoming novel *Lisho* and several conference papers co-authored with Carol MacKay.

ROBERT HEATH is a Professor of Biology at the University of California, Riverside, and a former dean. With George Slusser, he has taught classes examining science and science fiction.

SUSAN KRAY, Associate Professor of Communication at Indiana State University, publishes on film, television, and literature, with a special focus on representations of religious minorities, women, and technology in science fiction.

PEKKA KUUSISTO has published articles and has presented papers at several academic conferences, including the International Conference on the Fantastic in the Arts.

DAVID LEIBY has published an essay on time travel in the critical anthology *Intersections* and now works for the Highway Department of Orange County, with occasional forays back into literary criticism.

BRADFORD LYAU has taught at several colleges and universities and has published articles on both American and European science fiction.

CAROL MACKAY is Associate Professor of English at the University of Texas at Austin. She is the author of *Soliloquy in Nineteenth-Century Fiction* and editor of *The Two Thackerays* and *Dramatic Dickens*.

ERICA OBEY, who is currently teaching at the City College of New York, is studying nineteenth-century Gothic and supernatural literature.

JEFFERSON M. PETERS teaches English language and American literature at Fukuoka University. Since coming to Japan to work and live in 1993, he has studied manga and anime to learn Japanese language and culture.

RICHARD SAINT-GELAIS is an Assistant Professor in the Literature Department of Universite Laval, Quebec City. He is the author of an essay on fiction and reception theory and several articles about science fiction, detective novels, and contemporary fiction.

ANDREW SAWYER is the Librarian of the Science Fiction Foundation Collection and teaches in the M.A. in Science Fiction Studies offered at Liverpool. He is Reviews Editor of *Foundation: The International Review of Science Fiction* and co-edited a volume of essays entitled *Speaking Science Fiction*.

GEORGE SLUSSER, Professor of Comparative Literature at the University of California at Riverside, has written several books about science fiction authors and co-edited numerous critical anthologies. In 1986, he received the Pilgrim Award for his lifetime contributions to science fiction scholarship.

SUSAN STRATTON (formerly Susan Stone-Blackburn) is Professor of English and Associate Dean of Graduate Studies at the University of Calgary in Canada. Her current teaching and research interests include intersections of science and spirituality in "psience fiction" and feminist/ecological utopias.

GARY WESTFAHL, who teaches at the University of California at Riverside, is the author, editor, or co-editor of twelve books about science fiction and fantasy and writes a bimonthly column for the science fiction magazine *Interzone*.